Post-Charismatic 2.0
Rekindle the Smoldering Wick

POST-CHARISMATIC
2.0

REKINDLE THE SMOLDERING WICK

ROBBY MCALPINE

Post-Charismatic 2.0: Rekindle the Smoldering Wick - *Second Edition*

©2013 by Robby McAlpine

First edition published 2008 by David C Cook as *Post-Charismatic?*

ISBN: 978-0-9881304-7-0

Cover design and photography by Wendy McAlpine RPP, PPOC

DEDICATION

To Wendy, my beloved wife.

We've had all kinds of adventures, endured many twists and turns, and experienced both life's exhilarating highs and disillusioning lows. You have encouraged me, supported me, challenged me, and loved me though it all.

I love you more than words can say.

THE GENESIS CAFÉ: CONVERSATIONS ON THE KINGDOM

Robby has continued the fine and well-proven tradition of teaching by stories with *The Genesis Cafe: Conversations on the Kingdom*. Through the characters of the Elder, the Younger, and the Author you get a well thought out definition of what the Kingdom of God is and how it affects followers of Jesus today.

Robby has done an excellent job of expanding your understanding of the Kingdom of God and how it relates to you. It has been a long time since I have read something this good on such an important message.

John DiLullo

TABLE OF CONTENTS

PREFACE TO THE 2ND EDITION

Q: How many Charismatics does it take to change a light bulb?

A: Ten. One to change the light bulb, and the other nine to cast out the spirit of darkness.

(Insert boisterous, knee-slapping guffaws of merriment here.)

There are some things that we hear about in the Pentecostal, Charismatic, and Third Wave movements that we can laugh off easily. Just a few people with random silly ideas; they do not represent the mainstream of their movements. No harm, no foul.

This book is neither for, nor about them.

In growing numbers, people from charismatic backgrounds have fled churches that they once found to be sources of life. In almost every instance, what was ultimately behind the dysfunction that drove them away was some form of twisted theology.

Theology is simply our beliefs about God. What we think God is like directly impacts how we believe He interacts with us, what He expects of us, and how we are to interact with each other. Belief shapes behavior.

And if our beliefs are inaccurate, we will (even with the best of intentions and a sincere love for Jesus) behave in ways that aren't how God intended. Multiply the effect of bad theology and behavior throughout a local church, or an entire denomination, and the result is chaos.

"A bruised reed He will not break, and a smoldering wick He will not snuff out, till He has brought justice through to victory (Matthew 12:20)."

This book is for all the bruised reeds and smoldering wicks in the charismatic part of the Body of Christ. I hope that by reading this book, you will gain a deeper understanding of your own journey. But more than that, I pray you will find encouragement to continue to pursue the Spirit-filled life (but without the baggage).

Robby McAlpine
November 2013

Chapter One

CHARISMATICS ANONYMOUS

The metal door was propped open in defiance of the cool breeze, as it rustled through the few leaves remaining on the trees. The street-lamps had just flickered into life, bathing the concrete steps in light as dusk began to fall. In the bustle of the city's downtown, the weathered building was a small and almost unnoticed structure.

Inside the drafty room, under the quiet drone of the fluorescent lights, a few people were arranging the folding chairs into something resembling straight lines. At the front of the room stood a nondescript wooden lectern, flanked by a microphone on its stand. Off to one side, the room's few occupants gathered around a folding table adorned with a coffee urn and a collection of chipped ceramic mugs.

Sandra stood on the steps, waiting for her guest to arrive. Hands tucked into her jacket pockets for warmth, she smiled in welcome as people began to filter in past her. *I hope she doesn't change her mind,* Sandra thought to herself, as she scanned the pedestrian traffic for the familiar face of her friend.

Inside, Rick quietly went about his business of renewing acquaintances with some of the group's regulars, and making a point of welcoming anyone who seemed to be new or unsure of themselves. As the facilitator of the group, Rick was especially attentive to the need for creating a safe environment.

He was pleased to see Sandra enter the room, rubbing her hands together for warmth. She was with her guest, Justine; this was her first visit to the group. Like Rick, Sandra was a survivor who had completed the program, and was now "giving back" by reaching out to others with similar backgrounds and struggles.

There wasn't a large crowd tonight (it varied from week to week, but they were used to that), and Rick was tempted to set the microphone aside. From experience, he knew that some of those who might share later would be soft-spoken (and those in the back row would complain they couldn't hear), and chose to make use of the microphone anyway.

"Good evening, everyone," he began, as the stragglers quickly stirred their coffees and found their seats. "My name is Rick, and I am post-charismatic."

"Hello, Rick," came the gruffly chorused reply. A couple of the regulars chuckled at his choice of words.

"I want to welcome all of you to this meeting of Charismatics Anonymous," he continued, noting the diversity of facial expressions around the room. "And I want to make clear, as we do every week, that we do not consider ourselves to be *ex*-charismatics. Nor are we *anti*-charismatic. Our common ground is that we have all, in one way or another, been wounded and disillusioned by teachings and practices in our respective churches and denominations."

He paused for a moment, sensitive to the range of reactions among his listeners, given away by the scraping of a chair on the floor here, and an involuntary grimace or tearful eye there. Choosing his words carefully, he continued, "In some ways, it would be easier to simply choose to ignore the Holy Spirit, and be an *ex*-charismatic. I'll be honest: this has been a real temptation to me, more than once! But I just can't bring myself to be post-*Spirit*."

Rick could see the heads nodding in agreement among the regulars, and even some of the more skeptical of the newcomers seemed to understand. He could see Sandra whispering something (probably an explanation) to her nervous guest in the second-to-last row.

Trevor was sitting in the first row, although Rick mused that one could hardly call Trevor's posture 'sitting' – half on the chair, and half ready to either stand or bolt for the door. Trevor was a regular, and had been for several months now, but his church wounds were still very raw.

Motioning for Trevor to come to the lectern, Rick continued by way of segue, "Usually, the best thing is to simply begin to share our stories. We want everyone to feel the freedom to speak plainly, without fear of judgment, about your experiences."

Trevor immediately jumped out of his chair and all but ran to join Rick at the lectern, clutching a large, folded sheet of paper. Laughing nervously, his actions quick and edgy as was typical for him, Trevor unfolded his project and held it out for the rest to see.

"Hi, my name is Trevor, and I'm post-charismatic, too!"

"Hello, Trevor."

Gesturing to his creased art project, Trevor continued breathlessly, "I made this yesterday. I remembered what somebody said last week about making a fearless inventory, and it got me thinking: what if I made a list of 'You might be in a charismatic church if…' And then I just started drawing this."

And as people began to murmur approvingly, some even laughing out loud, Trevor read his list.

"You might be in a charismatic church if:

- "You avoid the 'positive confession cops' at your church, in case you have a cold that won't go away.

- "You've been told you have a 'religious spirit' because you asked the wrong question.

- "You finally figured out that 'touch not the Lord's anointed' really means SHUT UP!

- "People ask about your 'covering' and you know they don't mean the blanket on your bed.

- "You've confessed every sin you ever committed, and even a few you didn't, and you're still sick. So now you feel guilty, too.

- "Every prophet in town has promised you prosperity, fame, and a worldwide ministry, but you still work at a dead-end job and drive a '68 VW Beetle.

- "You are part of the Chosen Generation, because everybody over 26 failed to 'take the land' (but you still have to submit to them for some reason?)."

Sandra smiled at the creativity Trevor was using to deal with his sense of disillusionment, but she also wondered what effect it was having on her guest. Justine had smiled slightly at a few of the items, but appeared far closer to breaking down in tears at the memories that were stirred up.

Trevor even laughed at a few of his own favorites as he read the list out loud (for the sake of those in the last row), but his laughter faded and his expression shifted to one of discomfort as he finished. The large paper list shook slightly in his hand as he looked out over the group.

"Actually," he began, trying with obvious effort to control his emotions, "this list is only funny if it hasn't happened to you."

Pausing to clear his throat, Trevor straightened slightly and faced the group, clutching the list in both hands as he continued, softly but forcefully. "I agree with Rick. It would be a lot easier to just write sarcastic little lists and pretend like none of this really matters. Or maybe find a church that doesn't believe in the Spirit, except for on paper. Or just chuck everything to do with God and get on with my life. But I was reading in John 6 the other day, and Peter said 'Lord, where else would we go'? That's pretty much how I feel, too."

Much to her surprise, Sandra felt Justine stir beside her, as she leaned closer. "I want to say something," Justine whispered, "but I'm a little nervous. Will you come up there with me?"

"Of course," Sandra responded instantly. Taking Justine gently by the arm, they made their way to the front. As they approached, Trevor looked at them and nodded, making his way back to settle heavily on his front-row chair. The unexpected squeak of the metal legs on the tiled floor was jarring.

"Hello, everyone," Sandra said into the microphone, glancing around the room to make as much eye contact as she could. "My name is Sandra, and this is my friend Justine."

"Hello, Sandra. Hello, Justine," came the formal, yet surprisingly warm response. The regulars, of course, recognized Sandra as one of the sponsors who had completed the program. Her friend was obviously new; nobody could recall seeing her before, so they patiently waited with sympathetic concern as she tried to collect herself.

17

Justine stood silently for a long moment, head down, one balled-up fist pressed against her lips. After what seemed a small eternity, she looked up and began to speak

"I've only just left my church," she said at last. Speaking softly and haltingly at first, the words began to tumble out over themselves as she continued. "I am just so *scared* and *angry*. They said I would miss God's destiny for my life if I didn't stay submitted to our Apostle." The more she spoke, the sharper and louder her voice became. "I was terrified to question anything because I didn't want to speak against God's Authority. I didn't want people to say I was causing disunity. I knew something was wrong in our church, but I was too afraid to say anything."

Justine paused for a moment, as tears began slipping down her cheeks, in stark contrast to the angry tone of her voice. "Even tonight, when I first came in, I was scared that God would be angry because I was here. I keep thinking *what if my leaders find out?*"

She stopped abruptly, at a loss for words, an expression of anger, sadness and pain on her face. There was a profound moment of silence, before Sandra looked up to address the group.

"This is a difficult moment for me, as well," Sandra said softly, looking guilty. "You see, I was once a leader at Justine's church. I'm partly to blame for teaching her all those things. For Justine to reach out again to me now is… *humbling*, but also a very painful reminder of the damage that I've caused."

There were sympathetic nods and murmured affirmations throughout the small gathering. Rick took a deep breath, grateful for the caring atmosphere and yet grieved once again at the pain reflected in the two women together at the front, one trembling with pent-up pain and anger, and the other stricken with guilt.

How did this happen? He wondered, not for the first time. *How did it all go so wrong? What could we have done differently?*

Rick understood, of course, that the real problem wasn't *the people*. Not even the leaders who had taught, promoted, and defended unbiblical things. No, the real problem was the *teachings* that created and defended dysfunctional and unbalanced practices. A bad foundation inevitably results in the eventual collapse of the house.

A fragment of a Bible verse came to Rick's mind in that moment: "My people are destroyed from lack of knowledge..." *Hope I'm not taking that out of context*, Rick thought to himself. *But that about sums it up.*

Setting this train of thought aside for the moment, Rick crossed the floor to join Sandra and Justine, turning to address the whole group. The pause in the meeting brought on by Justine and Sandra's heartfelt sharing had only lasted a few moments, but it felt much longer. Rick wanted to tread carefully as he broke the silence.

"I realize that by even saying this, I may be conjuring up all sorts of emotions and memories for some of you," he began, scanning the faces before him. "But it's important, as we sort through everything, that we don't lose the most basic and precious things."

Laying his hand on Sandra's shoulder, Rick paused only a moment before gently asking, "Could we all pray for these two?"

Everyone could see Justine nodding her head, almost imperceptibly, but it was enough. There was a scraping and shuffling of chairs as the group stood to their feet. Some extended their hands towards the two women standing with Rick. Others simply bowed their heads, hands jammed into their pockets. Still others gathered around the three, although keeping a respectful distance.

And together, each in his or her own way, they prayed.

* * *

"Rather than watch our wounded brothers and sisters turn their backs on the faith or reject genuine spiritual experiences, those of us who identify with the charismatic renewal should determine to help rid our movement of its extra baggage."[1]

Post-charismatics find themselves wrestling to separate the chaff from the wheat.

Truer words have never been spoken. And more difficult words have never been spoken. Rooting out the problematic teachings and practices that have plagued Pentecostals, Charismatics, the Third Wave – and whatever new label emerges next – is much easier said than done. Some of the teachings seem to take on new life (and new terminology) with each successive generation, and many of them have built-in defenses to keep people from questioning or critiquing either the teachings or the teachers who promote them.

And as the fictional *Charismatics Anonymous* meeting illustrates, there are increasing numbers of spiritual casualties coming out of these movements. (You could also argue that people still trapped by false and abusive teachings are also spiritual casualties.) While there is no literal *Charismatics Anonymous* that I am aware of, the members could be described as *post-charismatic*.

Post-charismatics, as I am using the term, are those who find themselves caught between a rock and a hard place. Some have experienced emotional and psychological abuse because of unbiblical teaching and practices, while others have arrived at the conviction that much of what they've been taught is actually not supported by (or possibly contrary to) what the Bible teaches.

At the same time, they are "continuationists", which simply means that they believe that all the spiritual gifts listed in the New Testament continue to be available to Christians today (as opposed to those who believe that spiritual gifts have ceased – "cessationists"). As continuationists (an awkward word, yes), they cannot deny the Spirit's work, but they now find themselves wrestling to separate the chaff from the wheat, the baby from the bathwater, the sheep from the goats, or whatever metaphor appeals to you most.

I would generally agree with Jack Deere's statement in *Surprised by the Power of the Spirit*: "If you were to lock a brand-new Christian in a room with a Bible and tell him to study what Scripture has to say about healing and miracles, he would never come out of the room a cessationist."[2]

Of course, I would also suggest that this same person, after studying healing, miracles and the gifts of the Holy Spirit, would never come out of the room expecting to drop to the floor wailing as if they were in excruciating abdominal pain whenever they heard the word "intercession".

It is this weeding-out process which confronts post-charismatics. In some ways, post-*hype* might be a better description. "Burned out on hype and pulpit showmanship, weary of learning 95 ways to use spiritual gifts when they recognize more basic needs, these believers are in search of a deeper spirituality that emphasizes the fruit of the Spirit as much or more than the gifts."[3]

A quote widely attributed to Edmund Burke tells us: "Those who don't know history are destined to repeat it." Our first task in this weeding-out process will be to look at the historical roots of the modern Pentecostal and Charismatic movements. Understanding some of this history will be invaluable in providing a context for "how we got here from there".

After looking at the history, we will dig deeper into three areas of teaching that have contributed heavily to the current problems. Problems that have caused outsiders to mock, insiders to be used and abused, and many refugees to flee for their spiritual lives.

These three areas are so intertwined that it is difficult to separate them completely. One informs the other, which influences the next, which reinforces the first. Got it?

It is the difficulty in the sorting process that tempts many charismatics to throw up their hands in frustration, and give up. Many will simply skip being post-charismatic (weeding out the chaff to hold to the wheat), and jump straight into being non-charismatic.

And in the extreme, non-Christian.

These three areas of concern include:

1. The Latter Rain Movement (also called Kingdom Now or Dominionism),

2. Word of Faith (Prosperity, Health & Wealth), and

3. The Shepherding Movement (being 'under authority', submission to a 'covering').

We will look at how each of these sub-groupings came into being, what they taught, where things went sideways, and what a healthier, biblical response to each might be.

Each of these areas will be heavily footnoted, because it is my intent to present each group's teaching as accurately and fairly as possible. There is nothing to be gained from attacking a "straw man" that does not truly represent what these groups teach and practice. I believe that as their teachings are clearly laid out, and then compared to Scripture, the problematic areas will become evident.

My motivation for writing is the same today as when I wrote the first edition: I have many brothers and sisters who have been victims of some or all of these damaging teachings and practices. I cannot remain silent. I don't want to see people give up on their faith, nor settle for a 'safe' but ultimately sterile Christian life.

If these words can provide a context, and a way towards a healthier, biblical understanding of the Holy Spirit and His role in our lives, then I will have done what I can. While a single book could never pretend to function as the 'last word on the subject', I hope and trust that this will prove to be a redemptive starting point for current charismatics, post-charismatics, and anyone who desires more of the Spirit but wants to avoid the errors that led to the excesses.

With that in mind, let's take a look at our historical roots.

<u>CHAPTER NOTES</u>

1. Grady, J. Lee – *What Happened to the Fire?,* page 169.
2. Deere, Jack – *Surprised by the Power of the Spirit*, page 53.
3. Grady, J. Lee – *What Happened to the Fire?,* page 58.

Chapter Two

HISTORICAL ROOTS

Context is everything. When statements are taken "out of context", it almost always results in misunderstanding what the original writer was trying to communicate. When people have taken Scripture out of context, entire teachings and practices have been created that completely misunderstand the intent of the original Writer. And the inevitable result is spiritual casualties.

Before we can dig into some of the problematic areas currently affecting the charismatic movement, we need to understand their context. If we trace the history, we will gain important insights for the sifting process.

For example, the Pentecostal movement did not suddenly spring out of nothingness at the Azusa Street Mission in 1906. There is a historical context that predates that revival. Just as the Protestant Reformation had its roots in an ongoing cycle of reformation and revival long before Martin Luther nailed his 95 Theses on the doors at Wittenberg, so the Pentecostal movement has theological roots that go much further back. The same is true for the charismatic renewal of the 1960s, and any other revival movement. They all have roots in the past.

During the twentieth century, the Pentecostal, Charismatic and Third Wave movements comprised the fastest growing segment of Christianity. Some estimates place their combined numbers at above 600 million. Beyond their own church borders, their influence has been felt in many other churches and denominations as well.

In *The Churching of America 1776-1990*, church historians Roger Finke and Rodney Stark coined the term 'routinization of charisma'. This routinization follows a simple progression: (a) God sovereignly begins a work of revival and renewal among His people, (b) humanity asserts its tendency – within a generation or two – to institutionalize what began as a move of God, which then (c) calcifies into structural forms without power. This cycle has repeated itself in church history for centuries, and the Pentecostal and charismatic movements are not immune.

Charismatic author J. Lee Grady laments a sobering reality: "Too many times in this century, movements that were born of the Spirit ended up as spiritual miscarriages. And in every case, men and women were responsible for derailing God's holy purpose."[1]

There are many historical examples of Spirit-initiated revivals throughout the centuries, but for our purpose here, we will look primarily at the roots of the current Pentecostal and Charismatic movements.

JOHN WESLEY AND ENTIRE SANCTIFICATION

Perhaps the most significant roots of the Pentecostal story go back to the Great Awakening, and particularly the teachings of John Wesley. Of particular interest to our discussion is Wesley's teaching on "entire sanctification", contained in his booklet *A Plain Account of Christian Perfection*, published in 1766.

An important part of the Wesleyan background is the decidedly Arminian understanding that Wesley – and later Pentecostals and some charismatics – had of salvation and the ongoing work of the Spirit in the lives of Christians.

> **Aside**: I will not attempt to reconcile the Arminian/ Calvinist debate in this writing. The topic is far too immense. And I fully recognize that there are many nuances and emphases in both theological camps that will not be adequately articulated here. I will occasionally comment on one or both theological viewpoints only as much as it helps to lay the groundwork for looking at the post-charismatic question.

Wesley rejected the 'unconditional election' aspect of predestination, which Calvinists insist on. Wesley believed that human will and responsibility was involved as well in salvation. Wesley also wanted to avoid the opposite end of the spectrum (the heresy of Pelagianism), which taught that people could choose to follow Jesus based solely on their own decision without the necessity of God's intervening grace.

To answer critics who accused him of being Pelagian, Wesley appealed to the Arminian teaching on 'prevenient grace'. This simply meant that God has given grace for all humanity to respond to Jesus, but people must use their free will and choose to submit to Jesus as Lord. (Calvinists believe that man is incapable of seeking or finding God; everything rests on God's initiative and action.)

Why is this important to our discussion? The implication of having the free will to choose to follow Jesus also included the possibility of choosing to reject Him later, commonly called "losing your salvation". (This naturally clashed with the Calvinist doctrine of "perseverance of the saints".) If salvation could be lost, then the question of knowing if you were still 'in' (or not) becomes extremely important.

In Calvinist thought, free will (the power of contrary choice) is an illusion.

"Calvinism" is the name usually associated with the Reformed viewpoint, after the French theologian John Calvin (1509-1564) who best articulated his views in his book *Institutes of the Christian Religion*. Predestination is the doctrine that God decides (or better yet, has *already* decided) who will – and who won't – become Christians. In Calvinist thought, free will (the power of contrary choice) is an illusion.

(The following is admittedly an oversimplification of both Reformed and Arminian theology. My apologies to all parties who would have preferred that I invest more time in the nuances and range of opinion in both lines of thought. I only bring these up to briefly help set the historical context.)

The acronym T.U.L.I.P. is often used to identify the five main points of Calvinism:

- Total depravity (the imago Dei was completely obliterated when Adam and Eve sinned; humanity is incapable of seeking God).

- Unconditional election (God sovereignly chooses who will be saved, based solely on His grace).

- Limited atonement ("for God's good will and pleasure" – a favorite Calvinist phrase – the blood of Jesus is only effective for those who have been chosen (elected) by God; the non-elect have no option or alternative).

- Irresistible grace (those who are predestined *must* respond – they can do nothing else).

- Perseverance of the saints (sometimes called "once saved, always saved", but that hardly does the idea justice).

Arminian theology was developed from the writing of Jacobus Arminius (1559-1609). Known as 'the quiet Dutchman', Arminius emphasized that people have free will and personal choice in salvation. Later Arminian theologians developed a five-point synopsis similar to Calvinism's TULIP:

- Natural ability (the imago Dei is marred but not obliterated; however, humanity is dependent on the Holy Spirit for new birth).

- Election (based on God's foreknowledge of who would respond with free will to the gospel).

- Unlimited atonement (salvation is available to all, but effective only for those who respond).

- Prevenient grace (preparatory work of the Holy Spirit enabling humanity to respond to the gospel).

- Conditional perseverance (believers are empowered for victorious life, but are capable of turning from grace and losing salvation).

Part of the answer to the "losing salvation" question was Wesley's teaching on entire sanctification. For Wesley, this was a "second work of grace": a crisis event following salvation, where the believer was enabled to overcome sin in this present life. At the same time, Wesley freely admitted that absolute perfection was impossible this side of heaven.

This second work of grace meant that the believer was motivated by love for God and others, and any sinful actions or words which happened after this point would be minor mistakes and small slips. "Wesley did not believe that every Christian achieves this state (of perfection) during the course of this life. But he did believe it ought to be preached... for, he insisted, when salvation and the Christian life stand still, they erode."[2]

For many Methodists (those who followed John Wesley's teachings), this second crisis experience of entire sanctification (or "Christian perfection") became the crucial evidence that they were definitely headed for heaven. There was a lot of emphasis in early Methodism on "tarrying" (waiting on God), combined with a time of soul-searching and repenting of all known sin, before this second crisis moment would come.

> *Tarrying* is from the King James Version of Luke 24:49: "And, behold, I send the promise of my Father upon you: but tarry ye in the city of Jerusalem, until ye be endued with power from on high." *Tarrying* is not just some random charismatic phrase.

John Fletcher, one of Wesley's co-workers, was the first to identify this second blessing as the "baptism of the Holy Spirit", which was thought to bring inner cleansing and the ability to live in Christian perfection.

"Many Methodist holiness leaders already taught that on the day of Pentecost, the 120 were entirely sanctified in the Wesleyan sense."[3] This made it quite easy to equate the Wesleyan doctrine of Christian perfection with the baptism of the Holy Spirit.

HOLINESS & KESWICK HIGHER LIFE MOVEMENTS

Wesleyan theology later influenced what has been called the "Holiness" tradition in the mid- to late 1800s. Basically stated, the Holiness movement stressed that the fruit of the second blessing – or baptism of the Spirit – was a holy, separated life. The concept of tarrying and soul-searching expanded to suggest that the path of receiving this second blessing was purifying one's self of "worldliness".

Not surprisingly, several different views developed on the definition of 'worldliness', but there was a general trend towards extreme conservatism and not a little legalism. "They were overwhelmingly Arminian in their basic theology and strongly perfectionistic in their spirituality and lifestyle."[4]

In Great Britain, a movement called the *Keswick Higher Life* conference came to prominence in 1870, attracting many people from across a variety of denominations to their camp meetings. They tempered the Wesleyan teaching on entire sanctification in two ways:

1. The emphasis on the baptism of the Spirit shifted away from achieving entire sanctification, and focused more on receiving power from the Holy Spirit to live a Godly life and do good works.

2. Unlike their American Methodist cousins, they didn't believe that sin could be *eradicated* by this baptism of the Spirit. Instead, "they taught that sin was *counteracted* by the experience... allowing for a joyful and victorious Christian life *(emphasis added)*."[5]

Many of the participants in both the British and American Keswick meetings believed that the Holiness Movement would bring about true unity of the church, rather than the ecumenical efforts of the existing denominations. In contrast, there also arose a group that was identified as "a 'come-outer' movement led by radicals who abandoned any prospects of renewing the existing churches."[6] (Nothing new under the sun, is there?)

The effect of these splinter groups within the movement did not have an adverse effect on the basic message and emphasis of Keswick. The Higher Life movement, as part of the larger Holiness tradition, saw thousands of people claim to experience the second work of grace – the baptism of the Holy Spirit – during the last quarter of the nineteenth century. But for many, the question still remained: how can you know with certainty that you have received this baptism?

"I had such an experience of His love, I had to ask Him to stay His hand..."

Famous evangelists like Charles Finney (1792-1876) and Dwight L. Moody (1837-99, founder of Moody Bible Institute) contributed to the common understanding of Spirit baptism as a second work of grace, empowering believers for Christian life and service.

Finney at one point went so far as to question another pastor's ministry because Finney wasn't convinced his colleague had experienced the second blessing. "If he had ever been converted to Christ, he had failed to receive that divine anointing of the Holy Ghost that would make him a power in the pulpit... He had fallen short of receiving the baptism of the Holy Ghost, which is indispensable to ministerial success..."[7]

Moody's experience came in 1871 after two Free Methodist women confronted him after he had preached, telling him that he needed the power of the Spirit. Moody initially declined to let them pray for him, but later relented.

While in New York shortly afterwards, Moody "felt such an overwhelming sense of God's nearness that he rushed to a friend's house and begged for a room where he could lock himself in... and as he put it, 'I had such an experience of His love that I had to ask Him to stay His hand'."[8]

Moody's biggest influence on the American Keswick movement was his view that baptism in the Holy Spirit was primarily concerned with power for service, and not freedom from sin. This became the predominant understanding of those touched by the American Keswick movement.

Still, the answer to the question of what constituted "proof" of the Spirit's baptism remained elusive. Large numbers of people on two continents (and those who traveled from afar to attend the Keswick conferences) had been significantly impacted, with many claiming to have received the baptism of the Spirit. And yet, there was still the perceived need for what has been called "assurance of salvation".

The National Holiness Association arose in the late nineteenth century in America as a protest movement against the perceived stagnation of the churches there. The second blessing teaching was promoted here as well, and numerous well-known evangelicals were a part of this movement, including A.J. Gordon, Andrew Murray, A.B. Simpson (founder of the Christian and Missionary Alliance), and R.A. Torrey, who was the president of Moody Bible Institute at the time.

Torrey's view of the second blessing was similar to Finney's, as evidenced in his writing, "A man may be regenerated by the Holy Spirit and still not be baptized with the Holy Spirit."[9]

Unfortunately, the National Holiness Association became characterized by an extreme version of legalism. Sam Storms recounts that they "defined holiness as abstinence. On their list of taboos: the theatre, ball games, playing cards, dancing, lipstick, tobacco, alcohol, all forms of female make-up, the curling or coloring of one's hair, neckties for men, Coca Cola, chewing gum, rings, bracelets, or any form of worldly 'ornamentation', etc."[10]

While we may balk at this legalistic approach today, their insistence on repentance/holiness fits neatly with a view of sanctification where purifying oneself is required in order to receive the baptism of the Holy Spirit. This was also coupled in some circles with the lingering expectation that baptism in the Spirit would result in Christian perfection.

During these years, there were various splinter groups that also advocated the recovery of the charismatic gifts of tongues, prophecy, healing, etc. A number of these groups showed evidence in their early days of a genuine move of the Spirit. Sadly, these groups often degenerated into various elitist teachings and abuses which caused them to be shunned by the more mainstream expressions of the Holiness movement.

Significantly, the possibility of the charismatic gifts being associated with the baptism of the Holy Spirit had been introduced.

THE PENTECOSTAL MOVEMENT

Disclaimer: There are many well-known people in the Pentecostal movement whom you won't read about here. People like John G. Lake, Smith Wigglesworth, Kathryn Kuhlman, David DuPlessis (nicknamed "Mr. Pentecost"), and many others make for fascinating reading. But my intent in this section is to trace the developing theology and practices of the movement, not to write an exhaustive historical account.

In the years bridging the nineteenth and twentieth centuries, one of the more imaginative thinkers of the day, Benjamin Irwin, developed a series of baptisms that one might receive from the Holy Spirit. John Wesley's associate, John Fletcher, had already suggested the idea of multiple fillings by the Holy Spirit, but Irwin added a new twist.

The believer, according to Irwin, was "the potential recipient of multiple infusions of power, the baptism of the Holy Spirit and fire being but the first. Later blessings he characterized by various explosives: dynamite, lyddite, and oxidite."[11] Irwin's moral failings eventually led to the demise of the denomination he started, but among those who sat under his teachings was a man named Charles Fox Parham.

Parham's single greatest contribution to what would later be known as the Pentecostal movement was his teaching that the evidence of the baptism of the Holy Spirit was the gift of tongues. Parham's early emphasis was that these would be known languages (*xenoglossolalia*, as was the case in Acts 2) which he believed would result in a great missionary movement around the world.

What made Parham's group unique was their insistence that tongues were the necessary evidence of Spirit-baptism.

On New Year's Day 1901, one of Parham's students, Agnes Ozman, spoke in tongues (presumed to be Chinese), and was unable to speak or write English for three days afterwards. While Ozman was not the first person to speak in tongues in America – D.L. Moody saw tongues in evidence at some of his meetings, and they were reported during the Welsh Revival a few years later – "what made Parham's group unique was their insistence that tongues were the necessary evidence of Spirit-baptism."[12]

(Agnes Ozman would, years later, write of her disappointment that people put too much emphasis on tongues as *the* sign of the Spirit's baptism.)

William J. Seymour, a black Holiness preacher, had been influenced by Parham's teachings from the school hallway where he was forced, as a non-white, to remain while Parham was teaching. Seymour took the teaching of tongues as the initial evidence of the Spirit's baptism with him when he accepted a pastorate in Los Angeles. It is worth noting that, at the time, Seymour himself had not yet experienced the gift of tongues.

After some people began to speak in tongues at a Bible study Seymour was leading, space was rented at 312 Azusa Street in Los Angeles, and the movement called Pentecostalism was born. Nightly revival meetings ran for three years (1906-1909), and were attended by people from all walks of life.

Opposition was strong from some quarters: even R.A. Torrey, who had taught that the baptism of the Spirit was a second blessing experience, declared that Pentecostalism was "emphatically not of God"[13]. G. Campbell Morgan famously denounced the Pentecostal revival as "the last vomit of Satan".[14]

This strong reaction lent additional fodder to the come-outers, who saw this rejection as another evidence of the true work of God being shunned by a spiritually bankrupt institutional church. (This has been a common accusation repeated throughout the centuries in the cycle of revival, routinization and renewal.) This come-outer mentality will play into other areas that we will consider later.

The initial belief was that tongues were known languages, which would result in greater effectiveness in evangelizing the nations. This assumption quickly faded as eager missionaries discovered to their puzzlement that 'the nations' didn't understand a word they were saying. Alfred G. Garr, who had received his baptism experience at Azusa Street in the early days of the revival, arrived in Calcutta in early 1907, "only to find that he could not speak in what he thought was Bengali after all."[15]

Garr also taught that the gift of tongues was the initial evidence of the Spirit's baptism, but he focused more on the 'tongues of men and angels' (or 'prayer language') approach. His views caught on quickly among those who had genuinely experienced a baptism of the Spirit, but had later discovered that the language they had received was unknown.

It is useful to note that around this same time, near the end of the nineteenth century, non-charismatic theologians were developing an interpretive grid called Dispensationalism, which included what is known as "cessationism". This theological system, popularized by Benjamin Warfield in the late 1890s, believed that after the first century, the more obviously supernatural or "sign" gifts (tongues, interpretation, prophecy, healing, words of knowledge and wisdom, etc.) ceased (hence the term 'cessationism').

Cessationists taught that the purpose of these "sign" gifts was to authenticate the Apostles' ministry in spreading the gospel. Once the canon of the Bible was declared closed, the charismatic gifts were no longer necessary and therefore ceased. Any further occurrence of these gifts was therefore not from God.

In 1910, Charles Harrison Mason published his 'finished work' theology of gradual, progressive sanctification, which was instrumental to the formation of the Assemblies of God denomination in 1914. Today, this denomination is one of the largest Pentecostal denominations in the world.

An early controversy within the Pentecostal movement arose out of a group who claimed the doctrine of the Trinity was unbiblical. These "Jesus-only" proponents insisted that the proper formula for baptism was in the name of Jesus alone; the Trinitarian formula was misguided at best, and heretical at worst. Some groups required the re-baptism of anyone who had been baptized in the "name of the Father, the Son, and the Holy Spirit" (Matthew 28:19).

The Assemblies of God took a public stand against the Jesus-only teaching in 1916, which resulted in over 100 congregations leaving. The United Pentecostals are one of the largest Jesus-only (or Oneness) groups in America, and north of the border the

Apostolic Churches of Canada (started by Frank Small in Winnipeg during the 1920s) were their counterparts.

Small was a major proponent of the Oneness doctrine in Canada. Zion Apostolic Church, which he was instrumental in founding, is still active today, although the entire denomination has reverted to Trinitarian belief in recent years.

During the late 1940s and onward, a movement arose in Canada that became known as the Latter Rain. While the phrase "latter rain" was a common one among Pentecostals, referring to the outpouring of the Holy Spirit in the twentieth century, the movement that called itself by the same name developed many of its own unique teachings and practices.

William Branham, one of the major figures in the Latter Rain movement, was fiercely 'Jesus-only' in his theology, and insisted on re-baptizing any Trinitarian converts to his New Order of the Latter Rain. We will examine some of Branham's more controversial teachings – such as the "Serpent Seed" and "Manifested Sons of God" – as part of the Latter Rain discussion later.

The Assemblies of God and the Pentecostal Assemblies of Canada, among other prominent Pentecostal denominations, condemned the Latter Rain movement as heretical in 1949. However, many of Latter Rain teachings survived and re-surfaced in the charismatic renewal and continue to this day, so we will look at the Latter Rain's teachings and continuing influence in greater detail later.

For many Pentecostal/Holiness believers, the gift of tongues as the initial evidence of the Spirit's baptism became a vital link in their spiritual journey: now they at last had tangible evidence that they had indeed received the second work of grace. A.A. Boddy wrote in 1910 about knowing the "wondrous joy that the Spirit has thus sealed the believer unto the day of redemption."[16]

Please understand: I am not attempting to interact with all the theological nuances of these developments. They are simply important to understand in the trajectory that has led to the post-charismatics.

THE CHARISMATIC RENEWAL

It was in 1960 that the movement dubbed the Charismatic Renewal first became widely known, as a result of the much-publicized story of an Episcopal priest named Dennis Bennett. The difference from the existing Pentecostal movement – now established well enough that they were even accepted into the National Association of Evangelicals – was their emphasis on 'renewing' the mainline denominations: Episcopal, Lutheran, Anglican, Catholic, etc.

While the early Pentecostals were typically ostracized by existing denominations, the Charismatic Renewal developed predominantly *within* the mainline denominations. After some initial resistance, most of these denominations settled into allowing their charismatic members to co-exist with their more traditional congregations.

Dennis Bennett, while not the first person in a mainline denomination to speak in tongues, became a recognized name because he ventured to speak about it openly from the pulpit of his church in Van Nuys, California.

Although Bennett had received the baptism of the Holy Spirit and the gift of tongues in 1959, he kept it quiet initially, until rumors began to circulate and he knew he had to publicly address the situation.

"This he decided to do on Passion Sunday, April 3 1960. At all three morning services, Bennett explained in a quiet, unemotional way how he had been led to receive the power and the fullness of the Holy Spirit, and how this had included the 'gift of unknown tongues'. After the second service, an associate priest resigned, and a church officer called for Bennett's resignation. Bennett announced his resignation at the third service."[17]

The Charismatic Renewal developed predominantly within the mainline denominations.

Things might have faded quickly afterwards for Bennett, but an associate of his contacted the national magazines *Newsweek* and *Time*. Both magazines ran stories on Bennett's charismatic experience and the resulting turmoil in Van Nuys that forced his resignation. Bennett was transferred to a small, struggling parish in Washington State, which experienced explosive growth in numbers and a significant move of the Holy Spirit. This time, however, Bennett had the support and blessing of the local bishop.

The charismatic renewal multiplied quickly. "Within a decade, this movement had spread to all the 150 major Protestant families of the world, reaching a total of 55,000,000 people by 1990."[18] They were initially referred to as 'neo-Pentecostal', but "the word 'charismatic' came to be used to refer to folks from old-line denominations who were receiving the freedom of the Holy Spirit while continuing in their respective traditions."[19]

At the same time, "the Second Vatican Council, which concluded in 1965, created an atmosphere of openness to the charismatic work of the Holy Spirit"[20], and it was only two years later that charismatic experiences began to take place at Duquesne University in Pittsburgh. "In the more than 30 years since its inception, the Catholic charismatic movement has touched the lives of our 70,000,000 Catholics in over 120 nations of the world."[21]

Significantly, the Charismatic Renewal represented an adoption by many mainline denominations of Pentecostal theology regarding the baptism of the Holy Spirit and the initial evidence of speaking in tongues. Much of the existing liturgy, for example in the Anglican *Book of Common Prayer*, was easily compatible with this new experience of the Holy Spirit. This was a remarkable change from the ostracism that Pentecostals had endured only a generation earlier.

The *Jesus People Movement* of the late 1960s and early 1970s was another manifestation of the charismatic renewal, as literally thousands of hippies and other counter-cultural youth and young adults gave their lives to Jesus. The current Christian recording industry began out of the evangelistic efforts of early 'Jesus Music' groups, which were at first very controversial for their use of rock music (however tame they sound by today's standards).

Thousands of new believers, not always welcome at established churches, often ended up planting their own churches. In some cases, because of their isolation from the larger Body of Christ, these fledgling groups eventually became cultic and damaging. The need for discipleship among these often fiercely anti-establishment former hippies would become a serious issue in the early 1970s.

Ministry focusing on 'inner healing', or the 'healing of memories', began in this period, such as John and Paula Sandford's Elijah House ministry. Their books, such as *Healing the Wounded Spirit* and *The Elijah Task* put a stronger emphasis on the Holy

Spirit's role in counseling, as well as advocating the use of prophecy and words of knowledge with their clients.

The Shepherding Movement (also known as the Authority and Submission movement) arose in the 1970s, partly in response to the need for discipleship among young anti-establishment Christians. However, the movement created a serious crisis point for Pentecostals and charismatics alike, due to the extreme nature of some of their teachings on submission to spiritual leaders.

At the time, many charismatic leaders denounced the Shepherding Movement as authoritarian and abusive, but its influence – aided by the use of mass media – spread quickly across many denominational lines. Eventually, most of its main proponents abandoned their teachings in the 1980s, and one leader publicly repented with great remorse in 1989.

However, long after the demise of Shepherding as a 'movement' in the late 1980s, the concepts of "covering" and being "under authority" have survived and continue to this day. We will therefore examine this movement and its teachings separately and in greater detail later.

It was also during these years that the Word of Faith movement began to pick up steam. While it had already been around for some time, the advent of Christian broadcasting resulted in millions of people having access to what would become some of the most embarrassing and outlandish events on television.

Some of the most disturbing aspects of televised charismatic personalities (televangelists) steamrolled into the public eye in the late 1980s. One of the most cynically received was probably Oral Roberts' infamous prophetic word that God would "take me home" if Oral failed to raise $8,000,000 for his Faith Centre in Oklahoma. Oral managed to raise the money before the deadline (pardon the pun), but his Faith Centre closed permanently only two years later.

The Jim and Tammy Faye Bakker crisis occurred in 1987, when Jim was accused of having a sexual relationship with a church secretary. Jim was later sent to prison for financially defrauding his viewers via his PTL (*Praise the Lord*, later renamed *People That Care*) television show and theme park. Tammy Faye admitted to a drug addiction and divorced her husband. Jim came out of prison and wrote a book renouncing his former Prosperity (Health and Wealth) teachings, entitled *I Was Wrong*.

Probably the most devastating moment for many Pentecostal believers was the fall of Jimmy Swaggart in 1988. Swaggart was known for his fiery sermons and relentless attacks on Christian rock music in the mid-1980s, but when he was caught with a prostitute, he resigned from the pastorate with a tearful apology. Not long afterwards, Swaggart was discovered with a second prostitute. Swaggart had his ministerial credentials revoked by the Assemblies of God, and his influence went sharply down, although he later returned to ministry as an independent, non-affiliated speaker.

The cynicism felt by many of the emerging generations towards the extravagant lifestyles of televangelists – coupled with the increased focus on social justice and ministry among the poor – was compounded greatly by these events.

THE THIRD WAVE

The term 'Third Wave' was coined in the early 1980s by C. Peter Wagner to describe a growing number of "evangelical Christians who, while applauding and supporting the work of the Holy Spirit in the first two waves (classic Pentecostalism and the charismatic renewal), have chosen not to identify with either."[22] Some have suggested that the Third Wave is synonymous with the Vineyard movement begun by the late John Wimber, but that assumption is inaccurate. While it is true that many Vineyards would fit the classic definition of a Third Wave church, the Third Wave encompasses more than just the Vineyard.

The reasons for not completely identifying with the first two waves (Pentecostal and Charismatic) are largely theological in nature; one Pentecostal writer suggests that Third Wave churches tend to "disdain labels such as 'Pentecostal' or 'charismatic'"[23]. Third Wavers would agree that they have theological differences, but 'disdain' is probably a harsher word than is warranted.

"The 'third wave', therefore, is the embracing by evangelicals of the gifts of the Spirit while at the same time rejecting several of the classical Pentecostal and charismatic distinctives such as:

1. "The insistence that the baptism in the Holy Spirit is a distinct experience separate from conversion;

2. "The insistence that speaking in tongues is the initial physical evidence of baptism in the Spirit;

3. "The insistence that since 'healing is in the atonement' all believers may justifiably 'claim' complete physical health in this present age.

"The 'third wave' has also distanced itself from the errors of the Word of Faith movement as well as other forms of the so-called 'Health and Wealth' or 'Prosperity' gospel."[24]

During the Jesus People movement of the late 1960s and early 1970s, Calvary Chapel rose to prominence as literally thousands of hippies were baptized in the Pacific Ocean near Costa Mesa, California. Calvary Chapel's pastor, Chuck Smith, became one of most easily recognized leaders in a counter-cultural revival.

Another key figure in the Jesus People movement was the controversial figure of Lonnie Frisbee. Lonnie was a converted hippy, a passionate preacher and a tireless evangelist. He had a significant impact on Calvary Chapel, but found himself increasingly being set aside due to his unorthodox appearance and behavior.

Lonnie would surface again in the early days of the Vineyard movement, although until recently, Vineyard writings never acknowledged him by name. In most publications, these writers opted to refer to him as a 'young evangelist' or 'young preacher'. The landmark "Mother's Day Incident" in 1980 at John Wimber's Vineyard in Anaheim, which launched the Vineyard into its signs and wonders emphasis, came as a result of Lonnie preaching and inviting the Holy Spirit to fall on the young people in the congregation.

> **Arminianism says "If we, then God...", while Reformed believers would say, "Because God has, we will..."**

However, Lonnie's ongoing struggles with homosexuality (he died from AIDS in 1993) caused both Calvary Chapel and the Vineyard to distance themselves from him, despite the benefits of his ministry. At his funeral, he was charitably compared to Samson – an anointed person, but with crippling human frailty.

Another key doctrinal difference of the Third Wave is that the overwhelming majority of them are evangelicals from a Reformed (Calvinist) theological grid. What makes this significant is that Third Wave groups have generally *not* adopted the Holiness understanding of entire sanctification. Typically, they would assume that the filling of the Holy Spirit is a repeatable event to empower and equip believers for service.

"Arminianism says 'If we, then God...', while Reformed believers would say, 'Because God has, we will...'"[25] For the majority of those who consider themselves part of the Third Wave, there is a sense of polite bewilderment at the Pentecostal and charismatic insistence on tongues. The idea of tarrying or purging one's self of 'worldliness' in order to receive the Holy Spirit is equally foreign to their theology.

The Vineyard movement contributed its own fair share of controversy over the years, beginning with John Wimber's writings on what he termed *power evangelism*. (Keep in mind, as well, that during the 1980s *everything* was power-this or power-that, from power lunches to power neckties.)

Wimber's emphasis on power evangelism was to utilize the power of the Spirit – through prophecy, words of knowledge and particularly healing – as a door opener for sharing the good news of Jesus Christ. The Vineyard expanded quickly, and many evangelicals – with their predominantly Reformed theology – were introduced to spiritual gifts in a manner that was more easily accepted into their existing theology than classic Pentecostal/ second blessing teachings.

One of the Vineyard's main emphases was "everybody gets to play" – an attempt to practice the priesthood of all believers in terms of spiritual gifts. At the same time, Vineyard at one point embraced the Kansas City Prophets, another controversial group whose teachings included some of the rejected Latter Rain doctrines. The Vineyard's leaders, including Wimber, believed that they could bring correction to some of the Kansas City Prophets' more exotic teachings.

As time went on, however, the Vineyard distanced themselves from the Prophets, and with the departure of Metro Vineyard (now known as Metro Christian Fellowship) in 1996, the Kansas City Prophets era in the Vineyard ended. At the 1995 Pastors Conference, while speaking on the topic of leadership, John Wimber shared, "I came back to the Vineyard [leaders] in 1991 and apologized – repented, actually – of leading us into the prophetic era... I love the gift [of prophecy]; it was the packaging that I discarded."[26]

The Toronto Blessing began in 1994, and suddenly the Vineyard was once again in the middle of a controversial move of the Spirit. As other outpourings of the Spirit in history had already demonstrated – from Jonathan Edwards' concerns in the Great Awakening to Azusa Street – there was a mix of Spirit and flesh, and therefore a great need for careful discernment.

As the Blessing progressed, thousands of people from around the world boarded airplanes to make a pilgrimage to Toronto. From very early in the Blessing, concerns were raised within the Vineyard about some of the physical manifestations, and especially attempts by some to give these strange manifestations prophetic significance. As these concerns increased, Latter Rain teachings, so recently dealt with as a result of the Kansas City Prophets, began to surface again. In December 1995, the Toronto Airport Vineyard was asked to leave the Vineyard movement, and became Toronto Airport Christian Fellowship.

Similar events happened at the Brownsville Assembly of God church in Pensacola, Florida, beginning in 1995, but with a more Pentecostal flavor and theology attached to it. Many were comparing it to the Azusa Street beginnings of Pentecostalism.

In the early 21st century, the Lakeland Outpouring (as it became known) showcased a combination of televangelist extremes (heavy emphasis on money, claims of healing and people raised from the dead which later were revealed to be false), Latter Rain teachings, and more of the bizarre physical manifestations seen in the Toronto Blessing era. Leaders of the *New Apostolic Reformation* (a Latter Rain group), led by self-described "Presiding Apostle" C. Peter Wagner, anointed and blessed Todd Bentley to lead the Lakeland Outpouring in an elaborate service. Within a few days, they quickly distanced themselves from

Bentley as his moral failings were revealed and Bentley stepped down for a season.

The 'spiritual mapping' emphasis found its strength as the charismatic and Third Wave movements developed a stronger emphasis on world missions in the 1990s (the Pentecostals had been heavily involved in missions for many years already).

Toxic practices (spiritual abuse) are always rooted in toxic beliefs (false or misused teaching).

Spiritual mapping proponents sought to integrate their understanding of spiritual warfare and deliverance ministry into their missiology. The basic premise was that until territorial spirits were exposed and removed through what was called 'strategic level spiritual warfare', evangelism would be hampered.

Once these territorial spirits had been dealt with, the gospel would be received on a much wider scale. Predictably, this became another source of controversy, both inside the charismatic movement and out.

Dennis Bennett expressed his uneasiness with the Third Wave because it "denies that there is any experience of a baptism in the Holy Spirit following salvation, but that it all happens when we accept Jesus. It maintains that it is not necessary to speak in tongues in order to be baptized in the Spirit... This is mainly and usually because people have not themselves received the baptism in the Holy Spirit, and therefore sympathetic and well-meaning brothers and sisters are commenting on something they have not entered into."[27]

The suggestion that these recently Spirit-filled evangelicals are creating theology to explain their *lack* of experience was not embraced. Third Wave believers would describe themselves as "continuationists" (all spiritual gifts are still available today), but do not adhere to the tongues-as-initial-evidence theology of Pentecostals and many Charismatics.

The arc of the work of the Spirit in North America in the twentieth century began with the creation of a new wing in the church: the Pentecostals, who either chose or were forced to form their own denominational alliances. Later, the mainline denominations were touched by a similar move of the Spirit. And finally, conservative evangelicals (including many former cessationists) found their theological worldview expanding to include all the gifts of the Spirit.

ON THE EDGE

It may seem incredible, after all the evidence of the Holy Spirit moving with power in the previous century, that people are leaving and in some cases *fleeing* Pentecostal, Charismatic, and Third Wave churches in growing numbers. And yet, such an exodus has been underway for some time now, and if anything, is increasing.

Sometimes, if they had a previous affiliation with a non-charismatic church, they simply returned there and chalked up the whole experience as a sincere but misguided learning curve. Others find a meaningful connection to a more liturgical church system, while privately believing in and perhaps exercising charismatic gifts.

It grieves me to say that many of the younger generation simply gave up on their faith completely. They found the effort to discern the chaff from the wheat simply too overwhelming, often compounded by words of judgment and condemnation from leaders, family, and friends.

The bathwater simply became too toxic.

"Ideas have consequences," wrote Richard Weaver. As Christians, our beliefs influence our actions, whether we realize it or not. Toxic practices (spiritual abuse) are always rooted in toxic beliefs (false or misused teaching). Many people protest that they aren't interested in "doing theology". What they don't realize is that our thoughts and beliefs about God and how He works *are* theology.

Including bad or toxic theology.

My intent is to neither discredit nor applaud the charismatic movement. My goal is that we sift through some of the teachings (and resulting practices) and emerge on the other side with an approach to life that is Biblically-sound, Spirit-empowered, and without the unnecessary and damaging baggage of 'charismania'.

CHAPTER NOTES

1. Grady, J. Lee – *What Happened to the Fire?*, page 15

2. Gonzalez, Justo – *A History of Christian Thought Volume 3: From the Protestant Reformation to the Twentieth Century*, page 313

3. Christianity Today – *The Cleansing Wave*, page 3

4. Synan, Vinson – *The Origins of the Pentecostal Movement*, page 2

5. Christianity Today – *The Cleansing Wave*, page 3

6. Synan, Vinson – *The Origins of the Pentecostal Movement*, page 3

7. Storms, Sam – *Post-Reformation and Contemporary Developments in the Pentecostal and Charismatic Movements*, page 2

8. Christianity Today – *The Cleansing Wave*, page 4

9. Storms, Sam – *Post-Reformation and Contemporary Developments in the Pentecostal Movements*, page 4

10. Ibid., page 4

11. *The New International Dictionary of Pentecostal and Charismatic Movements*, page 727

12. Storms, Sam – *Post-Reformation and Contemporary Developments in the Pentecostal and Charismatic Movements*, page 5

13. Ibid., page 6

14. Ibid., page 6

15. *The New International Dictionary of Pentecostal and Charismatic Movements (Revised and Expanded Edition)* – page 787

16. Ibid., page 787

17. Ibid., page 479

18. Synan, Vinson – *The Origins of the Pentecostal Movement*, page 8

19. Bennett, Dennis – *God's Strength for this Generation*, page 2

20. Storms, Sam – *Post-Reformation and Contemporary Developments in the Pentecostal and Charismatic Movements*, page 10

21. Synan, Vinson – *The Origins of the Pentecostal Movement*, page 8

22. *The New International Dictionary of Pentecostal and Charismatic Movements (Revised and Expanded Edition)*, page 1141

23. Synan, Vinson – *The Origins of the Pentecostal Movement*, page 8

24. Storms, Sam – *Post-Reformation and Contemporary Developments in the Pentecostal and Charismatic Movements*, page 12

25. Jackson, Bill – *The Quest for the Radical Middle: A History of the Vineyard*, Vineyard International Publishing, 1999, (introduction)

26. Wimber, John – Leadership, 1995 Vineyard Pastors Conference, DVD #1, beginning at 15:39, www.vineyardresources.com

27. Bennett, Dennis – *God's Strength for this Generation*, page 8

Chapter Three
THE LATTER RAIN MOVEMENT

The evening session of the youth conference began normally. The band had led 1,500 conference attendees in worship for about 45 minutes, followed by a brief video presentation on the plight of Third World children. The money given in the subsequent offering was to go to these Third World children through the host church's missionaries.

We were really glad to be at this annual conference once again. It was a great opportunity, as youth leaders, to *not* be responsible for running an event for a change. We could simply enjoy building relationships and receiving ministry alongside the rest of our group. A side benefit was reconnecting with other youth leaders/ groups, and hearing their stories of God's faithfulness to them over the past year.

When the guest speaker for the conference began his sermon, we all settled down to listen. He was warm and witty in his introductory comments, sharing personal anecdotes as he developed a rapport with the audience. Several of our group had their notebooks out – they took notes on everything, and their journals were an intriguing combination of sermon notes, poetry, doodles, and written prayers. They were ready, pens in hand, to scribble down thoughts and insights from the speaker.

Then, almost as if an electrical switch had been thrown, something changed. The speaker's tone of voice, his facial expression, and his body language all morphed to something new. Gone was the relaxed, light-hearted, low-key sharing; the speaker's stance became more combative, his lower jaw jutted out, and his voice became strident and angry as he began to pace about the platform.

He was calling out the 'chosen generation' of youth who would "take the land that the previous generation failed to enter". We listened, somewhat taken aback, to a lengthy diatribe describing anyone over the age of 26 as a complete failure in the eyes of the God. The Lord's displeasure, it seemed, had something to do with their failure, through unbelief and lack of holiness, to 'take the land'.

After denouncing the older generation (meaning: myself, the worship team, and the leadership team of the host church), he launched into a rant about the lack of holiness in the lives of the youth. Apparently, Jesus Christ *really wanted* to come back, but He wasn't able to, because the youth were living compromised lives of worldliness. "You are *holding back* the Second Coming of Jesus", he yelled, shaking an accusatory finger at the audience. "If you would only get serious about holiness, then God will finally be able to use you, Jesus will see His will being done on earth, and you'll be worthy to take the land that the previous generation failed to."

We sat stunned on the floor; the pens that were poised for taking notes had frozen in mid-air or been put away. In the passionate, highly charged delivery of this message, something disturbing was taking place. I listened carefully, trying to discern what it was.

1. Holiness – well, like any student of the Word of God and disciple of Jesus, I was all for holy living.

2. The emerging generation stepping into what God was doing – hey, I was a youth pastor; my whole focus was on seeing youth giving their lives totally to Jesus.

3. And seriously, who *wouldn't* want to see the next generation even more passionate about Jesus than the current one?

Still, something just didn't sit right with the content of this speaker's message (his manipulative methodology is a whole 'nuther topic).

While none of us recognized it at the time, the entire conference was being introduced to classic Latter Rain teachings.

THE LATTER RAIN MOVEMENT

In the history of the Pentecostal, Charismatic and Third Wave movements, the *New Order of the Latter Rain* would normally be a small footnote. While it lasted as long as the Azusa Street revival of 1906 (three years), it was situated in a tiny, remote town in the northern prairies of Canada. However, as many made the pilgrimage to this small center, the influence of the Latter Rain has proven to be more far-reaching than its early beginnings would have otherwise indicated.

Many popular catch phrases that are still heard around charismatic circles had their origins in the Latter Rain movement. Most people are unaware of the doctrinal and practical baggage that is associated with these phrases. For example:

* As in the natural, so in the spiritual. Or, the natural speaks of the supernatural

* Joel's Army, Man-child Company, Overcomers, and more recently, Forerunners

* God offends the mind to reveal the heart

- The Joshua and Caleb Generation (they will possess the land that the previous generation failed to)

On the surface, these phrases appear reasonably benign. And to those who don't embrace the theological and eschatological package behind them, these phrases simply sound like the jargon that every group develops over time. Not everyone who uses these phrases is automatically Latter Rain in their theology (but you should probably double-check).

The Latter Rain movement occupied a brief time span (1947-49), originating in the Canadian Prairie province of Saskatchewan, in the town of North Battleford. Pilgrims from all over the world made the trip to North Battleford to observe and participate in the outpouring of the Spirit there, just as occurred during the Azusa Street revival in 1906, the Toronto Blessing in 1994, and most recently, Lakeland.

From all accounts, it was a genuine move of the Holy Spirit during those years. The infamy associated with the term 'Latter Rain' came later, as numerous troubling teachings emerged, which ranged from questionable to outright heretical.

Considering how brief the actual revival was, it is fascinating to observe how some of its more controversial teachings have survived and continue to spread decades later.

The uncanny persistence of Latter Rain teachings, long after the movement ended "officially", suggests that we invest some extra time examining the roots of the teachings more fully.

Two of the most prominent names associated with the Latter Rain movement are William Branham and George Warnock. While neither was present at the beginning of the revival in North Battleford, both of these men became linked to and were often identified as the main voices of the movement.

William Branham is usually known for his connection to the "healing evangelists" of the 1950s (for example, Oral Roberts and Paul Cain), and had already begun his itinerant ministry before the Latter Rain began. As word spread of an outpouring of the Spirit in North Battleford, Branham made a trip to be a part of it, and spread the word in his widespread ministry.

Branham's theology overlapped but was not typical of the entire Latter Rain movement. His "Jesus only" teaching didn't fit with the majority of the Latter Rain, which believed in the Trinity. One of Branham's most serious doctrinal departures, the "Serpent Seed" *(more later)*, was also not widely accepted in the Latter Rain. In a surprising contrast to the Wesleyan theology of the various Pentecostal denominations, many of the Latter Rain leaders were Reformed in their doctrine.

Many people who have been influenced by the Latter Rain would be shocked to learn the whole picture.

George Warnock became widely regarded as one of the chief writers in the Latter Rain movement. His most influential work, *The Feast of Tabernacles* – considered to be the "manual" of the Latter Rain – was published shortly after the Latter Rain revival ended its three-year heyday. Warnock was more directly involved long-term with the Latter Rain, while Branham continued his itinerant ministry, mostly in the United States, until his untimely death in an automobile accident.

The intersection of Warnock's and Branham's teachings was (1) their anti-denominational viewpoint, (2) their teaching on the "Seven Church Ages", and (3) the most controversial doctrine to arise from the Latter Rain movement, the "Manifested Sons of God".

TIMELINE

Key figures in the original outpouring at North Battleford included George and Ern Hawtin, P.G. Hunt, Herrick Holt and Milford Kirkpatrick. The common ground this group of friends and co-workers shared was a small school that they had started in North Battleford to train missionaries.

Originally, George Hawtin had begun *Bethel Bible Institute* in nearby Star City, but moved to Saskatoon in 1937 to affiliate the school with the Pentecostal Assemblies of Canada (PAOC). This process was finalized in 1945, ten years after the school's beginning.

However, "disputes between Hawtin and PAOC officials led to Hawtin's resignation under pressure in 1947; another Bethel teacher, P.G. Hunt, resigned in sympathy."[1] Together with Holt, Kirkpatrick, and Hawtin's brother Ern, they began a new work called *Sharon Orphanage and Schools* just down the road, in North Battleford.

"The Latter Rain Movement emerged at Sharon Orphanage and Schools in North Battleford, Saskatchewan, Canada, when about 70 students had gathered to fast, pray, and study the Word of God in November of 1947."[2]

As described by Ern Hawtin, "some students were under the power of God on the floor, others were kneeling in adoration and worship before the Lord... Soon a visible manifestation of gifts was received when candidates were prayed over, and many as a result began to be healed, as gifts of healing were released."[3]

As word of this outpouring began to spread, eager Christians began to flock to North Battleford. Many people favorably compared the early days of the Latter Rain to the events in Los Angeles 40 years earlier. This was significant for many Pentecostals, as "the movement was characterized by many reports of healings and other miraculous phenomena, in contrast to the preceding decade, which was described by Pentecostals as a time of spiritual dryness and lack of God's presence."[4]

"Thousands from both Canada and the U.S. attended the Sharon Camp Meeting in North Battleford on July 7-18, 1948, while reports of healings and the power of God were plentiful."[5] Invitations to speak came in from as far as Vancouver, and visitors from other cities who were impacted by the meetings carried the message and power back to their home churches. As time went on, new leaders emerged who became more identified with the Latter Rain movement than the original five leaders in North Battleford.

It is worth noting again that there were reports of genuine healings, and the attitudes of the participants were reportedly characterized by humility and a sense of 'brokenness' – noteworthy and positive attitudes. On the other hand, Stanley Frodsham wrote about his disgust that people were equating "this new revival which God is so graciously sending, where so many souls are being saved, where so many lives are being transformed, where God is so graciously restoring the gifts of the Spirit, with the fanatical movement of the past 40 years."[6] *(Referring rather uncharitably to the Pentecostals who had come before them, and exhibiting some of the elitist attitude that the Latter Rain became known for.)*

Controversy was not far behind, however, as numerous teachings and practices became associated with the Latter Rain. These controversial teachings led to the movement's eventual denunciation by the Assemblies of God, the Pentecostal Assemblies of Canada and other Pentecostal denominations in 1949.

As articulated by Bill Jackson in *Quest for the Radical Middle: A History of the Vineyard*, these biblically questionable teachings and practices included:

- **"Restorationism** – they argued that God had been progressively 'restoring' to the church NT truths that had been lost for centuries...

- **"Five-fold ministry** – the emergence of the five-fold ministry of Eph. 4:11, in particular the offices of apostle and prophet

- **"Laying on of hands**... for the purpose of imparting spiritual gifts was an important part of their practice

- **"Prophecy** – the prophetic gift was strongly emphasized, but often abused when employed to give directional (controlling) guidance to people

- **"Recovery of True Worship** – the restoration of David's Tabernacle as a model for true worship was stressed

- **"Immortalization of the Saints** – some in the movement taught that those who fully embraced the restoration would be blessed with immortality before the second coming of Christ. Although only a small minority taught this view, the entire movement soon became identified with it in the minds of its critics

- **"Unity of the church** – the church will attain an unprecedented unity in the faith before the return of Christ

- **"The Manifested Sons of God** – some associated with the movement embraced the idea that the church on earth is the ongoing incarnation of Jesus Himself..."[7]

After the decision in 1949 to reject the Latter Rain, you would expect that the movement would fade into obscurity, but this was not the case. Many churches left their respective denominations to align with Latter Rain leaders.

As time went on, the preaching of William Branham and the writings of George Warnock took on an increasingly come-outer paradigm, with Branham repeatedly telling audiences that all denominations were satanic in origin, and only those who accepted his teachings were the true Church.

The charismatic renewal of the 1960s and 70s saw elements of Latter Rain teachings resurface, and the Third Wave experienced similar inroads through the "Kansas City Prophets" in the early 1990s.

The recurring nature of some of the more controversial teachings, as taught by Branham and built upon by Warnock, require further investigation in order to understand how they are contributing to today's post-charismatic exodus.

Another key figure in the Latter Rain was Franklin Hall, whose book *Atomic Power with God through Prayer and Fasting* highlighted the practice of fasting and prayer as a key to spiritual power.

Like Branham, Hall was fascinated by the zodiac, and also spoke of the need for the "Manifesting of the Sons of God". His book on fasting and prayer also contains many ideas similar to the later Word of Faith (Health and Wealth) teachings, and so we shall look at Franklin Hall's influence in that section rather than this.

At the same time, we should make a cautionary note that many of those accused of holding Latter Rain doctrines in the present, actually fall into two categories: (1) those who knowingly have embraced and are promoting these teachings, and (2) those who have absorbed elements of the teachings (and jargon) but not the entire package.

Differentiating between the two is very important, so that genuine teachers and leaders are not arbitrarily denounced as false teachers. Indeed, many people who have been influenced by lingering Latter Rain doctrine would be shocked if they were to learn the whole picture of Latter Rain teaching.

Either way, it is important to again note the widespread influence of the Latter Rain's key figures in other controversies and movements.

WILLIAM BRANHAM

William M. Branham (1909-1965) was born in the hills of Kentucky, grew up in poverty and never received much in the way of formal education. His plainspoken Southern demeanor was engaging, and his commitment to personal holiness and a simple life-style was unquestioned. His "come-outer" message also connected powerfully with a generation of believers who were disillusioned with large, but seemingly compromised and lifeless churches and denominations.

Branham claimed to have had numerous angelic visitations since he was three years old, and also spoke of an angel that accompanied him onstage at his meetings, even instructing him on what to preach. Branham believed that the zodiac and the pyramids were part of God's revelation, in addition to the Bible. After his untimely death in 1965, his tombstone was constructed in the shape of a pyramid, with the names of the angelic Messengers of the Church Ages engraved on it. Branham's name appears on the pyramid's apex, as the angelic Messenger of Revelation 3:14 to the last Church Age *(more on this later)*.

Branham's teaching is not synonymous with Latter Rain in every detail, although much of Warnock's writing builds upon some of the foundations laid by Branham. And to be fair, some of the most damning quotes used to demonize Branham are taken out of context and trumpeted as 'proof' of his status as a false prophet.

Branham's followers (called 'Branhamites') have painstakingly transcribed his many sermons into text documents, which are readily available on the Internet. Today's Branhamites listen to his sermons and exegete them in the same way which Evangelicals exegete the Bible.

There were many reports of Branham's extraordinary prophetic gifts and the healings that happened in his meetings. While I cannot comment on what actually happened in his crusades, from reading his many sermons, I can appreciate that Branham:

- Had a profound commitment to personal holiness

- Was humble and self-effacing; he told his congregation that they shouldn't have named the church *Branham Tabernacle*, because he didn't want the glory for the ministry to go to anyone but Jesus

- Pointed out repeatedly that membership in a church did not equate salvation

- Had little time for the pomp and prestige of rich churches

- In a time when the civil rights movement was barely getting underway, Branham was very vocal about the equality of all races before God (although at the same time, he was against interracial marriage)

- Sought deeply to stay true to the things in the Bible that he had become convinced of; while we will not agree with many of his interpretations, he was a good example of standing firm even when it costs you friends and reputation

An example of an *inappropriate* use of a quote from Branham, which is used by many heresy-hunters as proof of false prophecy, is Branham's prediction of the End Times beginning in 1977. Obviously, the whole church did not go into apostasy at that time, as Branham predicted, which seems to lend credence to the arguments of the heresy hunters. However, to be fair, the quote needs a closer look.

Branham says: "Now, remember, 'predict', especially you listening at the tape. I don't say it will be, but predict that it will end by 1977, that the church will go completely into apostasy, and she'll be ousted out of the mouth of God."[8]

"You show me one place where one person was baptized in the name of the Father, Son, Holy Ghost, I'll raise my hands and say I'm a false prophet."

- William Branham

Yes, Branham used the word *predict,* but he also pointedly reminded the congregation "I don't say it *will* be, but predict..." It sounds as if Branham doesn't use "predict" in the same way we would – remember, he was an uneducated man who often used something less than the Queen's English. Perhaps he was contrasting "will be" (a certainty) with "predict" (a possibility). It is a quick and easy cheap shot to denounce him as a false prophet based on his use of the word *predict*, but not necessarily fair or accurate.

Do not assume that I'm defending Branham or the doctrines that he taught. Many of the teachings we will examine now are very disturbing to me. But we need to rise to a higher standard than misrepresenting people in order to discredit them with the label *false prophet/teacher*.

TEACHINGS PECULIAR TO BRANHAM

As mentioned earlier, not all of Branham's teachings reflect the mainstream of the Latter Rain. For example, Branham's insistence on the gift of tongues – which is not surprising in charismatic circles generally – was 'defended' in some very imaginative ways:

"Jesus died, speaking in tongues. They said He spoke, and He spoke in another language. Sure, He did. 'He spoke in Hebrew.' He did not. That's not Hebrew writing. He spoke in a heavenly language.[9]

"(St. Columba) would have nothing less... with speaking in tongues, the baptism in the Name of the Lord Jesus, carrying out the very things they started.[10]

"Each one of them that come out, come out with a Pentecostal blessing. That's exactly right. Even Martin Luther spoke in tongues.[11]

"Virgin Mary, being the mother of Jesus Christ... was among them hundred and twenty, had the baptism of the Holy Ghost, speaking in tongues and acting like a drunk woman out there, under the Spirit of God. And if the Virgin Mary had to do that in order to get into glory, how are you going to get in it anything less than that?"[12]

Branham was adamantly Jesus-Only in his theology, and insisted on re-baptizing any converts to his way of teaching. In his later years, this teaching became more and more a central part of his sermons – no matter what his subject matter, somehow his denunciation of the Trinitarian baptismal formula would come up.

"Tell him his baptism in Father, Son, and Holy Ghost is of the Devil and of the Catholic Church, watch what happens to him.[13]

"Now, what name did they use after they quit using Jesus' Name? Father, Son, Holy Ghost. And there ain't no such a thing. It's a dead theology.[14]

"You show me one place where one person was baptized in the name of the Father, Son, Holy Ghost, I'll raise my hands and say I'm a false prophet... Paul commanded them to be baptized over... And they had to do it before they received the Holy Ghost.[15]

"So, if we are teaching baptism in the name of Father, Son, and Holy Ghost, it's false prophecy."[16]

Branham also repeatedly denounced women with "bobbed *(short)* hair", who wore shorts or pants (since these were men's clothes) and used make-up. While this is not an uncommon viewpoint even today in some conservative churches, Branham's strident denunciations, coupled with his equally strong denunciation of the Roman Catholic Church as the whore of Babylon, are very extreme in their delivery.

"Now, remember, this is on tape too. A powerful woman, great woman, she'll either be President, or it'll be a woman representing the Catholic church (which I think it is) will take over here someday and she'll rule this country. This nation is a woman's nation. Flag was made by a woman, it's thirteen. She started out, thirteen stars, thirteen stripes, thirteen colonies. Everything's thirteen, thirteen, thirteen, right on down. Thirteen stars on her silver dollar now. Everything's thirteen. It's number thirteen, and appears in the 13th chapter of Revelations: completely thirteen. Everything is 'woman, woman, woman, woman, woman', right on down. She's took over Hollywood. She's took over the nation. She's took over the offices. She's took over everything there is; equal rights with the man, votes with the man, cusses like a man, drinks like man, anything else. And the... just bait for the Catholic Church, for the worship of a woman."[17]

"Also has been an evil thing done in this country; they have permitted women to vote. This is a woman's nation, and she will pollute this nation as Eve did Eden."[18]

"And by voting, they'll elect the wrong man some of these days. And you did at the last election. It was the woman's votes that elected Kennedy."[19]

"...by the woman's vote, the wrong man (Kennedy), which will finally be to full control of the Catholic Church in the United States; then the bomb comes that explodes her."[20]

Branham's low opinion of women may have been connected to his most controversial teaching: the "Serpent Seed". Branham taught that the Fall in Genesis 3 had nothing to do with Adam and Eve eating the fruit from the Tree of the Knowledge of Good and Evil. Instead, Branham insisted that 'original sin' was Eve having sex with Satan (!).

Based on this, Branham taught that there are two spiritual lineages at work in the world: God's and Satan's. God's descendants came through Seth (including King David and Jesus), and Satan's descendants came through Cain's lineage (including Judas Iscariot and the Anti-Christ).

"Now, here I've never had a preacher to agree with this yet... You know eating an apple, that wasn't what they did, made them realize they were naked. Certainly it wasn't. It had to come through sexually. It had to be, 'cause they realized they were naked when they taken this forbidden fruit. Ain't a woman a fruit tree? Aren't you the fruit of your mother? That was the fruit that was forbidden to be taken."[21]

"I believe, and can support it by the Bible, that it is the serpent that did it. The serpent is that missing person (link) between the chimpanzee and the man... he was the smartest thing there was, and the more like the human being than anything else that was on the field; closest to a human being. He was not a reptile."[22]

"He [the serpent] begin making love to Eve. And he lived with her as a husband. And she saw it was pleasant, so she went and told her husband; but she was already pregnant by Satan. And she brought forth her first son, whose name was Cain, the son of Satan."[23]

"She said, 'the Serpent beguiled me'. Do you know what 'beguile' means? Means 'defiled'. The devil never gave her an apple."[24] (Actual definition of 'beguile' at Dictionary.com: *to influence by trickery, flattery, etc.; mislead; delude.*)

While not all charismatics are anti-intellectual, the tendency is strong in many places.

"And then when Cain saw his holy-roller brother had been accepted before God, and signs and wonders was being taken place down there, he got jealous of him... He killed his brother. He was a murderer. Could you call God a murderer? Adam was God's son, and that jealousy and envy and everything could not come out of that pure stream. It had to come through another place. And it came through Satan, who was a murderer to begin with."[25]

"They *[Cain's descendants]* were smart, educated, intelligent people. Is that right? They were builders, inventors, scientists: Not through the seed of the righteous, but through the seed of Satan, the serpent... And they were scoffers at the seed of the woman: Noah, the righteous."[26]

"What was the seed of the serpent? Adultery. You follow it? Adultery with Eve."[27]

"Esau never harmed nobody, and Esau was of the devil. But Jacob, out of the same womb, was of God: the seed of the devil, the seed of the woman."[28]

"The serpent was twice as smart. His seed has always been twice as smart... Your pastor that gone down and got a lot of intellectual knowledge, and he stands up... Where does the seed of the serpent staying at? In the smart intelligent places like that: smart, shrewd scholars, that's where he is at."[29]

BRANHAM'S INFLUENCE ON THE LATTER RAIN

While Branham's Serpent Seed teaching was not widely accepted, some of his venomous attacks on the Roman Catholic Church were. Even to this day, you will encounter charismatics who revile Catholics on principle. And Branham's disdain for pastors and church leaders with religious education has too often been gladly perpetuated by charismatics everywhere. While not all charismatics are anti-intellectual, the tendency is strong in many places.

Branham was even more extreme in his diatribes against denominations. Many people today are questioning denominational structures, but Branham's teaching goes quite a bit further:

"They (Methodists) organized it, made an organization out of it, and God said, 'I hate the thing'...[30]

"Look what Billy Graham's had across the country. Oh, sure, a big regime, hired evangelists, paid song leaders.[31]

"Denominations was never ordained of God. It was ordained of the devil. And proved it by the Bible."
- William Branham

"As soon as a church goes into a denomination, it's dead. It never rises again... Martin Luther was all right, but when he organized, what did he do? Methodist was all right, when he organized, what did he do? Pentecost was all right, but when you organized it, what did you do? You hybrid it and bred it into the Nicolaitane Catholic church. Exactly what you done. Took up her form of baptism, took up her ways and actions, and the Bible said, 'You are a daughter to a whore, a harlot: a daughter of harlot.'[32]

"If any man will hear My voice and open the door... Not 'if any church, if any organization' – No, sir. He don't deal with them; they're dead and gone to begin with. He hates it. He always hated it. He said He hated it. He hates it yet tonight... the messengers to the church and the message to every church age condemned denominationism.[33]

"And there is never one time that God ever organized His church. The mother of organized churches is the Roman Catholic hierarchy... And as soon as the revival breaks in any Protestant group, they go right back and do the same thing. And the Bible said she was a whore.[34]

"We do not believe in denominations, because we find it in the Bible that denominations was never ordained of God. It was ordained of the devil. And proved it by the Bible."[35]

Branham's diatribes against denominationalism were second only to his attacks on Trinitarian baptism. When he came to one of his favorite topics – the Seven Church Ages – the themes of anti-Catholicism, baptism in the name of Jesus only, and his strong distaste for denominations came up in every sermon, almost in cyclical fashion.

Branham's teaching on the Seven Church Ages forms the backdrop against which George Warnock developed and wrote his most influential work, *The Feast of Tabernacles*, considered the manual or textbook on the Latter Rain's most well-known aberrant teaching, the "Manifested Sons of God" (MSOG). Branham refers to the MSOG teaching at various times, but it was Warnock who more fully developed it.

Branham based his Seven Church Ages teaching on the letters to the seven churches in Revelation 1-3. He taught that each church represented a different church age, and that the angel of each church was an anointed apostolic messenger to that church age. Each angelic (apostolic) messenger had been given a unique message from God for that church age, which must be obeyed.

Branham divided the Seven Church Ages as follows:

1. 53-70 AD – Ephesus; messenger was St. Paul; this was a relatively short 'church age' due to the church's unbelief

2. 70-312 AD – Smyrna; messenger was Irenaeus, who believed God more than anyone else

3. 312-606 AD – Pergamos; messenger was Martin, while the Babylonian religion infiltrated the church through the Council of Nicea (?!)

4. 606-1520 AD – Thyatira; messenger was Columba, while the church blasphemed the name of God through the papacy

5. 1520-1750 AD – Sardis; messenger was Martin Luther, who spoke in tongues and restored the truth of justification by faith to the church

6. 1750-1906 AD – Philadelphia; messenger was John Wesley, who restored the truth of entire sanctification and brotherly love

7. 1906 AD to date – Laodicea; messenger is William Branham, who comes as a latter day Elijah to turn the hearts of the children (church) back to the (Pentecostal) fathers

During his sermon on the Church Age of Pergamos, Branham shared a vision he'd had that placed him in the role of the seventh and final angelic messenger to the Laodicean Church Age:

"(The angel) said, 'You can't see Him now,' but said, 'soon He will come. We're waiting for Him. But when He comes, He will come to you first. And you'll be judged according to the Gospel you preaching, and we will be your subjects...'

"I said, 'What about Saint Paul?'

"Said, 'He'll be responsible for his age.'

"'Well,' I said, 'I preached the same Gospel he did.'

"And millions of voices raised, said 'We are resting upon that.' See? There you are, 'resting'.

"So the angel of God, the messenger to the church is responsible if he preaches not the Word."[36]

Part of Branham's theology regarding the Laodicean Church Age includes the MSOG teaching. These Sons would be revealed during this last church age. To introduce this doctrine, Branham taught his "three Bibles" view:

"As I've often made this remark and said God made three Bibles. The first one, He put it in the sky, the zodiac... He made the next one in the pyramid, back in the days of Enoch, when they made the pyramids... And the stone on the capstone never was found... Why? The Capstone was rejected; Christ, the Headstone (see?) was rejected... Now, and in the Bible, we're living in the last days, the top of the pyramid, the crossed fishes of the cancer age in the zodiac, in the time of the coming of Leo the lion, in the capping Stone, and in the days of the manifestation of the sons of God in the Bible. See?"[37]

In describing these Sons of God, Branham says:

"You give me this spotless church tonight, this group of people, perfectly, perfectly in the promise of God with the Holy Ghost, walking in the Spirit, I'll challenge any disease, or any affliction... and all of the unbelievers that there is, to bring any sickness of affliction in this door, and they'll walk out perfectly whole. Yes, sir. God gave the promise; only sin of unbelief can keep it away."[38]

Before we hand the baton to George Warnock to develop the MSOG teaching more fully, we should note that Branham had an interesting way of dealing with the critics of his teachings, particularly those who opposed his Serpent Seed and MSOG theories.

Most Pentecostals and charismatics do not believe that spiritual gifts are given by God to validate our theology. The charismatic gifts – *charismata* means 'grace gifts' or literally 'grace-lets' – are given solely based on God's grace towards us, not as rewards for spiritual maturity or to validate the messenger, only the Message.

Branham, however, takes the opposite approach:

"A lot of them say... 'I believe Brother Branham's a prophet, but let me tell you something. As long as the Spirit is on him, and he's discerning, he's the Lord's servant. But his teaching is rotten. It's no good.' Whoever heard of such tommyrot? It's either of God or it isn't of God. That's right. It's either all God or none God. That's the way it is."[39]

Branham's normal humility seems to have vanished in this statement. It's interesting to note that this same attitude of unaccountability will also be seen later in some of the abusive teachings of the Shepherding movement.

Branham's teachings have influenced the Word of Faith movement, the Shepherding movement, and the current revivalist movement. For an uneducated preacher, his influence has been far-reaching indeed.

GEORGE WARNOCK

George Warnock wrote many articles and books, several of which are considered classics for those in the Latter Rain movement. His most influential work was and is *The Feast of Tabernacles*, which outlined his most controversial teaching: "The Manifested Sons of God" (MSOG). A second influential book, *From Tent to Temple*, introduced the "Restoration of the Tabernacle of David"; another teaching that has survived to this day through the charismatic movement.

THE FEAST OF TABERNACLES

George Warnock wrote *The Feast of Tabernacles* in 1951, although the copy I was able to read includes a new foreword from Warnock dated 1980. He builds upon the same foundations that Branham taught regarding the Seven Church Ages, believing that we are in the Laodicean Age.

Warnock was much more eloquent than Branham, and also much more logical in his presentation on the MSOG. Like Branham, Warnock was strongly dismissive of denominations and higher theological education:

"When Jesus declared so emphatically 'I am the Truth', He there and then completely demolished the idea that Truth has anything in common with creeds and doctrines and theories about God and spiritual things... *[Truth]* will find little acceptance at the hands of the learned or the ecclesiastical."[40]

At the same time, Warnock invests a great deal of time and energy in the early part of his book in setting a historical and biblical background for his teaching on the MSOG, in order to validate his teachings as being well-reasoned and biblically logical.

Warnock's basis for the MSOG doctrine is the Feast of Tabernacles in the Old Testament, although his hermeneutical approach was almost completely allegorical, as we shall see. "The thesis of Warnock's book was that although the Feast of Passover was fulfilled in the death of Christ and although the Feast of Pentecost had had its fulfillment in the outpouring of the Holy Spirit on the Day of Pentecost, the third of Israel's great feasts, the Feast of Tabernacles, is yet to be fulfilled."[41] Warnock claimed that his insights into the fulfillment of this Feast came through direct prophetic revelations.

It is through Warnock that the phrase "the natural speaks of the supernatural" was first introduced, as it formed part of his rationale for using Old Testament feast typology to explain the meaning of Tabernacles. "It is important, therefore, that we should always observe that which is first, and natural, and from the natural learn to discern in what way it typifies the spiritual."[42]

> **"Truth will find little acceptance at the hands of the learned or the ecclesiastical."**
> - George Warnock

Warnock also claimed that applying Old Testament scriptures in unorthodox ways to justify his teachings was just following the example of the New Testament apostles.

"Then we care not in the least if orthodox theology forbids us to take Old Testament type and prophecy and apply them to the Church. The Apostles have already done so under the anointing of the Holy Spirit, and that is sufficient for men who believe in the verbal inspiration of the Holy Scriptures."[43]

"And if you want to know what Paul meant by 'rightly dividing the Word of truth', all one has to do is to examine his own epistles and see how he applied the Old Testament. Over and over and over again he takes an Old Testament scripture completely out of its 'context' as men would say, and applies it to some glorious Church truth which he is expounding."[44]

By claiming the 'right' to apply OT scriptures in whatever manner was consistent with his own prophetic insights, Warnock seems to have considered his writings on a par with Scripture. If someone voiced any concerns, Warnock's response is a classic:

"These things may sound fantastic to many Christians; but if so it is only because God's people in this modern age are so earthly-minded that they cannot appreciate nor understand the realities of the Spirit."[45]

Like Branham, Warnock viewed denominations as deceived and carnal, but he blamed this on lack of unity between denominations and the sin of unbelief. Those who refused to accept his teachings were likened to the children of Israel who refused to enter Canaan and wandered 40 years in the wilderness. Warnock applies this metaphor directly to the Pentecostal movement.

"The early generation of Spirit-filled people at the turn of the century took their journey from the blighting wilderness of denominationalism and encamped at their Kadesh-Barnea on the very doorstep of Canaan – but they too failed to enter in because of unbelief."[46]

As Warnock progresses in his development of the MSOG and the Feast of Tabernacles, this motif of "not possessing the land" (turning away because of unbelief) comes up repeatedly as a warning to embrace the Latter Rain teachings. Warnock also agrees with Branham that God is progressively restoring "lost truths" to the Church.

"And so from Reformation days and until now, God has graciously been restoring lost Truth; and the Reformation is by no means finished yet."[47]

Warnock takes John Wesley's theology of entire sanctification to a completely new level. Wesley prayed for a second work of grace (the baptism of the Holy Spirit) to enable him to live a life free from sin's domination (but still allowing for occasional slips and minor mistakes). In contrast, Warnock taught that *all* sin could be eradicated in this life.

"God is hastening the day and hour of Christian perfection... God will hear that prayer of sincerity and reveal the channel and means by which perfection shall be attained. *But prayer and repentance in themselves are not the means by which the saints are to be perfected.*"[48] (*emphasis added*)

"When we attain to this victory, there will be no need to formulate weak excuses why the victorious Christian can again fall into sin and suffer defeat – for this place in Christ knows no defeat... The promise, therefore, is held out to us at the ends of the ages, *as to no other people in any past dispensation.*"[49] (*emphasis added*)

Warnock also added a second component to entire sanctification: that unlimited spiritual power would be given to the 'overcomers' who turned their backs on dead denominations and embraced what God was doing through the Latter Rain movement.

"What then? Are there no limitations to the measure of power which the saints may appropriate? Yes, indeed, but they are limitations that they themselves erect in unbelief.[50]

"When the power and glory of the Feast of Tabernacles begins to dawn upon the Church, God's people are going to be clothed upon with such power and authority that the very nations themselves will have to bow in submission.[51]

"But those who will reach out and appropriate this new life, and are initiated into this 'secret' of which we have been speaking – theirs shall be the joy and delight of exploring the heavenlies long before they get there."[52]

Warnock emphasized that the need for this band of overcomers was not just for the sake of the denominations left on earth during the Great Tribulation (their punishment for not entering the land with the MSOG). Equally important, if not more, these overcomers were also to usher in the Second Coming of Jesus, who cannot return until the MSOG deal with Satan, the flesh and the denominational Babylon.

"And what is more, Christ is going to remain right where He is: at God's right hand until there shall arise a group of overcomers who shall conquer over all God's enemies... There must arise a group of overcomers who shall conquer and become absolutely victorious over all the opposing forces of the world, the flesh, and the Devil – before this dispensation draws to a close."[53]

"God has placed His only Begotten at His own right hand in the heavenlies, until all his enemies have been placed under His feet... There He shall remain, in obedience to the Word of the Father, until there ariseth a people who shall go in and possess their heritage in the Spirit, and conquer over all opposing forces of World, Flesh, and Devil."[54]

The task of getting the Bride ready for Jesus is an enormous one, according to Warnock, requiring complete unity in the Body of Christ before it can happen. Within our current denominational divisions, there is little hope. But the restoration of the offices of Apostle and Prophet – which had been "lost by" or "stolen from" previous generations due to their unbelief – would provide a divinely appointed governmental structure for this unity to take place.

Of course, this unity would require that people recognize the true Apostles and submit to their authority.

"Will they bring this unity to pass? To doubt it is to doubt God's Word. *It is not a case of rejecting man, because of his faults and failures, but to reject the God-ordained ministry is to reject God who gave him.* Many would much rather prefer to perfect themselves through prayer, fasting, reading the Word, and so forth. These have their place... but in themselves they will not produce this perfection. God has ordained ministries in the Body by which this perfection shall come to pass. To refuse the ministries, then is to say to Christ: 'I don't need your Ascension Gifts. I prefer to be perfected some other way'."[55] *(emphasis added)*

As *The Feast of Tabernacles* moves towards its final chapters, Warnock develops the details of how the MSOG will bring about unity, achieve sinless perfection, and receive immeasurable spiritual power and authority.

Warnock interprets the Revelation 12 passage a little differently from most theologians (but then again, Warnock discounts all theologians who don't recognize his prophetic revelations). Most interpreters see this passage as a description of Jesus being the male offspring who would "rule the nations with an iron rod" (a reference to Psalm 2). But Warnock believes that it refers to a group of Christians in the last days – the Manifested Sons Of God: "For the earnest expectation of the creature waiteth for the manifestation of the sons of God (Romans 8:19 KJV)."

For Warnock, the woman in Revelation 12 refers to the church, which will be enduring the Tribulation. The male son – called the "Man-child" in most Latter Rain circles, but also referred to as "Joel's Army" – is seen as a company of "overcomers", who will achieve sinless perfection, have authority over nations, overthrow Satan and his demonic hordes in the heavens, give comfort to the persecuted church during the Tribulation, and bring about the perfecting of the Bride that Jesus will return for.

"By this time this man-child company, this group of overcomers brought forth by the travail of the Church, is in a place of power and authority in the 'heavenliest', and the church that brought forth the man-child through much pain and spiritual travail, is left in the earth.[56]

"It is this wrestling with the spiritual hosts of wickedness in 'the heavenlies' that shall cause... Satan and his hosts to relinquish their kingdom into the hands of the Sons of God... And then into the very heavenlies shall they ascend, first of all in the Spirit, to take possession of the kingdom left vacant by the casting out of Satan, and his evil hosts. Then shall they be in a position to administer peace and life and blessing to a Church and a world that are in bondage and under oppression.[57]

"But the Dragon, having lost his kingdom, roams through the earth in great wrath, tormenting men, and attempting to persecute the Church which was responsible for bringing forth the overcoming man-child.[58]

"The great tribulation itself is going to be cut short because of the Sons of God... so the Sons of God, through the exercise of their royal priesthood, shall actually shorten the Great Tribulation. Jesus has declared that they would."[59]

The final section of *The Feast of Tabernacles* has to do with the entire body of Christ, out of which the MSOG are only a part – albeit an elite part.

Warnock proposed that since Jesus is considered the Head, and Christians are the body of Christ, then it only stands to reason that we complete Christ, and that without the body, the Head is only half a body (this teaching is sometimes referred to as the "Corporate Christ" doctrine).

"Christ the Head, therefore, is not complete without Christ the Body... And the ages to come are going to reveal, what is now revealed by the Spirit to those whose understandings have been quickened, that Christ is the Body – the whole Body, and not just the Head.[60]

"The Son of Man in heaven is not complete without the fullness of the Son of Man on earth, even the Body."[61]

While most Christians would agree that we are the body of Christ in that we carry out His mission in the world, Warnock takes it one step further, to suggest that we *are* Christ in a very real sense, and not merely in a representational sense. This is seen as a privilege for only a select few to understand and accept, which may mean that they are the potential MSOG.

"But a great secret in God's counsels was this: Christ was to appear twice, first in Incarnation, and secondly at the ends of the ages... Christ's first appearing was in the Head only, in one Man. Hence Elijah appeared in one man, even John the Baptist – for his spirit and power rested upon him. Now Christ will appear in His Church the Body. Hence the Moses-Elijah company, the fullness of Christ in many.[62]

> **When people ridicule these great truths – such ridicule is not against the saints, but it is against God Himself.**
> - George Warnock

"There shall come a day... when every eye shall see Him; when the same Jesus that was taken up into heaven, shall come in like manner as they saw Him go. But first there is the Appearing of Christ in the midst of His people by the Spirit, to establish the Kingdom of God within, and that is the hope of the Church."[63]

In other words, the second coming of Christ will be the perfected church.

Warnock concludes the *The Feast of Tabernacles* with great promises for those who will accept his teachings, warnings to those who oppose or question his teachings, and exhortations to seek to become one of the Manifested Sons. Aside from warnings against denominations and 'worldliness' in general, there is not much provided beyond the tantalizing prospect of being one of these all-powerful overcomers.

Warnock lists the benefits of being a Manifested Son in a long passage, which simultaneously mocks his critics:

- "A realm of the Spirit to such an extent that you live there constantly.

- "The 'mind of Christ' in any degree of fullness so that you can actually think His thoughts, and say His words, and perform His works, and live His very own life.

- "Enjoy real Divine health or Divine life to such an extent that your days will be lengthened excessively, without pain or feebleness or the abatement of your natural faculties.

- "To be so positively free from the sin nature that 'sin hath no more dominion' over you.

- "To go out to the nations speaking their language, with their accent, and understanding exactly what you say, and what they say.

- "Be caught away in the Spirit like Philip or Elijah in this day of modern travel.

- "Ascend up in the Spirit into 'the heavenlies' and literally topple Satan from his throne, and enter into the realm of power and authority 'in the heavenlies in Christ Jesus'."[64]

To those who question or reject Warnock's teachings, he warns: "When the people of God ridicule these great truths concerning the rebuilding of God's holy Temple, and the perfection of the saints into one, vital, united Body – such ridicule is not against the saints, but it is against God Himself."[65] (This tactic/threat continues to be used to silence critics and anyone with legitimate questions in many charismatic churches.)

The teachings of the Latter Rain continue to surface again and again in the charismatic movement. Whether called Kingdom Now, Dominion Theology, Joel's Army, the Man-child Company, the

Joshua and Caleb Generation, or the original Manifested Sons of God, this is a teaching that just will not fade into obscurity.

With words that echo many charismatic conferences today, Warnock sums up his admonitions to the readers of *The Feast of Tabernacles* with a rallying call:

"The whole question resolves itself into this: Are we going to remain in the condition of those who have been saved and baptized with the Holy Spirit? Or are we going to arise from the dusty sands of this great and terrible wilderness and follow our Joshua across the Jordan into real, triumphant, overcoming power in the Spirit of God?

"Thank God there ariseth a new generation that has caught the vision. A few Calebs and Joshuas have survived the blight and the dearth of the wilderness, and are leading the saints in the power of the Spirit into realms of glorious victory."[66]

THE TABERNACLE OF DAVID

Warnock's second influential teaching was the "Tabernacle of David", in his book *From Tent to Temple*. Central to Warnock's teaching, which was very much a part of the Latter Rain in general, was that truly biblical worship needed to follow the pattern of Davidic worship as found in the Tabernacle of David.

The Old Testament passage often used as a scriptural basis is Psalm 22:3: "Yet you are enthroned as the Holy One; you are the praise of Israel." If the wording doesn't sound familiar, it's because that was the NIV rendering.

The preferred rendering – really, the *necessary* rendering in order to use this verse as a foundation for the Tabernacle of David – is from the King James Version: "thou that inhabitest the praises of Israel". This is the foundational verse for 'Davidic worship':

God is seeking a place where His glory can dwell permanently, as it did in the Tabernacle of David.

It should also raise a red flag of discernment when a teaching is dependent on the wording of one translation of Scripture.

It is important to recognize that this phrase is found in the middle of the famous passage, which Jesus quoted from the cross, "my God, my God, why have You forsaken me?". The context of the verse clearly shows that it is not written to give us instructions on how worship should be done in order to experience God's presence. It's a prophetic lament at God's seeming distance from David, and later, Jesus Christ on the cross.

It should also raise a red flag of discernment when a teaching is dependent on the wording of one translation of Scripture.

Warnock also taught that the tabernacle Moses made, as per God's instructions, was replaced in importance by David's tabernacle: "It was a center of worship which stood in sharp contrast to the solemn worship of Moses' tabernacle. Instead of the sacrifices of animals, the sacrifices offered at David's tabernacle were the sacrifices of praise, joy and thanksgiving."[67]

Warnock writes: "We do not know how long the cloud of glory rested on the Tabernacle *[of Moses]*. But we have good reason to believe that it gradually faded away..."[68] (What "good reason"? Warnock is never specific.)

In common Latter Rain manner, the assumption is that the current church (in all of its denominational forms) had grown cold and lifeless, and that in order for God's presence to return, the church must purify itself and make itself ready to be a people worthy of receiving His presence.

"There is a Hannah in the world today. She cries out in the distress of her spirit for a son... a 'manchild'... a people who will come forth in the full image and likeness of Christ out of a dying religious order, and who will be God's oracle to a confused Church..."69

Bill Jackson sums up this expectation by noting, "He (God) is looking for a resting-place and He will one day find it in a people that finally get serious about the things of God."70

Holiness was a key, alongside praise, for the church to become the kind of gathering God would be pleased to inhabit. This emphasis on holiness (and who wouldn't be desirous of seeing more holiness in the church?) often ended up in a restrictive legalism, but in the beginning stages of the Latter Rain, it was a genuine passion for serving God in the hearts of broken and repentant people.

The assumption of the Tabernacle of David teaching is that there was a set pattern of worship that must be followed, or the presence of God would not come and dwell. The pattern included: (1) Levites (worship leaders) who were set apart, highly skilled, and who alone could carry the Ark of God's Presence, (2) joyful praise and celebration, and (3) finances released to pay the Levites for their non-stop 24/7 praise.

While many Tabernacle of David advocates argue that the Davidic worship replaced the sacrifices of the Jewish faith – the 'sacrifice of praise' was seen as the new sacrifice – the Bible does not support this idea. These same advocates suggest that the sacrifices prescribed in the Pentateuch stopped once the ark of God's presence was brought into David's tabernacle – and that any true revival in the Old Testament record included a rejection of the Mosaic system and return to the Davidic.

The wording "sacrifice of praise" is problematic in that most translations render it as "giving thanks". The idea of the sacrifice of praise being a model for New Testament worship only works if you prefer one (English) translation against another. In fact, the "sacrifice of praise" in the Psalms (and Jeremiah) is dependent on the King James Version of the Bible. The phrase appears in the New Testament in Hebrews 13:15, where it is found in the context of confessing Jesus' name, doing good and sharing with others.

Just as he had earlier in the *Feast of Tabernacles*, Warnock warned his critics that they were comparable to Uzzah, whom God struck dead for steadying the Ark of the Covenant when it was in danger of falling off the cart. (2 Samuel 6:3-8)

"The 'new cart' is man's device to keep the move of the Spirit steady – free from error, free from false doctrines – and to keep the ark of His presence and glory from going on the rocks... It is really man's attempt to keep things under control, to keep the revival from falling apart, to keep the doctrines pure, to keep the people from getting scattered, but in the long run it hinders what God is doing, and brings it to a halt."[71]

The true mark of spiritual leadership in the Davidic tabernacle was determined by 'the anointing' of the leader, which Warnock placed at odds with those concerned with doctrine: "For we need no other credentials for ministry in the House of God, apart from the Anointing."[72] Warnock used 'anointing' as his justification of taking Old Testament passages out of context in order to support his teachings, citing the example of the apostle Paul. Warnock's assumption was that under the 'anointing', his words were as authoritative as those of the New Testament writers.

Warnock emphasized the need for the church to recognize the authority of the new apostles and prophets, and submit to them. As in the *Feast of Tabernacles*, Warnock's conclusion is that the Davidic worship – which will provide a place for God to inhabit the praises of his people – will lead to the "corporate Christ" being manifested: "And as we submit to the law of the seed, and the law of the egg, and the law of the cocoon, we shall see – and those about shall see – the living Christ walking once again in the midst of men, in the corporate Body of Christ in the earth."[73]

Warnock's writings, particularly *The Feast of Tabernacles*, have been and continue to be very influential in charismatic circles. The *Tabernacle of David* teaching is part of an approach to Scripture that surfaced repeatedly in the charismatic renewal of the 1960s and 1970s, and continues to inform many expressions of Spirit-filled churches to this day.

We have invested quite a bit of time on the teachings of the Latter Rain. Since they have so deeply influenced the charismatic renewal, the Word of Faith movement, the prophetic movement, International House Of Prayer (IHOP), and provided the foundation for the Shepherding movement and the New Apostolic Reformation, I felt it necessary to invest time investigating the Latter Rain's more controversial teachings.

It is up to all of us, as discerning people, to evaluate what we're being taught. The Berean Christians of Acts 17:11 did two very wise things:

1. *They listened with great eagerness.* This means they were open and teachable, not suspicious and hard-hearted. We would do well to stay teachable, and not confuse discernment with a critical, nit-picking attitude.

2. *They searched the Scriptures, to be sure that what Paul was teaching lined up with Scripture.* They had teachable attitudes, but that didn't mean that they were gullible and naively swallowed whatever they heard. They were willing to consider new ideas, but not to go beyond the boundaries of Scripture.

THE PROPHETIC MOVEMENT

We could discuss many different personalities and ministries at this point. Some would immediately think of Rick Joyner's Morningstar Ministries; others would suggest the Kansas City Prophets (Bob Jones, Paul Cain, John Paul Jackson), and still others may point to International House of Prayer (IHOP) founder Mike Bickle (a pastor who promoted and is associated with the Kansas City Prophets).

But once you start trying to chase down all the recognized prophetic voices today, where do you stop? The list would be both exhaustive and exhausting.

In the prophetic movement, like any movement, there is a range of theological positions on various non-essentials, as well as a range of maturity. Just because someone says in a sermon: "God is raising up the emerging generations" doesn't mean that they are preaching MSOG – although you might want to ask them to clarify what they meant. Ask, don't attack.

The Kansas City Prophets (KCP) were a controversial group who are probably the most well known example of Latter Rain teaching in recent years. To be accurate, the phrase 'Kansas City Prophets' was not a title they gave themselves; it was given by others. But because of their notoriety, and continued influence, we will briefly look at them.

A common prophetic theme of the Kansas City Prophets had to do with the 'nameless and faceless army' that God was going to raise up (often called Joel's Army). This became a staple in prophetic conferences, and was widely repeated through many charismatic churches and denominations.

Bill Jackson notes the irony: "It is interesting that even as the vision was shared that God wasn't going to use superstars any more, the entire Restorationist premise was built on God raising up end-time apostles and prophets."[74]

Another of the repeated prophecies that made the rounds had to do with the 'emerging generations', often referred to as the Joshua and Caleb generation, among other names. The premise was that the previous generation of believers (the Baby Boomers) had failed to enter the land, so God was going to use their children (Generation X) instead. This, of course, is exactly the same idea that the Latter Rain had proposed back in the late 1940s. (The idea continues to this day, but with the "Millenials" as the latest "chosen generation".)

The Kansas City Prophets (Paul Cain, Bob Jones, and John Paul Jackson) as well as Mike Bickle, the pastor of the Kansas City Fellowship, became the center of more controversy in 1990, when Ernie Gruen, another charismatic pastor in Kansas City, published his 233-page report, *Documentation of the Aberrant Practices and Teachings of Kansas City Fellowship (Grace Ministries)*.

The use of prophetic words to establish doctrine was also a troublesome issue during the Latter Rain movement.

In this report, Gruen and his staff documented many of KCF's teachings (from KCF's recorded sermons), and the verdict from Gruen et al. was "heresy from false prophets".

Several Christian leaders were involved trying to sort things out, when John Wimber of the Association of Vineyard Churches stepped in. Wimber offered to bring KCF into the Vineyard family in 1990, and provide some instruction and accountability for the church and the prophets.

POST-CHARISMATIC 2.0

At the time, it was widely reported that Gruen withdrew many of his charges against Bickle and the Kansas City prophets, apologizing and referring to himself as "deceived and a deceiver". Gruen vehemently denied having ever withdrawn his critique, and to his death called the story of his supposed retraction "total lies".

The Vineyard publicly dealt with several issues arising out of KCF's ministry, most notably "allowing prophetic people to teach who were not gifted in teaching, and the attempts by some of the prophets to establish doctrine based on prophecy".[75] The use of prophetic words to establish doctrine had also been a troublesome issue during the Latter Rain movement.

The Kansas City Prophets had already influenced the Vineyard movement, even before they officially joined the Vineyard. And yet almost exactly one year later, the Vineyard began to distance themselves from the prophetic movement. The Vineyard's methodology had always been to equip the saints to do the ministry, and the 'end times army' motif ran against that. The contrast was significant, as noted by Bill Jackson: "Ministry was in the hands of the new breed and dread champions. John *[Wimber]* had always taught us that everyone gets to play – we just have to play nice and share our toys. Dread champions we were not."[76]

Tom Stipe is a former Vineyard pastor who left the movement around the same time the Vineyard was beginning to distance itself from the KCP. His comments in the introduction to Hank Hannegraaf's *Counterfeit Revival* about the influence of the prophets on the Vineyard were less than complimentary.

Stipe had some specific allegations that are hard to prove – you just have to take his word for it. However, some of the things he listed sounded very familiar when I first read them:

- People moving to new places/churches at prophetic direction that turned out to be wrong – they blamed God

- Teenagers who were promised stardom (mostly musicians who would 'go to the nations') but then nothing happened

- People in local churches who had been promised special ministry becoming angry when their pastors didn't recognize and release them into their 'new anointing'

- Pastors and leaders became afraid to lead, if by doing so they weren't doing what the prophets had instructed

By 1995, the Vineyard had come to a much stronger conclusion regarding the Prophets: while recognizing and embracing prophetic ministry in general, there was a consensus that the pendulum had swung too far, and needed to come back into balance.

"At the Pastors Conference in the Vineyard's new facility in Anaheim Hills in 1995, Wimber told the movement that he regretted leading the Vineyard into the prophetic era, saying that it did, indeed, get us off track."[77] In a Vineyard-released DVD from the same conference, Wimber goes so far as to use the word "repent" to describe his change of heart.

Mike Bickle voluntarily removed his church from the Vineyard movement in 1996, citing a need to be faithful to the prophetic themes that had characterized his church since its beginning: Intercession, Holiness, Offerings, and Prophetic. These four 'banner themes' were the basis for its acronym IHOP (later: International House of Prayer). Six years later, Bickle felt the Vineyard had not adopted the IHOP banner themes, which was one of his stated reasons for leaving the Vineyard.

(Bickle also suggested that the Vineyard had offended the Holy Spirit during the Toronto Blessing by asking TACF to leave the Vineyard movement.)

Of the three most well known prophets, Bob Jones was removed from ministry for sexual sin in 1991. Bob has since returned to ministry, although the Vineyard does not permit him to minister in their churches.

John Paul Jackson began Streams Ministries in New Hampshire, where he continues to teach on the dread champions that will be raised up, and offers dream interpretations for visitors to his website.

Paul Cain was "outed" by his prophetic colleagues Rick Joyner and Jack Deere for an unrepentant addiction to alcoholism and homosexuality. Cain confessed publicly and began a process of restoration, but publicly retracted his confession during the Lakeland events a few years later.

IHOP has since published a list of 'Affirmations and Denials' on its website, which includes the following: "Some have wrongly identified our ministry today with the false teachings that were popularized by some in the Latter Rain movement. At no time in the past did we have any relationship with this movement."[78]

Such a statement is mind-blowingly deceptive, although *technically* true.

1. No, they were not in relationship with the Latter Rain movement. Not "officially", anyway. The Latter Rain movement ended "officially" in the early 1950s. IHOP had its genesis in Mike Bickle's Kansas City Fellowship in the early 1980s, some thirty-plus years later.

2. But for years, and to this day, Mike Bickle and his associates have boldly and clearly taught Latter Rain doctrines.

I have no desire to engage in "calling names" or attacking anyone's personal testimony. But IHOP's denial of any connection to the Latter Rain's teachings is *simply untrue*. (I write these words with a sense of profound sadness.)

THE NEW APOSTOLIC REFORMATION

In the late 1990s and into the 21st century, a new movement, called the New Apostolic Reformation (NAR), has been steadily rising in numbers and influence. C. Peter Wagner is recognized as one of its main proponents due to his prolific writing ministry which has devoted several titles to this movement: *ChurchQuake!*, *The New Apostolic Churches*, *Spheres of Authority*, *Apostles and Prophets: The New Foundation for the Church*, and so on. Wagner describes himself as the "Presiding Apostle" in the International Coalition of Apostles, which he founded.

In his book *Spheres of Authority*, Wagner presents a stunning revisionist approach to church history. Central to the New Apostolic Reformation is the Latter Rain belief that God is restoring the "offices" of apostle and prophet. These "offices" became lost due to prejudice in the church.

Wagner writes: "The Latter Rain embraced the ministry of apostles and prophets. Not surprisingly, they were condemned by their first cousins, so to speak, the Assemblies of God because they threatened the status quo."[79]

Wagner agrees with Australian Assemblies of God minister, David Cartledge, who dismissively labeled the American Assemblies of God "Pentecostal cessationists". Wagner makes no mention whatsoever of the heretical doctrines that led to the rejection of the Latter Rain, and instead turns the movement into a sort of martyr for the NAR cause.

Perhaps it's best to keep our focus on the *theology* underlining the problematic practices. Like the prophetic movement, once you start trying to say who currently promotes Latter Rain teachings and practices – and who doesn't – where do you start and where do you end?

Suffice it to say that the New Apostolic Reformation is currently the most influential group of churches and leaders that embrace and promote Latter Rain theology. They do not try to hide it, although they sometimes use updated terms. But underneath, their theological beliefs are classic Latter Rain.

The most well known church in the New Apostolic Reformation is perhaps Bethel, with its *School Of The Supernatural* and recording artists *Jesus Culture*.

Bill Jackson, in *The Quest for the Radical Middle*, offers the following advice as a grid for sorting through prophetic ministry, which would also serve as a good filter for Latter Rain emphases:

"We should embrace the gifts and outpouring of the Holy Spirit but refrain from any kind of apocalyptic exegesis and fervor...

"We need not to get so caught up in a particular interpretation that we lose sight of the fact that we could be wrong.

"We should never try to establish doctrine from prophecy. Doctrine is derived from the exegesis of Scripture...

"We should beware of any kind of elitist attitude in connection with prophetic ministry...

"We need to affirm that our pastoral call is to equip the saints for the work of ministry... not needing to wait either for the anointed apostle or prophets or for the coming revival...

"We need to be careful about our motives in pursuing prophecy... While we are to encourage prophecy in the local church, let us beware of fostering a climate that is no different than why people pursue astrologers..."[80]

SO NOW WHAT?

If there was anything positive in the Latter Rain movement, it was their genuine emphasis on personal holiness. This was at least partially motivated by the belief that they would be better equipped to usher in Jesus' second coming by being part of the Joshua and Caleb generation. But they were also reacting against a perception of spiritual coldness among their Pentecostal churches.

"The question posed by the Latter Rain had to do with the role of human obedience in helping or hindering the sovereign plan of God. On what basis or for what motive do we serve Him? How does revival come?"[81]

And our quest for holiness is part of the larger topic of spiritual maturity; how do we "grow" in Christ, becoming more like Him, and "work out (our) salvation with fear and trembling (Philippians 2:12-13)"?

The other issue raised by the Latter Rain was the so-called "Five-Fold" ministries of apostle, prophet, pastor, teacher and evangelist as found in Ephesians 4:11-16. According to the Latter Rain, end-time prophets and apostles are the new foundation for the end-time church. We have seen modern Latter Rain proponents such as the New Apostolic Reformation create a hierarchy that places Apostles (as recognized and endorsed by the International Coalition of Apostles) as the ultimate leaders that everyone else – including the other four "offices" – must submit to.

(The issue of 'submission' will be dealt with further when we look at the Shepherding Movement. The Latter Rain's influence was also very prominent there, which makes it difficult to separate the topics.)

First, let's take another look at the so-called "five-fold offices".

FIVE-FOLD RECONSIDERED

The term 'five-fold' ministries/offices, or 'Ascension Gifts' are all man-made labels for the gifts mentioned in Ephesians 4. Labels aren't necessary a negative thing – like most jargon, a label can function as a sort of verbal shorthand. But it is helpful to keep in mind that the Bible doesn't call anything in Ephesians 4 'five-fold' or 'offices'. When people begin by insisting on these terms, they may be using these labels in order to steer the discussion into their preferred viewpoint.

All spiritual gifts, including the 'five-fold', are given by and through the Holy Spirit. Before jumping directly into the Ephesians 4 passage, we should first look at a little background on the Spirit who gives the gifts.

During the same evening when Jesus washed the disciples' feet, we also find His most direct teaching regarding the work of the promised Holy Spirit, who would soon be poured out at the Feast of Pentecost.

The Bible doesn't call anything in Ephesians 4 'five-fold' or 'offices'.

Jesus had mentioned the Spirit before: when He warned the Pharisees about the unforgivable sin of attributing the work of the Spirit to Satan (Matthew 12:22-32; Mark 3:20-30), and also at the end of His parable about the neighbor who comes at night with a request for food (Luke 11:13). But this evening, the Last Supper, would mark a much fuller disclosure from Jesus about the work of the Holy Spirit.

The Holy Spirit empowers individual Christians in a remarkable way. In the Old Testament, we read of people who were anointed by the Spirit at different times and for different reasons (Samson, Solomon, David, Samuel, Elijah and the rest of the Major and Minor Prophets, for example). But once the Holy Spirit would be sent (at the Feast of Pentecost, as we know now), from that point on *all* Christians would be empowered by the Spirit.

At the Last Supper, Jesus describes the Holy Spirit repeatedly with the Greek word *parakletos* (transliterated as *paraclete*), a word meaning "one who comes alongside". Various Bible translations have given different synonyms for this term, including counselor, helper and comforter.

While all of these meanings are possible – and perhaps it's best to simply say that *all* the possible definitions are simultaneously accurate – what stands out is the "coming alongside" nature of the Spirit's work. Jesus remains the Head of the body, and the Spirit – while indwelling us – is also in some way "alongside" us, pointing to Jesus, empowering us to follow Him, purifying us, and gifting us to co-operate in the advancing of the Kingdom.

During the Last Supper, Jesus tells His disciples that the Spirit will be the Spirit of truth. The Spirit of truth will teach the disciples and also bring to remembrance what Jesus had already taught them. This would come in handy as the disciples obeyed Jesus' instruction in Matthew 28:20 to teach "all that I have commanded you" to new disciples.

Jesus also reminded His disciples that His leaving was necessary before the Spirit was sent (John 16:5-15). Already, the circle of those who were commissioned to preach, heal, and deliver people from demonic bondage had been widened from twelve (Luke 9:1-6) to seventy-two (Luke 10:1-17). The coming of the Spirit to indwell all believers was necessary for widening that circle indefinitely to include every follower of Jesus.

Jesus lists several aspects of the Spirit's work: convicting people of sin and righteousness, guiding the disciples into truth, speaking to us what He hears from the Father, and bringing glory to Jesus by sharing His thoughts and plans with us. This tied neatly into Jesus' earlier declaration that His disciples are friends, not servants, "because a servant does not know his Master's business" (John 15:15).

Spiritual gifts are from the Spirit. (Profound, yes?) But the Spirit is the *paraclete* – the One who comes alongside – and the gifts that He gives will operate in the same manner. Jesus came as the Servant who washed His disciples' feet (John 13:1-17), and He sent His Spirit as one who comes alongside.

The Ephesians 4 gifts are for bringing the body to maturity in Christ, but they do so in the same manner as the Spirit: coming alongside. Ephesians 4 was not written as a blueprint for a hierarchical leadership structure requiring submission. This is also in keeping with Jesus' command that the disciples should never seek to lord it over each other (Matthew 20:25-28).

The gifts of apostle, prophet, and teacher are also included in two other gift-lists in the New Testament: Romans 12:6-8 and 1 Corinthians 12:28.

The Romans 12:6-8 passage is interesting, as the gifts of prophecy and teaching are clearly placed on the same level as gifts of serving, encouraging, giving and mercy (apostle isn't mentioned in this list). There is nothing that suggests a hierarchical or 'office' function. In Romans, the emphasis is on exercising the gifts by faith, and with humility.

The context of the Romans gift list begins with a very well known introduction: "Offer your bodies as living sacrifices, holy and acceptable to the Lord; this is your spiritual act of worship." (Romans 12:1), and to "not conform any longer to the pattern of this world" (Romans 12:2).

In the context of this passage, it isn't possible to interpret this to mean that the prophet or teacher was somehow given authority or preeminence over others. "But because the pagan idea of leadership pervades our churches, many of us are in constant pursuit of celebrity status in the Kingdom of God...[82] All of us in the charismatic renewal need a swift return to these simple truths of self-denial. We need to learn humility."[83]

The emphasis in 1 Corinthians 12:28-29 is that *all* of the gifts are necessary, and that since *all* of us are (equally) parts of the body, none of the gifts has even a hint of elevated importance in the body. "Position and prestige" do not go hand-in-hand with being given a certain gift.

True, Paul begins the list in verse 28 by saying that God has appointed "first apostles, second prophets, third teachers", followed by miracles, healings, helps, administration and tongues, which has been used to suggest that the highest gift is to be an apostle.

The following verse, however, reveals a key element to understanding these gifts as *parakletos*: not everyone has all the gifts, and all are necessary. There is no indication that some gifts are more necessary than others. Paul's teaching on the body in 1 Corinthians 12 also makes this abundantly clear.

In many charismatic churches, the Ephesians 4 passage has been (mis)-used to create and defend a structure of hierarchical authority and submission by labeling these gifts as 'offices' (with the implication that governance is part of the 'office').

If I may be kind and blunt at the same time, that kind of thinking is completely inconsistent with the rest of the New Testament's teaching regarding spiritual gifts, and especially the nature of the Spirit who gives them.

EPHESIANS 4:11-16

As we unpack this passage of Scripture, it would be helpful to keep in mind, as blogger Brent Toderash (aka *Brother Maynard*) reminds us, "the gift is not given to an individual, but to a corporate group, the church."[84] This is an important distinction! Spiritual gifts are *expressed* through individuals, but they are given to the *church*.

The Corinthians were a status-obsessed and highly competitive group.

Perhaps the main reason that people want to interpret these gifts as 'offices' of authority is because of the inclusion of *apostle* in the list. Even the Reformer John Calvin considered this passage to mean 'offices' in his commentary on Corinthians, although he only accepted that those of pastor, teacher, and evangelist were valid after the first century.

The word 'apostle' in Greek is *apostolos*, and can be translated in several different ways – delegate, envoy, messenger, agent – and all of these interpretations are found in the New Testament.

Referring to the Greek *apostolos*, Grudem notes, "In the broad sense, it just means 'messenger' or 'pioneer missionary'."[85] In this regard, there is biblical evidence that there can be ministry that is apostolic in nature without necessarily being an Apostle in the same sense as the Twelve. It is no accident when Luke 10 records Jesus sending out the seventy-two, that the word 'sent' is *apostellō*, the verb form of *apostolos*. To be an apostle is to be sent.

"The early church did use the word apostle from time to time for other than those who had witnessed the Resurrection. However, the term is used in these cases in its generic sense of dispatching representatives on an official mission on behalf of the senders."[86]

It becomes apparent that there are the twelve 'Big A' apostles, as well as a larger number of 'small a' apostles in the New Testament. The original disciples (minus Judas) were seen as the 'Big A' apostles. They were eyewitnesses of Jesus' resurrection (as were over 500 others who were not considered apostles in the same sense). They had authority to make decisions on behalf of all Christians (e.g. Acts 15:1-31), and in some cases, under the inspiration of the Holy Spirit, wrote parts of the New Testament.

"However, besides the Twelve, the New Testament text appears to clearly designate such persons as Paul, James the brother of Jesus (1 Corinthians 15:7; Galatians 1:19), Barnabas (Acts 14:14), Andronicus and Junias (probably a woman) who were 'outstanding among the apostles' (Romans 16:7)."[87]

While there is some debate whether Andronicus and Junias were actually apostles, or simply held in high esteem by the apostles, it is clear that Paul, Barnabas and James the brother of Jesus *were* considered apostles. None of them were part of the original twelve, so we now have clear biblical record of at least *fifteen* apostles, and perhaps more.

Some have also suggested Epaphroditus because Paul used the word *apostolos* in Philippians 2:25 in reference to Epaphroditus being a 'messenger'. Still others have claimed that Timothy was not a pastor but an apostle, because Paul refers to the two of them as "we" when mentioning Paul's rights as an *apostolos* of Christ. In both cases, the idea that Epaphroditus and/or Timothy were anything more than 'sent messengers' would be a bit of a stretch.

Caution: The biggest problem at the church in Corinth was elitism and pride. Paul's first epistle to them comes back to this problem over and over again. From factions based on who they followed (Paul, Apollos, Peter, Jesus), to greediness and gluttony at the Communion table, to claiming superiority based on what spiritual gifts they had – the Corinthians were a status-obsessed and highly competitive group of people. ("Spiritual pride" has to be the most glaring oxymoron of all time.)

Paul reminds them that apostles should not be viewed as super-leaders, but rather as *servants* to the church (1 Cor. 4:1). Even during his biting and sarcastic rant in 1 Corinthians 4:8-13, the emphasis is on refuting the arrogant posturing of an elitist group within the Corinthian church. (Interesting: the Greek word for 'false apostle' literally means: "lying messenger".)

The Twelve hold a special place in the history of the church. They are described as twelve foundations of the New Jerusalem (Revelation 21:14). They are also considered the foundation, along with the prophets, upon which the church was established (Ephesians 2:20).

The other apostles in the New Testament, even the apostle Paul, functioned differently from the Twelve. Even the seventy-two that Jesus sent (*apostellō*) in Luke 10 are viewed differently than the Twelve.

"The fundamental problem with the hierarchical understanding of the office gifts is that it misunderstands the nature of service in the Kingdom. Jesus was among us as one who serves, and He was demonstrating how Kingdom leadership works: not to lord it over, but to serve. Rather than taking a title or position, Jesus exhorts leaders to humble themselves and become the least among those they serve."[88]

The function of the five-fold gifts, according to the passage in which they are listed, is "to prepare God's people for works of service, so that the body of Christ may be built up" (Ephesians 4:12). "The five-fold ministries are not here equated with elders, nor are they charged with leading or ruling the church – just equipping them."[89]

The Greek word for 'equipping' is *katartismos*, which has also been translated as 'preparing' (NIV) and 'perfecting' (KJV). It is used only once in the whole New Testament, and means "complete furnishing, equipping". Equipping for what? According to Ephesians 4:12, it was for "works of *diakonia* (service)".

"When the Jerusalem Council resolved the schismatic debate over whether the Gentiles should keep the Jewish law, the issue was decided by 'the apostles and elders' (Acts 15:4,6,22)."[90]

It wasn't just the Apostles who decided this issue when the inclusion of Gentile believers brought about a cultural identity crisis for the fledgling church. The apostles, together with a number of anonymous leaders referred to only as elders, made a group decision. If any group of apostolic people had the "right" to make an autocratic decision, it would have been the original Apostles, yet they worked in concert alongside the elders in the Jerusalem church.

"Prophets, while never appointed to ruling functions in their capacity as prophets like overseers/elders, did exercise spiritual influence with the apostles and elders in the belief and practice of the Early Church."[91]

What cannot be ignored is that, in a body where Paul wrote that he wished everyone could exercise the gift of prophecy (1 Corinthians 14:1, 39), he never appointed prophets, nor instructed any of his church planters to appoint prophets or apostles. Elders were appointed, but they appear to be the only ones given any mandate for governance.

Ironically, one of the responsibilities of an elder was to safeguard the church from false apostles who would attempt to draw people away to follow them. Today, elders would have the same responsibility to safeguard their churches from Latter Rain-influenced 'apostles'.

HOLINESS AND SPIRITUAL GROWTH

The Wesleyan/Pentecostal view of the second blessing, with or without the accompanying evidence of tongues, has long created a subtle mindset that spiritual growth (sanctification, holiness, maturity) revolved around crisis moments of the Holy Spirit's intervention.

And to be fair, there are many charismatics – and also post-charismatics – with exciting stories of their encounters with the Holy Spirit. These experiences were often quite profound, resulting in feeling humbled, comforted, accepted, strengthened, penitent and overjoyed – all at the same time.

This understanding of the Spirit's work was the impetus behind the weekly practice of 'altar calls' or 'ministry time' at the end of each and every gathering of the church. Anyone who has experienced a genuine touch from God during these prayer times can attest to the immediate effects in their own lives (i.e. an assurance of God's love).

Some critics have made mocking remarks about charismatics having a "may God zap you" approach to spiritual growth. And truthfully, they do have a point. The emphasis *has*, at times, been heavily weighted towards a crisis moment with the Spirit, and church gatherings were designed primarily as vehicles for these moments.

At the same time, many charismatics have looked at things like 'spiritual disciplines' *(more on this later)* as being simply works-based striving in our own strength. Their (understandable) concern is that we will cease to be truly Spirit-led, and instead put our faith and trust in our own efforts to better ourselves.

Post-charismatics run the opposite risk. In their disillusionment with what Brent Toderash once called 'the weekly crisis event at the front of the church', they can place too much emphasis on spiritual disciplines. As a result, the Holy Spirit is reduced to an administrative role, instead of a vibrant presence whenever two or three are gathered in Jesus' name.

It is human nature to swing from one extreme to another as we try to correct perceived imbalances. Developing a 'both/and' approach to being Spirit-led while also embracing spiritual disciplines will go a long way in balancing out the pendulum swing.

Discipleship is a word that once had a rich heritage, but has lost much of its attractive meaning. Many today have substituted the phrase 'spiritual formation'. Regardless of what term is used, the root remains the same: it refers to *sanctification* – the process of becoming more Christ-like in our character, attitude, words and actions over time.

Holiness is another word that has suffered from misuse, to the point that people cringe at the caricatures that come to mind whenever they hear it. They are often reacting to groups that have used holiness as a hoop to jump through in order to get what they want from God.

We would be in error to not put as much emphasis on holiness as the New Testament writers do.

To be blunt, the Latter Rain's approach to holiness is ultimately self-centered, and tends towards a mercenary pragmatism. We pursue holiness, in this approach, in order to get something from God: health, financial blessings or to be a part of Joel's Army.

We have come a long way from Jesus' words: we are only unworthy servants who have the awesome privilege of being included in God's work of redemption throughout history (Luke 17:7-9). Many of the saints of yesteryear understood that holiness and sanctification were to be sought simply for their own sake, and not because of what we might 'get' for it. Bernard of Clairvaux (1090-1135) wrote:

"On the lower plain of action, it is the reluctant, not the eager, whom we urge by promises of reward. Who would think of paying a man to do what he was yearning to do already? For instance, no one would hire a hungry man to eat, or a thirsty man to drink, or a mother to nurse her own child. Who would think of bribing a farmer to dress his own vineyard, or to dig about his orchard, or to rebuild his house? So all the more, *one who loves God truly asks no other recompense than God Himself.*"[92] *(emphasis added)*

By one sacrifice He has made perfect for ever those who are being made holy.
(Hebrews 10:14)

It is this understanding of holiness and sanctification – that God is both the source and the reward of those who are His followers – which we need to recapture. Our goal is to follow in the footsteps of saints in centuries past, who learned to live all their lives in the presence of God, and not just during meetings, conferences, and church services. Brother Lawrence of the Resurrection (author of *The Practice of the Presence of God*) stands as but one of many examples:

"Everything was the same to him – every place, every employment. The good brother found God everywhere, as much while he was repairing shoes as while he was praying with the community. He was in no hurry to make his retreats, because he found in his ordinary work the same God to love and adore as in the depth of the desert."[93]

Our motivation for sanctification is not to twist God's arm to do something for us or to usher in revival, although God may sovereignly do these very things in the midst of our journey. We are pursuing a deeper relationship with Jesus *that results in us changing.*

There are two ways to view Jesus' words: "If you love me, you will obey what I command" (John 14:15). On one hand, obedience is proof of our love for Jesus. On the other, love provides the *motivation* for obeying Jesus. Yes, obedience does not depend on love. For example, when a parent asks (commands) one of their teenagers to take out the trash, the teenager may obey, but their motivation may merely be a desire to borrow the family car, not a sense of love and devotion.

Jesus taught that loving God is the highest priority for all Christians. Obedience out of duty or in recognition of Jesus' Lordship is better than disobedience, to be sure, but it is not the ideal that Jesus Christ invites us to step into. Obedience rooted in our deepening love of Jesus is the healthy soil that maturity in Christ will best grow in.

While we do not treat holiness as a prerequisite for God's blessing, we would be in error to not put as much emphasis on holiness as the New Testament writers do.

Throughout the New Testament, the Greek word that is most often translated *holy* is *hagios*, which simply means "a most holy thing; a saint". It is the same Greek word used in 'Holy' Spirit, and also the favorite word of Luke, Paul, Peter, John, and the writer of Hebrews when referring to Christians as 'saints'. Most famously, John uses *hagios* when he writes, "Day and night they never stop saying: 'Holy, holy, holy is the Lord God Almighty, who was, and is, and is to come'" (Revelation 4:8).

One of my favorite passages on holiness is Hebrews 10:11-14:

"Day after day every priest stands and performs his religious duties; again and again he offers the same sacrifices, which can never take away sins. But when this priest [Jesus] had offered for all time one sacrifice for sins, He sat down at the right hand of God. Since that time He waits for His enemies to be made His footstool, because by one sacrifice *He has made perfect for ever those who are being made holy.*" (*emphasis mine*)

It is this last phrase that so succinctly summarizes this section: "...because by one sacrifice he has *made perfect forever* [past tense] those who *are being made holy* [ongoing tense]". We can stop agonizing over whether or not Jesus is pleased with our performance – He considers us perfected already. At the same time, we can deliberately choose to co-operate with the Holy Spirit in the process of maturing (sanctification), as we are being made holy.

The word in this phrase that is translated 'perfect' is *teleioo*, which means "to make complete, to bring to a proposed goal". It is the same Greek word that James employs when speaking of faith being made perfect by works in James 2:22. The word, when used in Hebrews 10:14, refers to the finality of our holiness in God's view.

The word that is translated *holy* at the end of Hebrews 10:14 is *hagiazo*, which is from the root *hagios* that we've been looking at, and is usually translated as 'holy' or 'sanctified'. The King James rendering of this verse reads "...he hath perfected (*teleioo*) for ever them that are sanctified (*hagiazo*)."

As one Reformed theologian, who is also a continuationist, notes: "If we grow in sanctification we 'walk by the Spirit' and are 'led by the Spirit' (Galatians 5:16-18; cf. Romans 8:14), that is, we are more and more responsive to the desires and promptings of the Holy Spirit in our life and character."[94]

The meaning of sanctification in Hebrews 10:14, when *hagiazo* is translated as 'holy' (*sanctified*, KJV), is being dedicated to

God's purposes, rather than our own or those of the world. Theologian Millard Erickson comments on *hagiazo*:

"In this sense holiness refers to a state of being separate, set apart from the ordinary or mundane and dedicated to a particular purpose or use... It is in this sense that the New Testament so frequently refers to Christians as 'saints', even when they are far from perfect."[95]

The good news is that we don't have to become legalistically paranoid about our personal holiness. And the other good news is that if loving Jesus is truly our pursuit –with all of our heart, soul, mind and strength (Mark 12:30) – then we will actively co-operate with the Holy Spirit in His transforming work of sanctification. As the late John Wimber wrote:

"Spiritual growth, then, is a product of the initiating, empowering work of the Holy Spirit, *and* of our active co-operation. He engages our minds, wills and emotions, and He expects us to respond. If *either* divine initiative or human response is missing, we will not grow."[96] *(emphasis in original)*

The both/and dynamic of co-operating with the Holy Spirit will free us from a legalistic approach to holiness and sanctification. It will also allow us to be Spirit-led as we include spiritual disciplines and genuinely Spirit-initiated 'impartations' in our journey's repertoire.

SPIRITUAL DISCIPLINES

"But solid food is for the mature, who by constant use have **trained themselves** to distinguish good from evil" (Heb. 5:14).

"No discipline seems pleasant at the time, but painful. Later on, however, it produces a harvest of righteousness and peace for those who are **trained by it**" (Heb. 12:11).

"For this very reason, **make every effort** to add to your faith goodness; and to goodness, knowledge; and to knowledge, self-control; and to self-control, perseverance; and to perseverance, godliness; and to godliness, brotherly kindness; and to brotherly kindness, love. For if you possess these qualities in increasing measure, they will keep you from being ineffective and unproductive in your knowledge of our Lord Jesus Christ" (2 Peter 1:5-8).

The topic of spiritual disciplines can evoke strong opinions, usually ranging somewhere between viewing disciplines as *the* key to spiritual maturity, or looking at them as fleshly striving or 'salvation by works'.

But if we take a both/and approach, we can view spiritual disciplines as co-operating with the Holy Spirit in the process of sanctification. In we keep that balance, we won't fall into the trap of seeing spiritual disciplines as either the magical cure-all, nor as legalistic striving based on human effort.

Our goal in using any spiritual discipline is that we become more 'set apart' for God's use. We've been redeemed, but we are still in need of maturity.

Grudem notes, "Although Paul says that his readers have been set free from sin (Romans 6:18) and that they are 'dead to sin and alive to God' (Romans 6:11), he nonetheless recognizes that sin remains in their lives, so he tells them not to let it reign and not to yield to it (Romans 6:12-13)."[97]

When we also consider the verses listed at the beginning of this section (Hebrew 5:15, 12:11 and 2 Peter 1:5-8), we see the recurring theme of being 'trained' and choosing to 'make every effort'. Bishop Todd Hunter (Anglican Mission in America) provides a very insightful way of viewing spiritual disciplines as 'training':

"Apple trees easily and naturally produce apples. But no matter how hard they may try, no matter how much they may sincerely groan and 'religiously' agonize over it, they cannot produce pumpkins... The disciplines are 'indirect effort'. In practicing them, we do what is currently under our control with the intent, hope and expectation that they will enable us to do what we dream of in our idealistic language. Watch *The Karate Kid* with this in mind. You will see how Daniel-san learns karate in very indirect ways. By doing what he can – scrub floors, paint fences and waxing cars – he becomes the kind of person who can naturally and easily defend himself from even expert karate punches and kicks. Lesson: we cannot 'try' to be good (remember the apples and pumpkins); we must 'train' ('store up good in us') to be good."[98]

Many times, by exerting our own willpower, we can approximate and imitate spiritual growth. We try harder, work harder and pray harder, and think (for example) that we have learned self-control and kindness as we relate to those around us. Then, out of nowhere, somebody cuts us off on the highway, and our reaction – whether verbal, our utilization of a symbolic and universally-recognized gesture involving a certain finger, or even just the internal 'road rage' that wells up within us – gives away what is truly beneath our carefully crafted spiritual veneer.

This should serve as a reminder that this is a co-operative effort with the Spirit; it is not dependent on our own efforts, although we are involved in the process. Richard Foster, whose *Celebration of Discipline* stands as a modern classic on the subject of spiritual disciplines, says it well:

"Willpower has not [*sic*] defense against the careless word, the unguarded moment. The will has the same deficiency as the law – it can deal only with externals. It is incapable of bringing about the necessary transformation of the inner spirit."[99]

Grudem concurs on the need for the Spirit's work on a deep level: "To be dead to the ruling power of sin means that we as Christians, by virtue of the power of the Holy Spirit, have power to overcome the temptations and enticements of sin."[100]

Many of us are painfully aware that Paul spoke for everyone when he wrote in Romans 7: "I do not understand what I do. For what I want to do I do not do, but what I hate I do... For what I do is not the good I want to do; no, the evil I do not want to do – this I keep on doing... What a wretched man I am! Who will rescue me from this body of death" (Rom. 7:15-24)?

But let's take care that we don't overlook Paul's conclusion to his honest confession of struggle: "Thanks be to God – through Jesus Christ our Lord (Rom. 7:25)! Therefore, there is now no condemnation for those who are in Christ Jesus, because through Christ Jesus the law of the Spirit of life set me free from the law of sin and death" (Rom. 8:1-2).

Yes, we each understand that we continually wrestle, as Paul did in Romans 7. Yet by keeping Romans 8:1-2 in mind, we can stop beating ourselves up for our failures, because God has already declared that there is no condemnation. Learning to walk in forgiveness (no condemnation) is a discipline itself for many Christians.

"Just as prayer for daily bread provides a model for a prayer that should be repeated each day, so the prayer for forgiveness of sins is included in the type of prayer that should be made each day in a believer's life."[101]

It's often been said that prayer is a two-way street, and charismatics – with the theological understanding that God still speaks today – have no problem with this idea. But as many critics inside and outside of the charismatic realm have noted, a certain lack of biblical literacy has (at times) resulted in some pretty bizarre teachings and practices, based on "God told me".

Foster writes, "In prayer, real prayer, we begin to think God's thoughts after Him: to desire the things He desires, to love the things He loves, to will the things He wills. Progressively, we are taught to see things from His point of view."[102]

The most effective way to 'test' or 'weigh' what we think God is speaking to us is to know what His written Word says. If Scripture is in conflict with what we (or anyone else) thinks God is saying, stick with Scripture. Of course, in order to have this safeguard in place, we will need to practice the spiritual discipline of Bible study.

When many people hear an admonition recommending *Bible study*, they often envision a dry time spent legalistically slaving over the Bible. However, the exact opposite is true, if we approach reading and studying (understood as "becoming fascinated with") the Bible as a trustworthy grid for understanding and putting into action what we feel the Spirit is saying to us.

As we learn how to partner with the Holy Spirit, we will discover an increasing desire to co-operate more fully. It's not unlike a brilliant guitarist, who invests many hours doing scales and finger exercises. As a result, the guitarist develops a repertoire of skills and instinctual fretboard knowledge that comes almost automatically during an improvisational solo. The hours of practice are forgotten in the joy of playing with ease and excellence.

As Todd Hunter mentioned above, spiritual disciplines are an 'indirect effort' that will pay off when we most need to respond 'automatically' in a Spirit-led way.

For example, it will certainly be more beneficial to anyone we are praying for if we are at ease and supernaturally natural in our prayer. There is not much benefit if we are stumbling around, searching for the right words to say, as it becomes obvious that prayer is something we talk about, but don't do much of.

SUFFERING AS SPIRITUAL DISCIPLINE

This has never been a popular thought in Christian circles, including (maybe *especially*) among charismatics. We are far more likely to rebuke the devil than to remember that God already told us that suffering is unavoidable. Jesus *promised* us 'trouble' (John 16:33), after all! Fortunately, He also promised to be with us.

> **Even as we cooperate with Him, we are not setting the agenda – the Holy Spirit is.**

We have all heard some variation of the old joke: "God, give me patience – *right now!*" For those who appreciate irony, the epistle of James already tells us *how* God develops patience in us: by sending trials our way (James 1:2-4). Yet when the trials come in answer to our prayer for patience, we panic, rebuke the devil, and try to pray the trials away.

Part of our 'training', according to Hebrews 12:7-11, includes hardship and trials. It is 'discipline' if we learn and grow through it; if we fail to learn, and mature, then it will only feel like punishment.

It is interesting – and no doubt significant – that James prefaces his chapter on faith and works by talking about enduring trials and temptations (James 1:2-4, 12) as part of being 'perfected' and 'not lacking anything' (James 1:4).

There seems to be certain areas of our lives where we don't mature during good times. Trials and temptations, which drive us deeper into faith and dependence on God, are somehow able to accomplish this much more effectively.

The saints of Hebrews 11 were praised for their great faith in spite of *not* receiving what they were waiting and believing for. We should also take note that these saints – of whom it is written: "the world was not worthy" (Hebrews 11:38) – also endured a dark list of terrible things as part of their faith resume. As they walked in faith, they experienced mistreatment, torture, execution, imprisonment, flogging, stoning, being sawed in two, persecution and death by the sword. They didn't receive what they had faith for, but they *died believing.*

The author of Hebrews wrote about these saints in order to inspire us to embrace the race that we are running, and accept that part of the race will include suffering. Paul had his famous 'thorn in the flesh' (whatever it was), which didn't go away despite his prayer of faith, because God had a purpose for that thorn: to keep Paul humble (2 Corinthians 12:7-10).

Recognizing that hardships are sometimes part of God's maturing process should put our fears to rest that, somehow, any and all troubles we encounter are the result of our own actions. This was the assumption of the disciples with the man born blind (John 9:1-3). Their assumptions shaped their question: whose sin led to the man's blindness? But Jesus refuted that idea, saying that the man's healing (to God's glory) was the focus, not finding someone to blame.

At the same time, Paul warns us in Galatians 6:7-8 that we reap what we sow. We do not have a 'get out of jail free' card that exempts us from the consequences of our choices. We *do* have the promise of forgiveness and restoration, fortunately! An important part of sanctification is learning how to "sow to the Spirit" (Galatians 6:8).

Peter later wrote that suffering for God was praiseworthy, but if we're suffering because we're jerks, then it's not (general paraphrase of 1 Peter 3:17 and 1 Peter 4:12-16).

Delving into the question of the existence of evil is outside the scope of this writing, but suffice it to say that in an imperfect world, where all of creation is groaning (Romans 8:22), as Jesus promised, we will 'have trouble'. However, there is good news as well: "I have told you these things, so that in Me you may have peace. In this world, you will have trouble. But take heart! I have overcome the world (John 16:33)."

(WELCOMING) SURPRISES

A healthy understanding and practice of spiritual disciplines will help us avoid the "may God zap you" approach to spiritual maturity. However, if the pendulum swings too far, we may find ourselves caught in a performance-based approach to discipleship that is entirely dependent on our own efforts.

> "I often saw a discrepancy between what Christians believed and what they practiced."
>
> - John Wimber

The Holy Spirit is the One with whom we are co-operating in this process. Even as we cooperate with Him, we are not setting the agenda – the Holy Spirit is. And we should not be surprised when the Holy Spirit sometimes does the unexpected. In fact, we should anticipate and expect that God will do "immeasurably more than all we ask or imagine, according to his power that is at work within us" (Ephesians 3:20). Paul was not exercising exaggerated poetic license when he wrote this.

In one sense, the Holy Spirit is always present, because one of God's attributes is His *omnipresence*. And He is always present simply because every follower of Jesus has the Spirit indwelling them. On the other hand, there are also many biblical examples where the awareness of the omnipresent Spirit's presence went beyond what was considered *normal*. These times, where the Holy Spirit's presence becomes more tangible and demonstrative, are often referred to as the 'manifest presence' of the Spirit.

The Holy Spirit is not some abstract force. He has personality, a will of His own, and is co-defined as *Lord* and *God* in the Trinitarian parts of the early church creeds. The Nicene Creed reads, in part, "We believe in the Holy Spirit, the Lord, the giver of life, who proceeds from the Father and the Son, who with the Father and the Son is worshipped and glorified..."

Making use of spiritual disciplines is a good thing, but if we neglect the ongoing role of the Holy Spirit in both personal and corporate transformation, we will become 'functionally cessationist'.

To be a *functional cessationist* is to give lip service to the reality of spiritual gifts, yet by either neglect or deliberate choice, never use them.

John Wimber made a wise observation about this. I believe the same principle applies to the practice of all spiritual gifts, and even our expectation for the Spirit's manifest presence:

"Many of these people were not offended by the *theory* of divine healing; it was the *practice* of healing prayer that offended them. I was not entirely surprised by their reaction. As a church consultant I often saw a discrepancy between what Christians believed and what they practiced."[103] *(emphasis in original)*

There are many biblical stories of God showing up unexpectedly in people's lives:

* Abram (later Abraham) didn't anticipate being called out of Haran (Genesis 12:1-5).

* Moses wasn't expecting God in the burning bush (Exodus 3:1-4).

- Gideon was hiding in a winepress and when 'called' by the "angel of the Lord", used the opportunity to complain about how God was treating Israel (Judges 6:11-13).

- Samuel thought it was Eli calling him during the night (1 Samuel 3:1-18).

- The apostle Paul thought he *was* doing God's work, till Jesus knocked him off his donkey with a new revelation and new marching orders (Acts 9:1-19).

These are but a few examples of God interrupting peoples' normal routines with His manifest presence. It should also be noted that the encounters listed above turned out, over time, to be significant turning points in their lives and the lives of those around them.

Some refer to the Spirit's manifest presence as 'God showing up'. While critics have at times suggested that saying 'God showed up' is proof of theological heresy (denying God's omnipresence), such an accusation falls flat on its face if you read the Bible.

For example, Solomon would have anticipated that dedicating the Temple would be a spiritually momentous event, but were any of those present prepared for what actually happened? "When the priests withdrew from the Holy Place, the cloud filled the temple of the Lord. And the priests could not perform their service because of the cloud, for the glory of the Lord filled his temple" (1 Kings 8:10-11).

One of the most well-known New Testament passages in charismatic circles is Acts 2, the watershed moment which even non-charismatic theologians agree marks the starting point of the church age.

The disciples had been instructed by Jesus to stay in Jerusalem until the Spirit was given (Acts 1:4-5). Although they were doing just that, they had no idea what it would look like. They were expecting power to be Jesus' witnesses, but the rushing wind, the tongues of fire, speaking in other tongues, and the resultant three thousand people becoming followers of Jesus in a single day was far beyond what they would have imagined.

Paul and Barnabas were sent on the first of Paul's many missionary voyages when the Spirit interrupted one of the meetings of the church at Antioch: "While they were worshipping the Lord and fasting, the Holy Spirit said, 'Set apart for me Barnabas and Saul for the work to which I have called them'" (Acts 13:2).

And in the final book of the New Testament, the Revelation, we find John recording the beginning of his experiences with the simple words, "On the Lord's Day I was in the Spirit, and I heard behind me a loud voice like a trumpet..." (Revelation 1:10). Whether John was praying, worshipping or whatever, he says he was 'in the Spirit' and then the Revelation began.

Church history is full of many instances of the Holy Spirit 'showing up'. John Wimber, in his book *Power Evangelism*, provides a partial list of well-known leaders from early church history who wrote of their Spirit-initiated encounters, including Justin Martyr, Irenaeus, Tertullian, and Augustine. Significantly, it is worth pointing out that Augustine initially *rejected* overt manifestations of the Holy Spirit, but later changed his mind, writing in *The City of God* that Christians *should* expect the miraculous intervention of the Holy Spirit.

John Wesley's journals reveal numerous times where, during prayer times, the Spirit would profoundly move: "About three in the morning, as we were continuing instant in prayer, the power of God came mightily upon us, so that many cried out for exulting joy and many fell to the ground. As soon as we were recovered a little from that awe and amazement at the presence of His majesty, we broke out with one voice, 'We praise Thee, O God, we acknowledge Thee to be the Lord.'"[104]

The historical list could go on almost indefinitely. The point is simply that throughout post-Acts 2 history, the Holy Spirit has been continually working in His people to advance the Kingdom.

The question worth pondering is whether or not it is better to be "surprised by the power of the Holy Spirit" (the title of Jack Deere's book), or if we should actively *anticipate and pray* for the Spirit's manifest presence and ongoing ministry through the Body of Christ.

It's easier, in some ways, to focus entirely on the crisis moments at the altar, and to bury ourselves in endless revival meetings, waiting in anticipation for the next great move of the Spirit, as many charismatics presently do. It's equally easy for us to embrace a more hands-on approach via spiritual disciplines and doing acts of mercy and justice, but relegate the Spirit to stories of the old days.

It's much more of a stretch to co-operate with the Spirit in our sanctification; to embrace that we are viewed by God as holy even as we are being made more holy; to train ourselves via the spiritual disciplines *and* continue to not only expect and welcome, but to yearn for the manifest presence of the Holy Spirit.

CHAPTER NOTES

1. *Dictionary of Pentecostal and Charismatic Movements (Burgess, Stanley M., editor)*, page 831

2. Storms, Sam – *Post-Reformation and Contemporary Developments in the Pentecostal and Charismatic Movements*, page 8

3. *The New Dictionary of Pentecostal and Charismatic Movements*, page 831

4. Ibid., page 830

5. Storms, Sam – *Post-Reformation and Contemporary Developments in the Pentecostal and Charismatic Movements*, page 8

6. *The New Dictionary of Pentecostal and Charismatic Movements*, page 832

7. Jackson, Bill – *The Quest for the Radical Middle: A History of the Vineyard*, Vineyard International Publishing 1999, condensed list found in chapter: *Introducing the Prophets*

8. Branham, William – *The Laodicean Church Age*, (43)

9. Branham, William – *Five Definitive Indications of the True Church of the Living God*, (106)

10. Branham, William – *The Thyatirean Church Age* (25)

11. Branham, William – *The Pergameum Church Age* (188)

12. Branham, William – *The Laodicean Church Age* (277)

13. Branham, William – *The Sardicean Church Age* (65)

14. Ibid., (101) Branham, William – *The Serpent Seed* (5-1)

15. Ibid., (7-1)

16. Branham, William – *The Laodicean Church Age* (49)

17. Ibid., (52)

18. Branham, William – *Condemnation by Representation* (5-2)

19. Branham, William – *The Laodicean Church Age* (47)

20. Branham, William – *Condemnation by Representation* (6-1)

21. Branham, William – *The Serpent Seed* (19-3)
22. Ibid., (21-3,5)
23. Ibid., (23-4)
24. Ibid., (23-8)
25. Ibid., (24-5)
26. Ibid., (26-5)
27. Ibid., (30-1)
28. Ibid., (35-4)
29. Ibid., (3-5)
30. Branham, William – *The Laodicean Church Age*, (124)
31. Ibid., (143)
32. Ibid., (204)
33. Ibid., (261)
34. Ibid., (290)
35. Branham, William – *The Serpent Seed*, (1-5)
36. Branham, William – *The Pergameum Church Age*, (290-300)
37. Branham, William – *The Manifested Sons of God*, (49)
38. Ibid., (35)
39. Ibid., (197)
40. Warnock, George – *The Feast of Tabernacles*, page 2
41. *The New Dictionary of Pentecostal and Charismatic Movements*, page 831
42. Warnock, George – *The Feast of Tabernacles*, page 10
43. Ibid., page 9
44. Ibid., page 57
45. Ibid., page 102
46. Ibid., page 3
47. Ibid., page 17

48. Ibid., page 39
49. Ibid., page 37
50. Ibid., page 62
51. Ibid., page 100
52. Ibid., page 96
53. Ibid., page 63
54. Ibid., page 90
55. Ibid., page 47
56. Ibid., page 31
57. Ibid., page 85
58. Ibid., page 32
59. Ibid., page 69
60. Ibid., page 41
61. Ibid., page 42
62. Ibid., page 94
63. Ibid., page 99
64. Ibid., page 61-62
65. Ibid., page 76
66. Ibid., page 62
67. Ibid., page 101
68. Ibid., page 62
69. Warnock, George – *From Tent to Temple,* page 2
70. Jackson, Bill – *The Quest for the Radical Middle: A History of the Vineyard,* page 186
71. Warnock, George – *From Tent to Temple,* page 6-7
72. Ibid., page 8
73. Ibid., page 20
74. Jackson, Bill – *The Quest for the Radical Middle: A History of the Vineyard,* page 200

75. Ibid., page 231

76. Ibid., page 234

77. Ibid., page 239-240

78. http://www.ihopkc.org/about/affirmations-and-denials/

79. Wagner, C. Peter – *Spheres of Influence,* chapter 2

80. Jackson, Bill – *The Question for the Radical Middle: A History of the Vineyard,* page 249-240

81. Ibid., page 187

82. Grady, J. Lee – *What Happened to the Fire?,* page 160

83. Ibid., page 161

84. Toderash, Brent (aka Brother Maynard) – *Servant Leadership and the Five-Fold Ministries: Ephesians 4 Gifts Reconsidered*

85. Grudem, Wayne - *Systematic Theology,* page 911

86. Assemblies of God Position Paper: *Apostles and Prophets (2001),* page 5

87. Assemblies of God Position Paper: *Apostles and Prophets (2001),* page 4

88. Toderash, Brent (aka Brother Maynard) – *Servant Leadership and the Five-fold Ministries: Ephesians 4 Gifts Reconsidered,* page 4

89. Ibid., page 5

90. Assemblies of God Position Paper: *Apostles and Prophets (2001),* page 6

91. Ibid., page 9

92. Bernard of Clairvaux – *On Loving God*

93. Brother Lawrence of the Resurrection – *The Practice of the Presence of God,* page 53

94. Grudem, Wayne – *Systematic Theology* 1994, page 754

95. Erickson, Millard – *Christian Theology,* page 968

96. Wimber, John (with Springer, Kevin) – *The Dynamics of Spiritual Growth,* page 144

97. Grudem, Wayne - *Systematic Theology,* page 748

98. Hunter, Todd – *Spiritual Disciplines*

99. Foster, Richard – *Celebration of Discipline,* page 17

100. Grudem, Wayne – *Systematic Theology,* page 747

101. Grudem, Wayne – *Systematic Theology,* page 751

102. Foster, Richard – *Celebration of Discipline,* page 33-34

103. Wimber, John (with Springer, Kevin) – *Power Healing,* page 49

104. Telford, John – *Life of John Wesley,* The Epworth Press, London UK (1947), page 394

Chapter Four

WORD OF FAITH

Shortly after we were married, Wendy and I took a group of teenagers to a Christian music festival west of Toronto, where we spent five days enjoying leaky tents, mostly-cooked campfire food, and a lot of great Christian bands.

During the festival, we ran into friends whom we hadn't seen in a while, and it was a great time of catching up, as well as building deeper relationships with the teenagers who had accompanied us.

On the third day, the weather was grey and overcast, and as we sat on the grass about twenty yards from the main stage, we were remarking on the threatening sky. Thunderstorms in southern Ontario, after all, can be quite intense.

A friend from summer camp, Carolyn, looked up at the heavy clouds and commented in an off-hand manner, "Man, I sure hope it doesn't rain."

A woman seated a few yards away whirled around to face us, quite agitated. "Don't talk like that!" she rebuked Carolyn. "Don't you know your words have power, and the demons can make it rain because of your bad confession?"

We thought she was joking at first. We had never heard anyone speak this way in person; televangelists, sure, but we weren't expecting this at a Christian music festival. "Oh, and I suppose you believe God wants us all rich and healthy, too?" asked Carolyn.

"Of course!" the woman exclaimed, looking at us as if she wondered if we were truly Christians. "As your faith is, so be it unto you!" And with that, she abruptly turned on her heel and quickly departed.

We all looked at each other, eyebrows raised, and then collectively shrugged and went back to waiting for the next concert to begin.

"I still hope it doesn't rain," said Carolyn, with a mischievous grin. (It didn't.)

For years, some conservative evangelicals have used the "health and wealth" or "positive confession" teachings as a warning against the entire charismatic movement. They mistakenly believed that this doctrine – properly known as "Word of Faith" – was normative for the mainstream of the charismatic movement.

(There are also other, less-complimentary terms that are used by some Christians to describe this movement. The more Christ-honoring response, even where strong differences of opinion exist, is to call people what they have named themselves. In this case, Word of Faith.)

What may come as a surprise to many conservative evangelicals is that some of the strongest criticisms of the Word of Faith movement have come from within the charismatic realm itself.

"Years before the Jim Bakker/PTL scandal, many believers in America were so repulsed by money-grubbing TV preachers that they returned to their denominational churches in disgust."[1]

Many theologically conservative evangelicals have avoided the charismatic movement because of their disdain for Word of Faith teachings and the extremes of televangelism. Today, it is also not uncommon to hear post-charismatics point to the Word of Faith movement as one of the reasons that they now wish to distance themselves from being called charismatic.

There have been several accusations made against the Word of Faith movement's original writers that we need to address before digging deeper into the teachings themselves.

KENNETH E. HAGIN: PLAGIARIZER?

Evangelical authors have written numerous books exposing the Word of Faith teaching; the most well known would include John MacArthur's *The Charismatics (1978)*, *Charismatic Chaos (1992)* and *Strange Fire (2013)*, Hank Hannegraaf's *Christianity in Crisis (1993)*, and D.R. McConnell's *A Different Gospel (1988)*.

McConnell's book created quite a stir when it was first published. In it, McConnell accused Kenneth E. Hagin, the acknowledged father of the Word of Faith movement, of plagiarizing the earlier works of E.W. Kenyon. McConnell's book included a side-by-side chart comparing segments from books by Kenyon with Hagin's writings. The evidence is damning, despite Hagin's protestations that he had developed his teaching long before he had even heard of Kenyon. Hagin does concede, however, that he may have come across some of Kenyon's sermons or writings but had not recalled this fact when he wrote his own material. "Reading or hearing something once was all that was necessary for him to recall it verbatim."[2]

Joe McIntyre is the president of the Healing Rooms ministry, as well as Kenyon's Gospel Publishing Society, and is the current publisher of Kenyon's writings. McIntyre has authored a book entitled *E.W. Kenyon and His Message of Faith: The True Story*. In it, McIntyre concedes that the similarities between Hagin's and Kenyon's work are too obvious to ignore, but contends that Kenneth Hagin (called "Dad" Hagin by many in the movement) had a photographic memory, which could account for his verbatim wording.

While acknowledging the plagiarism, McIntyre does not think this constitutes a serious issue between Hagin and Kenyon. According to McIntyre, "from his vantage point in heaven, Kenyon is probably delighted that Kenneth E. Hagin has been so successful in getting the message of faith, so dear to Kenyon's heart, out to so many in the world in this generation."[3]

Whatever the reason behind the similarities between their writings, what remains is that McIntyre – as the inheritor and promoter of Kenyon's written legacy – confirms that their message is one and the same. Ultimately, whether or not the charges of plagiarism are warranted, we need to examine the *content* of their joint message.

THE NEW THOUGHT CONNECTION

The other common accusation regarding E.W. Kenyon was his connection to what was called 'New Thought' during his university years. As the *Dictionary of Pentecostal and Charismatic Movements* puts it:

"Conceptually, the views espoused by E.W. Kenyon can be traced to his exposure to metaphysical ideas derived from attendance at Emerson College of Oratory in Boston, a spawning ground for New Thought philosophical ideas. The major tenets of the New Thought movement are health or healing, abundance or prosperity, wealth, and happiness."[4]

McIntyre takes exception to McConnell's stating that the New Thought movement influenced Kenyon in any way: "Kenyon wasn't actually in Boston during the time McConnell believes he was... As to Kenyon's being influenced at Emerson College, when Kenyon went there for the one year he attended, he was not walking with the Lord and was not seeking any kind of religious training."[5]

While McIntyre may be able to prove, historically, that Kenyon was not at Emerson College when the main proponent of New Thought (Ralph Waldo Trine) was there, the argument that therefore Kenyon wasn't influenced still seems weak. Even if Kenyon was "not walking with the Lord", that doesn't mean that he would therefore be impervious to any New Thought concepts that he was exposed to.

Some of the strongest criticisms of the Word of Faith movement have come from within the charismatic realm.

Again, as with the evidence of Hagin's plagiarism, the similarities between New Thought and Word of Faith are striking. While this doesn't necessarily prove a common root, it cannot be ignored either.

Regardless of whether one believes McConnell or McIntyre on the issue of New Thought roots in the writings of E.W. Kenyon, the point remains: how does the teaching itself stand up?

E.W. KENYON

Essex William (E.W.) Kenyon (1867-1948) hailed from upstate New York, and much of his early ministry years were spent in the New England area. After numerous pastoral positions, he started the Dudley Bible Institute – which soon moved to Spencer Massachusetts and was renamed Bethel Bible Institute – where he served as president for twenty-five years. The school moved again some years later, and became Providence Bible Institute.

When Kenyon later relocated to Los Angeles, he became a pioneer in the area of radio broadcasting there and later in Seattle.

"Kenyon later devoted himself more fully to itinerant ministry and writing... Although he was not Pentecostal, his work *The Wonderful Name of Jesus* (1927) was widely read among Oneness Pentecostals. His writings have had a broad acceptance in the Deeper Life and charismatic movements."[6]

For someone who was not Pentecostal himself (all of his churches were Baptist), Kenyon has had a profound impact on the charismatic movement. One of those influenced heavily by Kenyon was W.J. "Ern" Baxter, who went on to become William Branham's manager, a participant in the Latter Rain movement, but would become best known in later years as a member of the "Fort Lauderdale Five" who gave leadership to the Shepherding Movement.

Others who have been influenced by Kenyon's writings include Kenneth Copeland, Don Gossett, Charles Capps, and of course, Kenneth E. Hagin and Kenneth Hagin Jr.

Kenneth E. Hagin

Kenneth Hagin is widely considered to be the father of the Word of Faith movement, by friends and critics alike. Certainly, through his Rhema Bible Training Center in Tulsa OK, his daily radio program 'Faith Seminar of the Air', over 50 million copies of his 125 books, monthly tapes, and his half-million-subscriber *The Word of Faith* magazine, Hagin is one of the most influential and well-known proponents of Word of Faith teaching.

Hagin was born with a heart condition from which he was not expected to survive, although he was fifteen before his health failed to the point of making him an invalid. During his sixteenth year, "during a ten minute period, his vital signs failed three times. On each occasion, he witnessed the horrors of hell. This led to his conversion on April 22, 1937."[7] By the time Hagin turned seventeen he had been healed of his heart condition, and began a ministry mostly among Baptist congregations. After experiencing a baptism in the Holy Spirit at age twenty, Hagin began to minister among Pentecostals, and pastored numerous Pentecostal churches.

Hagin's itinerant ministry as a Bible teacher and evangelist began twelve years later, in 1949. "During the following 14 years he had a series of eight visions of Jesus Christ, who in the third vision granted him the gift of discerning of spirits, enabling him to pray more effectively for the healing of the sick."[8]

Richard Riss charitably writes, "Kenneth Hagin emphasizes the message of uncompromising faith in God's desire to bless, in every area of life, all who do not doubt him... his message emphasizes the need to pray only according to God's principles as found in the Judeo-Christian Scriptures."[9]

LEGAL/COVENANT FOUNDATION

The main thrust of the Word of Faith teaching, or "Positive Confession" as it is sometimes called, is that our words have the power to determine our quality of life. A positive confession – speaking only words of health, prosperity and success – will result in our lives being characterized by health, prosperity and success. Contrarily, a negative confession – which is interpreted to be lack of faith or the presence of doubt – can bring the opposite upon the undiscerning believer. "As your faith is, so be it unto you" was a popular slogan to summarize this concept.

Kenyon typically used legal terminology to explain his views: "Christianity is a legal document... You have as much right to demand healing as you have to demand the cashing of a cheque at a bank where you have a deposit."[10] This kind of approach is foundational to understanding the Word of Faith worldview.

Kenyon's premise is that God has promised healing, prosperity and success, and that the only thing that believers need to do is just claim these promises. Hagin concurs when he writes, "That's how it is with our rights and privileges in Christ. Healing belongs to us. God has provided it for us. But we have to possess it."[11] And the key to possessing healing (and prosperity) is the spoken word of positive confession.

Echoing this 'legal' viewpoint is Kenneth Copeland, another prominent figure in the Word of Faith movement. Copeland uses the term *covenant* rather than Kenyon's reference to a *legal document*, but his meaning is the same: "Discipline everything you do, everything you say, and everything you think to agree with what God does, what God says, and what God thinks! God will be obligated to meet your needs because of His Word."[12]

These words sound uncomfortably strong – demand, possess, obligate – but to the Word of Faith movement, they would only be arrogant and presumptuous *if God had not already promised these things.*

From their theological vantage point, they are simply choosing to be obedient and believe all that God has promised in Scripture. In their view, the rest of the evangelical/charismatic church has been guilty of ignoring and possibly suppressing biblical truth.

"The Church took spiritual blessing and left the prosperity and healing portions of the promise. It is true that spiritual redemption is a greater blessing than prosperity or healing, but God never asked you to choose...

"He held out the new birth, prosperity and healing. The Church took the new birth and disregarded prosperity and healing."[13]

In the Word of Faith view, salvation *includes* healing and prosperity. One of the most well-known verses that the Word of Faith is fond of quoting is Isaiah 53:5: "But He was pierced for our transgressions, He was crushed for our iniquities; the punishment that brought us peace was upon Him, and by His wounds we are healed." This is basis for their belief that 'healing is in the atonement'. Consider Hagin's words:

"The sinner does not need to beg God to save him. The work's already been accomplished. All he needs to do is accept it and thank God for it – then it becomes his.

"The believer doesn't need to ask God to heal him because Jesus has already borne our sickness. All the believer needs to do is know that healing belongs to him."[14]

Most Word of Faith adherents that I know personally are honestly and deeply concerned that other Christians don't accept their teaching; to them, the rest of the Church is failing to truly believe God. Kenyon writes: "How glad the Father would be, if we would arise and take our Legal Rights... A literal translation would read: 'If ye shall demand anything in my name, that will I do'... In the face of this mighty Fact, poverty and weakness of spirit are criminal."[15]

> **God will be obligated to meet your needs because of His Word.**
>
> - Kenneth Copeland

This approach to interpreting the Bible becomes the lens through which Word of Faith proponents view all of Scripture. This places Christians into the position of holding God accountable for promises in His Word – even promises which He may not have actually made. "The self-defined phrase 'confessing the Word of

God' takes precedence over hermeneutical principles and rules for biblical interpretation. This approach not only does violence to the text but forces the NT linguistic data into artificial categories that the biblical authors themselves could not affirm."[16]

USE OF RHEMA

Another key to the Word of Faith approach is their concept of the Greek words *rhema* and *logos*. Simply put, they define *logos* to be the written word of God and *rhema* as the 'living word' or the 'now' word of God. "The major premise of *rhema* doctrine is that whatever is spoken by faith becomes immediately inspired and therefore dynamic in the particular situation or event to which it is addressed."[17]

Many Christians have had the experience of reading a well-known passage of Scripture, and suddenly, a certain verse or phrase seems to jump off the page. The reader (probably correctly) concludes that the Holy Spirit is speaking through that verse or phrase.

On the surface, this may sound similar to what Word of Faith teaches, but after looking more closely at their beliefs, the differences will become clearer.

The Word of Faith teachers take this idea much further than a verse being highlighted during a Christian's Bible reading. Word of Faith applies the *rhema* principle to the words *spoken by Christians*. It goes beyond *rhema* as a 'now word' from the Holy Spirit and instead becomes a way of speaking into existence the desires and thoughts of the individual Christian.

"The positive confession emphasis has a tendency to include statements which make it appear that man is sovereign and God is the servant... This puts man in the position of using God rather than man surrendering himself to be used of God."[18]

Word of Faith teachers are quick to stress that any positive confession must be based on the word of God. Some try to distance themselves from the idea that people choose to make their 'confession' based on their own greed or wants. For example, Kenneth Copeland makes a point of urging generosity as the basis for making a positive confession of prosperity: "Now you can see that the basic reason for the operation of faith is to meet the needs of mankind. You may not need much money to be happy and successful in your own life, but people are starving and dying throughout the world. Someone must provide for them."[19]

(In my own area, one of the local Word of Faith churches is well known for its generosity to families who are struggling financially, as well as to the street community. Give them credit: they are generous towards the poor and disadvantaged in our community.)

Copeland's appeal to a generous motivation for claiming prosperity is commendable. However, the problem behind the prosperity emphasis is the assumption that it is God's will that *all* believers live in total health and material prosperity. "God has established His covenant – for salvation, for healing, for deliverance, for prosperity – and these provisions of the covenant are set out in God's Word."[20]

In order to validate this use of *rhema*, Word of Faith teachers point to Romans 10:8: "But what does it say? 'The word is near you; it is in your mouth and in your heart,' that is, the word of faith we are proclaiming..." For Word of Faith proponents, to "proclaim the word of faith" is the active participation of Christians, speaking forth the promises found in God's word. This particular verse has become a signature catchphrase to encourage positive confession.

It is helpful to read Romans 10:8 in its context, which aids greatly in understanding what Paul meant by the phrase 'the word of faith we are proclaiming':

"But what does it say? 'The word is near you; it is in your mouth and in your heart,' that is, the word of faith we are proclaiming: *that if you confess with your mouth, 'Jesus is Lord,' and believe in your heart that God raised him from the dead, you will be saved.* For it is with your heart that you believe and are justified, and it is with your mouth that you confess and are saved." (Romans 10:8-10, emphasis added)

In context, this verse is about saving faith in Jesus Christ, not to a positive confession leading to prosperity and/or healing. Of course, Word of Faith teachers will quickly point out that the definition of the Greek word for 'salvation' *(sozo)* includes wholeness, healing and peace, as well as the normally understood saving function of faith. The emphasis in the Romans passage, however, is not on the power of the believer's confession to claim prosperity. Paul is proclaiming the message (word) of faith that the Romans can be saved by faith in Jesus.

Finally, in the New Testament, the words *logos* and *rhema* are used almost interchangeably. "In the case of the Septuagint, both *rhema* and *logos* are used to translate the one Hebrew word *dabar*, which is used in various ways relative to communication... The Word of God, whether referred to as *logos* or *rhema*, is inspired, eternal, dynamic, and miraculous. Whether the Word is written or spoken does not alter its essential character."[21]

In the story found at the beginning of this section, the agitated woman was concerned about the effect of our 'negative confession' on the weather. The most common basis for this kind of thinking comes from Proverbs 6:2: "If you have been trapped by what you said, ensnared by the words of your mouth..." This verse is used as a proof-text to defend the idea that negative words have power to bring destruction into a believer's life, or at the very least cause us to lose promised blessings. A friend of mine who was raised in the Word of Faith movement can recount stories about the 'confession cops' who thrived on rebuking others in their church for 'negative confessions'.

E.W. Kenyon writes: "The enemy *[Satan]* will try to make you deny your confession. He will try to make you confess weakness and failure and want..."[22]

"We do not come with that quiet assurance that we would if some banker had given us his word in regard to our financial standing at the bank. This leads to weakness, to doubt and fear. It makes a vacillating type of faith."[23]

Hagin explains it further: "I began by telling them it is unscriptural to pray, 'If it be Thy will' concerning anything which God's Word has already promised us. When you put an 'if' in your prayer, you are praying with doubt."[24]

Copeland echoes the same theme: "I have prayed with people and when I finished said, 'It is done and it will come to pass.' Then the other person who was supposed to be agreeing with me would say, 'I certainly do hope so, Brother Copeland.' At that point I am forced to say, 'Well, it won't. I agreed... you hoped.'"[25]

But if we return to the Proverbs 6:2 passage, we will see a different application arising from the plain meaning of the verse when read in context:

"My son, if you have put up security for your neighbor, if you have struck hands in pledge for another, if you have been trapped by what you said, ensnared by the words of your mouth, then do this my son, to free yourself, since you have fallen into your neighbor's hands: Go and humble yourself; press your plea with your neighbor!" (Proverbs 6:1-3).

In context, Proverbs 6:2 has nothing to do with a negative confession. This is a father giving advice to his son on how to extricate himself from a hasty pledge that the son finds himself unable to fulfill. The advice is for the son to humble himself and negotiate with the neighbor with whom he made the hasty vow.

The use of the hermeneutical approach to Scripture known as *eisegesis* – lifting verses or fragments of verses out of context – is grounds for holding the positive/negative confession teaching at a healthy distance. The immediate context of the verses suggests that the Word of Faith understanding is not based on sound biblical exegesis, and the broader witness of Scripture also does not back up the Word of Faith teachings.

> 1. **eis·e·ge·sis** [ahy-si-jee-sis] – noun; An interpretation, especially of Scripture, that expresses the interpreter's own ideas, bias, or the like, rather than the meaning of the text.
> 2. **ex·e·ge·sis** [ek-si-jee-sis] – noun; Critical explanation or interpretation of a text or portion of a text, especially of the Bible.

"When the positive confession teaching indicates that to admit weakness is to accept defeat, to admit financial need is to accept poverty, and to admit sickness is to preclude healing, it is going beyond and is contrary to the harmony of Scripture[26]... When the positive confession doctrine indicates a person can have whatever he says, it fails to emphasize adequately that God's will must be considered."[27]

The last area of concern with how the *rhema* doctrine is used is the idea that our words can have the same creative power as God's. Kenyon states:

"We can bind Demons, bind disease, and habits, and bind men so that they cannot go on in the will of Satan; or use fearsome power to deliver souls over to Satan for the destruction of the body[28]... We see Peter striking a man and woman dead for lying.

Awful power this is; power to heal and power to slay. They were walking in the omnipotence of the authority given them by Jesus."[29]

Contrary to Kenyon's suggestion, Peter only *foretold* the deaths of Ananias and Sapphira. The Bible does not say that Peter was the one who struck the two of them dead. While Jesus *has* given authority to individual Christians, to describe it as 'omnipotence' is treading on thin ice. Omnipotence is one of the incommunicable attributes of God: He shares it with no one. *(And Jesus did not give us authority to kill other Christians!)*

Hagin has advanced a similar idea – that we are able to 'bind' people to God's purposes:

"I raised my Bible in one hand, lifted my other hand to Heaven, and said, 'In the Name of the Lord Jesus Christ, I break the power of the devil over my brother Dub's life and claim Dub's deliverance. That means deliverance from the devil and full salvation in Jesus' Name. Amen.

"And this is a critical point on salvation, on faith, and on receiving whatever you need from God: As long as Satan can hold you in the arena of reason, he will whip you every time – in every battle, every conflict."[30]

Earlier, I mentioned that several televangelists got into some controversy for claiming that Christians are "little gods". However, this idea is not isolated to a few televangelists.

Kenyon wrote: "John 10:10: 'I came that they may have life, and may have it abundantly.' What is Life? Life is the Nature of God. You may have the Father's Nature abundantly."[31] Christians would normally agree that we are partakers of the divine nature (2 Peter 1:3-4), but this is usually understood in terms of the imputed righteousness of Jesus and empowerment for living a holy life. To equate the 'abundant life' of John 10:10 with possessing God's nature is a stretch, to say the least. And as unworthy servants who have the undeserved privilege of partaking in the divine nature, humility would be a more appropriate and fitting response (Luke 17:10).

The famous revivalist John G. Lake was more succinct: "Man is not a separate creation detached from God; he is part of God Himself... God intends us to be gods. The inner man is the real governor, the true man that Jesus said was a god."[32] (Lake's ideas were influenced by Phineas P. Quimby, a progenitor of New Thought in the mid-1800s, whose writings also influenced E.W. Kenyon, as well as William Branham.)

Even after the outcry against some of the televangelists who promoted the "little gods" theology, the teaching continues to circulate. "*[Archibishop]* Earl Paulk of Atlanta wrote recently, 'Just as dogs have puppies, and cats have kittens, so God has little gods. Until we comprehend that we are little gods and we begin to act like little gods, we cannot manifest the Kingdom of God.'"[33]

Hagin's terminology is not as controversial, but his understanding is very much in keeping with Paulk: "Notice that through Jesus, we have been made righteous. We believers (we who have been born again) don't have to try to become righteous – because we are righteous."[34] If by this Hagin meant that we are declared righteous because of the finished work of Christ on the cross, we could agree with this statement. However, in the Word of Faith understanding, it goes beyond God declaring us righteous, and becomes part of possessing God's nature as "little gods", who now have the power of the creative spoken word.

A more nuanced view would be the position taken by the Assemblies of God: "When believers recognize the sovereignty of God and properly become concerned with the will of God, they will not talk in terms of compelling God or using God's power. They will speak of becoming obedient servants."[35]

HEALING

Very early on, Kenyon set the course for the belief that healing is a God-ordained right for all Christians: "We have come to believe that it is just as wrong for a believer to bear his sickness when Jesus bore it, as it is for him to bear his sins when Christ bore them."[36] This concept of healing being synonymous with salvation is repeated today in Word of Faith circles.

Hagin writes: "I can't push a button or pull a lever, so to speak, and make the gifts start working. They operate as the SPIRIT wills. Yet we are instructed not to wait for Him, since He has already done something about our healing at the Cross[37]... Likewise, it is not a matter of God healing an individual; it is a matter of the person accepting the gift of healing God has already provided."[38]

Copeland puts it this way: "When the Word says you are healed, you are healed! It doesn't matter what your body says about it. If you will believe this and operate accordingly, then the covenant you have with God – His Word – will become the absolute truth in your situation, and your physical body will come into agreement with the Word[39]... God has established His covenant – for salvation, for healing, for deliverance, for prosperity – and these provisions of the covenant are set out in God's Word."[40]

Word of Faith believes that physical healing and wholeness is bound up in our salvation. Healing is part of the 'legal document' that Kenyon speaks of, and the 'covenant' of Copeland's writings. It is this approach that gave rise to the unflattering but generally accurate phrase "name it and claim it".

"In the mind of the Father, you are healed. Jesus knows that He bore your diseases. How it must hurt Him to hear you talk about bearing them yourself. Learn to say: 'I am healed because He did that work and satisfied the Supreme Court of the Universe.'"[41]

If you speak with Word of Faith people, they are genuinely puzzled, and at times deeply concerned with other Christians who believe that suffering might be a part of God's plan/will for a believer. To them, not claiming the healing that is promised in salvation is, at best, foolishness, and at worst, the sin of unbelief.

To suggest that suffering might be a part of God's will for a believer's life is seen as a misrepresentation of God's character; some would go as far as labeling it blasphemy.

The Word of Faith movement has been described as having an "over-realized eschatology". Poverty, disease and sin *will* be eradicated at the return of Jesus to usher in the Kingdom. There is no debate about that. The question raised by the Word of Faith is how much of that Kingdom reality is available in the here and now.

Kenyon's passionate declaration fits this over-realized eschatology: "The hour will come when you will awaken to the fact that he *[Satan]* cannot put disease upon you, that he cannot give you pain and anguish in your body. The hour will come when you will know that want and poverty are things of the past as far as you are concerned."[42]

PROSPERITY

Pentecostals and Charismatics believe in divine healing, although they would differ from the emphasis of the Word of Faith movement. However, saying that "it is God's will that you be rich" provokes an even stronger reaction than the idea of 'claiming' healing.

The Word of Faith understanding is that prosperity, like healing, is an implied part of our salvation. Many Word of Faith teachers link financial prosperity to God's original plan at the creation of the world. Gloria Copeland, Kenneth's wife, puts it this way:

"God's will for Adam was abundance and plenty. Poverty and lack came only after Adam changed gods and began to operate under Satan's dominion... Since His will does not change, God's will for His people today is abundance (James 1:17)... From the beginning of time, He has provided financial prosperity for His people through obedience to His Word."[43]

This view of prosperity as a part of God's will is found in Kenyon's writings, although not as prominently as his admonitions to claim healing: "This Redemption is real. Satan is defeated, disease is outlawed, and want *[poverty]* is banished."[44]

A popular verse that is applied to prosperity (aside from Old Testament passages about the covenant with Abraham), is 3 John 2: "Beloved, I wish above all things that thou mayest prosper and be in health, even as thy soul prospereth" (KJV).

The word translated 'prosper' in this verse is the Greek word *euodoo*, which can be translated to mean:

1. To grant a prosperous and expeditious journey

2. To grant a successful issue, to cause to prosper

3. To prosper, be successful

Word of Faith contends that this is a clear statement that financial prosperity is to be the norm for Christians everywhere.

"John was a wise old man, strong in the Lord, and he said, 'I wish above all things that you prosper and be in health.' Through our traditional ideas, we have been led to believe that prosperity is bad or ungodly. However, John writes that we should prosper and be healthy."[45]

It is interesting to note that the emphasis attached to 3 John 2 by Word of Faith teachers is dependent on the King James Version. If we were to look at the same verse in a different version, we find a different note being sounded:

"Dear friend, I pray that you may enjoy good health and that all may go well with you, even as your soul is getting along well" (NIV).

"Dear friend, I hope all is well with you and that you are as healthy in body as you are strong in spirit" (NLT).

> "You can have what you say! You must realize that it is God's will for you to prosper."
>
> - Kenneth Copeland

If we refer to any of the three possible definitions for the word 'prosper' (Greek *euodoo*), the plain sense of the NIV or NLT translation makes better contextual sense than the Word of Faith's interpretation. John is writing a personal greeting to Gaius (the recipient of the original letter), and this phrase should not be taken as anything other than a good friend's well-wishing. This brief verse serves as the introduction to the real meat of John's letter, not as a doctrinal statement on prosperity.

The Word of Faith movement has difficulty accepting the notion that adverse circumstances could be a part of God's plan. Hagin notes: "People will say about someone, 'Well, God used that tragedy to bring him to salvation.' But that kind of thinking is not in line with the Bible."[46]

The emphasis is on God's love and covenant promise to bless – physically, spiritually, and financially – Christians who understand and have faith to believe God's covenant. Poverty, or even humble circumstances, is seen as un-biblical.

Copeland writes: "You won't find a Jew who believes in poverty because poverty is not in the Old Covenant. It is in religion, not in the Bible. It was put into Christianity as a religion during the Dark Ages when the Word was taken from the people and put away in monasteries. Poverty oaths were fed into Christianity when the religious hierarchy took over. The men operating it were not born-again men."[47]

Knowing God's covenant is the key to getting what you are promised (prosperity): "He cannot establish His covenant in your life without prospering you. The man who holds to poverty rejects the establishment of the covenant... The covenant cannot be established in your life unless you believe God's Word concerning prosperity. Let there be no doubt about God's will. God's will is to establish His covenant in the earth. Prosperity is a major requirement in the establishment of God's will."[48]

Unbelief, then, or lack of understanding this covenant, leads to tragic results, according to Word of Faith reasoning:

"Moses went forth in the name of the covenant, performed miracles by the power of God in the face of Pharaoh, and led God's people out of bondage. They could have gone free 400 years before, but they didn't know their covenant!"[49]

Nowhere in Scripture are we told that God's people could have gone free earlier, simply by claiming the covenant. Moses didn't teach that to the people, nor did God mention it during the time at Mount Sinai when He gave the Law to Moses.

The Assemblies of God summarized it this way: "This view advocates that God wants believers to wear the best clothing, drive the best cars, and have the best of everything. Believers need not suffer financial setbacks. All they need to do is to tell Satan to take his hands off their money. The believer can have whatever he says whether the need is spiritual, physical, or financial."[50]

Kenyon echoes this same sentiment: "There is no excuse for the spiritual weakness and poverty of the Family of God when the wealth of Grace and Love of our great Father with His power and wisdom are all at our disposal."[51]

Copeland agrees: "You can have what you say! Remember, we said earlier that all the material substance you will ever need is already in the earth. Everything you need is already here. The confession of your mouth will cause you to possess it. God will see to that[52]... You must realize that it is God's will for you to prosper (see 3 John 2). This is available to you, and frankly, it would be stupid of you not to partake of it!"[53]

FRANKLIN HALL (LATTER RAIN WRITER)

Another influential proponent of the prosperity doctrine was Latter Rain writer Franklin Hall, who wrote *Atomic Power with God through Prayer and Fasting*.

Like William Branham, Franklin Hall was involved primarily in the Latter Rain (Restorationist) churches. Although he was not a part of the Word of Faith movement itself, some of his ideas overlapped and influenced the Word of Faith approach.

Like Branham, Franklin Hall was fascinated with the Zodiac, and likened Scorpio (a scorpion) to the sex drive, which he believed was also connected to life and death in God's economy. He also shared the Latter Rain viewpoint that the church had 'lost' many vital teachings after the days of the apostles:

"They *[the early Christians]* not only failed to have power to do the impossible, but after the days of the apostles the church became powerless, and eventually began to say that the days of healing were over; that the miracles were not for them anymore; the Holy Spirit, after the Bible pattern, was forsaken, and the power of the apostolic age was lost."[54]

An extremely judgmental attitude towards all denominations – another common Latter Rain theme – is also continued in Hall's writings, as is his belief that the Manifested Sons of God will set things right.

"The cripples, the sick, the suffering, the insane asylums filled with the distressed, and hospitals running over with sick and wounded, the groanings of suffering humanity everywhere, all is because the Sons of God do not have the vision, and know not how to manifest. The Laodicean, denominational, bound Church has so much riches, comfortable pews, stained-glass windows. But the CHRIST is left outside."[55]

Remember Hagin's words? "As long as Satan can hold you in the arena of reason, he will whip you every time."[56] Franklin Hall agrees:

"While reason is nervous, excited, and troubled; faith is patient, relaxed, and calm. It is necessary to be founded on the Word of God and believe the Word of God to retain our healing... We would be healed, but if our faith was not definitely established in the WORD OF GOD, there would be a possibility of the return of the ailment."[57]

Finally, Franklin Hall proposes the same idea that healing and prosperity are linked to salvation which Kenyon, Hagin, Copeland, etc. also share:

"If Jesus did not redeem the whole man, including his physical body and his material welfare, then Christ did not redeem any part of a man! It is a disgrace and a shame that Christians can have every kind of sickness that a sinner can have, and die a Devil's painful death in the same manner as a person without God can die and still claim salvation!"[58]

Hall's influence in the charismatic renewal of the 1960s, through his writings and those who had absorbed them earlier, sheds some light on why Word of Faith teachings continue to proliferate among churches that are not generally associated with the rest of the Word of Faith movement.

POST-CHARISMATIC REACTION

Late one autumn, one of our local church pastors was diagnosed with cancer. During the following winter and spring, he battled the disease, made some progress, and then suffered a setback, followed by more progress and then another setback.

During this season, hundreds of people were praying for his healing. He was well known around the city, and numerous churches sent their entire staff and eldership teams to anoint him for healing. Some pastors came to him, as he lay in his hospital bed, to repent for their attitudes towards him in previous years, and they would pray for each other.

The summer was looking better, and anyone who visited him in the hospice room set up in his house could be sure of two things: (1) a warm welcome, and (2) he would pray for *you* after you prayed for him. Such was his pastoral heart for others, even as his physical body suffered.

Hope and faith for healing continued to ride high, but as August drew to a close, another setback reared up, and by the end of September, he was gone.

It was, understandably, a devastating time for everyone who knew him, especially his wife and children. The grieving process had barely begun, when one of his teenagers was confronted by a group of students at one of the Christian high schools.

They were brief, but devastating, in their remarks. Your father, they stated unequivocally, died because your church failed to claim his healing. If your father had been at a Word of Faith church, they said, he would still be alive today. It was therefore inappropriate for the family to ask the Spirit to be their Comforter, because the Spirit was offended by their failure to claim the healing that could have been.

Needless to say, these words brought no comfort or encouragement to a grieving teenager. While more mature Christians in the Word of Faith camp would not be as crassly callous in their remarks, the underlying assumptions would remain.

Many people outside of the charismatic movement have avoided it based on the perception that Word of Faith teachings are typical of all charismatics. Examples such as this one only serve to reinforce that decision.

Post-charismatics also point to the excessive lifestyles of televangelists, the performance-orientation of always having to 'check their confession', and the negligence towards the poor to explain their decision to distance themselves from their charismatic backgrounds.

The emerging generations have been raised in a much more globally aware society than previous generations. By globally aware, I mean also that they are more aware of their *responsibility* in the world. They possess a strong sense of social justice for the suffering in other nations.

Organisations such as World Vision, the Voice of the Martyrs, Make Poverty History, and others have served to heighten the average Christian's awareness of global opportunities to alleviate suffering and carry out Jesus' commands to care for the poor.

When the apostle Paul went to Jerusalem to meet with the other apostles, he wanted to plainly set forth the message that he had been preaching among the Gentiles (as recounted in Galatians 2:1-10). The leaders in Jerusalem, including James, Peter and John, approved of Paul's presentation of the gospel, and agreed that Paul and his companions should continue as they had been among the Gentiles. They had only one suggestion for Paul in his ministry: "all they asked was that we should continue to remember the poor, the very thing I was eager to do" (Galatians 2:10).

Many are asking the legitimate question, "What are we doing for the poor?" and not finding any satisfactory answers. The Word of Faith response tends to place the blame on the poor themselves, because their lack of faith is responsible for their poverty. Only by claiming their inheritance in the covenant could they extricate themselves from their current economic situation.

Many in the emerging generations would read verses like Isaiah 58:6-7 as a rallying cry: "Is not this the kind of fasting I have chosen: to loose the chains of injustice and untie the cords of the yoke, to set the oppressed free and break every yoke? Is it not to share your food with the hungry and to provide the poor wanderer with shelter – when you see the naked, to clothe him, and not to turn away from your own flesh and blood?"

Younger charismatics are looking at New Testament passages such as James 2, which clearly advocates a 'faith and works' dynamic, and feeling as though they have just discovered a missing jewel in their Christian experience.

"Suppose a brother or sister is without clothes and daily food. If one of you says to him, 'Go, I wish you well; keep warm and well fed,' but does nothing about his physical needs, what good is it?" (James 2:15-16).

Many are also weary of the constant pressure to check their positive confession (and avoiding the 'confession cops') to ensure that they aren't negating their confession by admitting weakness, doubt, pain or lack of finances. A helpful read is the Assemblies of God document *The Believer and Positive Confession,* published on their denominational website, which puts positive confession into a biblical perspective:

- "Paul admitted weakness and then stated that when he was weak, he was strong because God's strength is made perfect in weakness (2 Corinthians 12:9-10).[59]

- "It was after the disciples recognized they did not have enough to feed the multitudes and admitted it that Christ marvelously provided a more than adequate supply (Luke 9:12-13). It was after the disciples admitted they had caught no fish that Jesus directed them to a most successful endeavor (John 21:3-6).[60]

- "Paul even went so far as to glory in his infirmities instead of denying them (2 Corinthians 12:5-10).[61]

- "Paul had been shown he would suffer (Acts 9:16). Later he rejoiced in his sufferings for the Colossians."[62]

To many Christians, the Word of Faith teachings neglect the very real existence of suffering. And in the real (fallen) world where we live, bad things can sometimes happen to good (even faith-full) people. A more balanced and biblical viewpoint would say: "God promises to supply the needs of believers, and He knows how to deliver the godly out of temptation; but reigning in life as Christ did may also include suffering. The committed believer will accept this. He will not be disillusioned if life is not a continual series of pleasant experiences."[63]

One of the most famous missionary stories of the twentieth century was that of Jim Elliott and his five companions, who were murdered by the Auca Indians (whom they had hoped to evangelize). Jim's widow, Elizabeth Elliott, returned later to the same area, and eventually many of the tribe were converted to Christianity, including some of her husband's killers. *Through Gates of Splendor* was written by Elizabeth to chronicle the events that led to the conversion of many Auca Indians.

It goes without saying that Word of Faith teachers would *not* use this story as an example of the spread of the gospel, as it contradicts their assertion that God does not use misfortune to bring people to Himself.

After Judas' suicide, all but one of the original twelve disciples died a martyr's death, as did the apostle Paul. Only John lived to a ripe old age – in exile on the penal island of Patmos. Paul's ministry "resume", found in 2 Corinthians 11:23-28, included beatings, imprisonment, shipwrecks, knowing thirst and hunger, and going without food many times. His life was certainly not characterized by ongoing prosperity and triumph – from a human standpoint. And yet at the end of this 'resume of pain', Paul concludes: "If I must boast, I will boast of the things that show my weakness" (2 Corinthians 11:30).

One of several televangelist scandals in the late 1980s was the fall and imprisonment of Jim Bakker for defrauding his viewers of millions of dollars. While in prison, Bakker had a lot of time to think and study Scripture, and came to the conclusion that the prosperity doctrines that he had taught were, in fact, unbiblical.

J. Lee Grady quotes Bakker as saying, "There is no way, if you take the whole counsel of God's Word, that you can equate riches or material things as a sign of God's blessing... I have asked God to forgive me and I ask all who have sat under my ministry to forgive me for preaching a gospel emphasizing earthly prosperity."[64]

The Assemblies of God position paper also noted that the prosperity teachings were unique to an already-affluent North American culture: "Does the teaching have meaning only for those living in an affluent society? Or does it also work among the refugees of the world? What application does the teaching have for believers imprisoned for their faith by atheistic governments? Are those believers substandard who suffer martyrdom or grave physical injury at the hands of cruel, ruthless dictators? The truth of God's Word has a universal application."[65]

Grady cites this as a corroborative example: "In 1993 healing evangelist Benny Hinn stunned some of his followers when he announced that he was washing his hands of the so-called 'prosperity gospel'... God would not permit him, he said, to stand before the poverty-stricken people of Manila and promise them that if they gave in the offering, God would bless them with more money. If the prosperity message should not be preached in the Philippines, Hinn decided, it should not be preached in America. 'It is not a message from God,' he said."[66]

Sadly, even a cursory look today at Hinn's website today shows that he has once again embraced the prosperity gospel.

Finally, the performance-orientation of the Word of Faith movement is exhausting for many, and to those who have already dealt with issues of striving and works-based sanctification, it is anathema (cursed). The idea that our reality is shaped by our positive or negative confession puts all the responsibility on human effort, and precludes God's grace (unmerited favor) being active in our daily lives. "The disciples of Kenyon speak of prosperity as a 'divine right' and have formulated laws of prosperity to be rehearsed daily by persons seeking health and wealth."[67]

This wariness of performance-orientation is compounded by Franklin Hall's idea that fasting was a way of coercing God to perform: "Jesus fasted in order to secure His perfect faith from His humanity side... Jesus received the Holy Spirit, but this did not seem sufficient. It requires fasting and prayer to operate the Holy Ghost."[68]

Sadly, this just sounds like more works-based performance. And the unspoken (and sometimes spoken) assumption is that if prosperity, health and victory are *not* apparent in a Christian's life, the problem is (obviously) their faulty faith. This judgmental accusation usually serves to destroy whatever faith the person might have had, if they have been convinced that: "All of God's blessings and provisions are conditional. He gave us His Word to let us know what conditions must be met in order for us to receive these blessings."[69]

155

The truth of God's word is that He *does* provide for our needs, and instructs us to pray for our daily bread. But this is not based on a contractual obligation that God is forced to honor, if we can just muster up the right kind of faith. Throughout the Bible, there are many stories of God's miraculous healing power, as well as miracles of financial provision, but nowhere does Scripture teach us that these things are our 'rights'. They are, as everything else we receive from God, gifts of grace that flow out of His will.

SO NOW WHAT?

At a deeper level, the Word of Faith movement challenges us with the question of how faith is supposed to work. If we reject the Word of Faith emphasis, have we then reduced faith to an intellectual assent to the propositional statements of doctrine that define salvation? If Martin Luther's rallying cry of the Reformation still rings true – "the just shall live by faith" (Romans 1:17) – what does that look like?

Perhaps the first thing to address is our understanding of our role in the Kingdom of God. Many people seem to unconsciously hold to the idea that, in the final analysis, "it's all about me". We would never say this out loud, of course, because it would sound as presumptuous as it actually is. If you were to ask any group of Christians, everyone would enthusiastically agree that it's all about Jesus, and perhaps even quote Matt Redman's thoughtful song, *The Heart of Worship*.

For many of us, however, the reality is that too often we are unconsciously adding Jesus to **our** story. We may even naively use phrases like 'making' Jesus Lord of our lives (as if He needs our endorsement to be *Lord*). We say this innocently, not realizing that we have bought into a way of thinking that in our busy and important lives, we've graciously allowed Jesus some space as well.

I'm stating this somewhat provocatively in order to make a point: when we become followers of Jesus, we are stepping into a mighty, rushing river of God-history – the Kingdom of God – that predates us by literally thousands of years. We are not the center of the story; Jesus is. In reality, we are being added to *His* story, and not the other way around.

If the story *did* revolve around us, then the Word of Faith approach would not seem so strange. We could talk in terms of "operating the Holy Spirit" (Franklin Hall), of our "right to demand healing" (E.W. Kenyon), or that "prosperity is a major requirement in the establishment of God's will" (Kenneth E. Hagin).

When we become followers of Jesus, we are stepping into a mighty, rushing river of God-history.

Assuming that the story revolves around us will result in an unbalanced approach to prayer and faith from the very foundation of our understanding of God. The Assemblies of God summed it up this way: "This puts man in the position of using God rather than man surrendering himself to be used of God."[70]

After a conversation with David Watson about the state of the charismatic renewal in 1980, John Wimber wondered, "Have we entered a post-charismatic era, or is the charismatic movement entering a new stage in its development?"[71] (Note: Wimber was equating *post*-charismatic with *non*-charismatic, not as we have been using it here.)

One of John Wimber's signature phrases as he led the Vineyard movement was "everybody gets to play". Wimber simply meant that there should be no super-stars doing all the work while the majority sat and watched. In a post-charismatic scenario (in the sense that I have been using the term), the role of faith is vitally important, if we really believe "everyone gets to play".

During His earthly ministry, Jesus preached about nearness of the kingdom of God, healed people, performed miracles, cast out demons, and taught anyone who would listen, but He also modeled an interesting dynamic for His followers. Jesus showed us what living in dependence on the Holy Spirit looked like.

For example, Jesus emphatically stated that He only did what He saw His Father doing, or said what His Father was saying. Jesus lived in a radical dependence on His Father, and taught His disciples to emulate that example.

"Jesus gave them this answer, 'I tell you the truth, the Son can do nothing by Himself, He can do only what He sees his Father doing, because whatever the Father does the Son also does'" (John 5:19).

"By myself I can do nothing; I judge only as I hear, and my judgment is just, for I seek not to please myself but Him who sent Me" (John 5:30).

While speaking to the Pharisees, Jesus further stated, "When you have lifted up the Son of Man, then you will know that I am the one I claim to be, and that I do nothing on My own but speak just what the Father has taught Me... for I always do what pleases Him" (John 8:28-29).

And at the Last Supper, Jesus used similar terminology: "I am the vine; you are the branches. If a man remains in Me and I in him, he will bear much fruit; apart from Me you can do nothing" (John 15:5).

This sense of radical obedience to His Father's leading is not only a pattern for us to follow – since we claim to be "followers" of Jesus – but is also perhaps an explanation of why Jesus only healed one person at the pool of Bethesda in John 5:2-9.

The Pool of Bethesda, near the Sheep Gate in Jerusalem, was reputed to have healing qualities for the first person able to get into the waters after they were stirred up supernaturally. John tells us that a 'great number' of blind, lame and paralyzed people were lying around the pool, each hoping to be healed.

Despite the number of people hoping for healing around the pool, Jesus approaches only one of them: an invalid who had been waiting there for 35 years. During this prolonged wait, the invalid had become embittered and self-pitying as a result of his futile attempts to be the first into the pool.

Even when Jesus asks him, point-blank, if he wants to be healed, the invalid doesn't give him a straight answer. All that came out was a frustrated explanation about why he couldn't be healed.

This man clearly showed a *lack* of faith, yet Jesus healed him anyway. This is a remarkable contrast to other occasions when Jesus healed because of the faith of the sufferer (blind Bartimaeus – Mark 10:46-52) their family (Jairus – Luke 8:40-56), employers (the Roman Centurion – Luke 7:1-10), and friends (the roof-wreckers of Mark 2:3-12).

And then Jesus promptly left. There is no biblical evidence that Jesus healed anyone else in a place where "a great number" (John 5:3) were waiting and hoping for healing.

Jesus is recorded elsewhere as healing 'all' who came to Him (Matthew 8:16; Mark 6:56; Luke 6:17-19). It seems striking that He apparently chose to ignore the needs of the crowd around the Pool, and healed only one (apparently weak-in-faith, high-on-self-pity, no-positive-confession) invalid.

Unless, of course, that for reasons that only the Father knows, Jesus was acting exactly as the Father had instructed Him to. We don't know what the rationale would be for performing only one healing in such a needy place, but if we believe that God's thoughts and ways are truly above our thoughts and ways (Isaiah 55:8-9), then our inability to explain the purposes of God should come as no surprise.

How does this tie into our discussion on the role of faith? Simply this: we have to reconcile two opposite extremes: (a) a Word of Faith paradigm that demands that God perform healings (and financial blessings) on a contractual basis in response to our faith, or (b) negating any reliance on faith, and run the risk of "doin' the stuff" in our own strength and without genuinely being led by the Holy Spirit.

Jesus offers us a third way, a middle ground: taking great risks of faith, but only the risks that the Father is telling us to take, as a response to the initiating of the Spirit.

FAITH IS SPELLED R-I-S-K

Throughout the New Testament, the Greek word that we translate 'faith' (*pistis*) occurs over and over again. In some places, it is also used for 'believe' or 'believed'. For example, "So again I ask, does God give you his Spirit and work miracles among you by the works of the law, or by your believing *(pistis)* what you heard?" (Galatians 3:5).

Pistis has two meanings, the first being that of conviction or belief, while the other meaning has to do with fidelity or faithfulness. Both meanings are generally applicable to the New Testament use of *pistis*; for example, the same word is used throughout the famous 'Hall of Faith' in Hebrews 11, as well as in the discussion of faith and works in James 2 (which we will explore soon).

When Christians discuss the topic of faith and how it relates to salvation, there has been an unfortunate tendency to devolve into endless debates surrounding the age-old question of predestination versus free will. When this happens, our efforts to understand "living by faith" are often obscured.

When the discussion of faith focuses only on how salvation occurs, then certain Bible verses are hijacked or explained away, depending on one's convictions on the predestination/free will continuum.

Some of these verses include Romans 14:23, where Paul, as he concludes his discussion on whether or not Christians are allowed to eat meat sacrificed to idols, makes this comment: "But the man who doubts is condemned if he eats, because his eating is not from faith; and *everything that does not come from faith is sin.*" *(emphasis added)*

This is a provocative piece of Scripture. If we only view faith as being involved with our salvation, or specific instances where we are praying for divine intervention (healing, provision, deliverance, etc.), we run the risk of missing what "living" by faith means.

To keep this verse in context, we need to remember that Paul is addressing the question of eating meat sacrificed to idols. Paul's instruction emphasizes that those whose faith is strong (mature), for whom the meat is a non-issue, need to be aware of the effect of their actions on those whose faith is weak (immature). This passage has often been used – or misused – to address such 'grey areas' as the consumption of alcohol, 'secular' music and body art (piercings and tattoos), to name a few.

The context of this verse is that faith – weak and strong, immature and mature – was being expressed *in community*. Faith has a personal element to it, of course, but the idea of "living by faith" takes place best in the Body. Living in a community of faith takes faith. The risk lies in the choice to remain open and welcoming in spite of the pain that happens when imperfect people deal imperfectly with other imperfect people. Even King David once lamented: "Even my close friend, whom I trusted, he who shared my bread, has lifted up his heel against me" (Psalm 41:9).

We are in danger of losing what it means to "live by faith" if there is no element of risk-taking.

Another verse that speaks of living by faith, but is often over-shadowed by the predestination/free-will debate, is Hebrews 11:6a: "And without faith it is impossible to please God." The rest of that verse suggests that it is tied to salvation, since it speaks of God rewarding those who seek him; Arminians nod enthusiastically at this verse, while Calvinists quickly page over to Romans to counter the idea that anyone seeks God.

As is often true, it is the context of this verse in Hebrews 11 that gives us a clue as to what it means to *live* by faith, as well as being *saved* by faith. All of the saints listed in Hebrews 11 lived in light of what they believed God had promised, even without any physical evidence to back it up. "Now faith is being sure of what we hope for and certain of what we do not see" (Hebrews 11:1). It was not just an intellectual assent to propositional statements regarding the faith; it was a certainty in God that enabled them to make life decisions that would make no sense to a non-faith mind.

Noah building the Ark, Abraham leaving his homeland and later almost sacrificing his son Isaac, Moses refusing a life of ease in Pharaoh's palace in order to lead the cantankerous Israelites through the wilderness, Rahab risking her life to hide the Israelite spies in Jericho, and Gideon's army of 300 taking on thousands of

Amalekites (to name just a few) – all have something in common: their faith caused them to do outrageous things in the eyes of others.

Many charismatics have long understood that "Faith is spelled R-I-S-K", and yet much in today's church could be viewed as being done in the strength and ingenuity of people, with or without the Holy Spirit. When Pastor Bob Girard looked around his church in the late 1960s, his heart-breaking assessment was: "It wasn't *Acts*. It was a testimony to the good things people can do – *all by themselves*."[72] *(emphasis in original)*

The very real danger, as we detox from charismania, is that our communities of faith will be merely communities, whether faith is involved or not. By that, I do not mean that salvation by faith won't be important to these groups. My concern is that we are in danger of losing what it means to live by faith if there is no element of risk-taking in our communities. For example, most if not all spiritual gifts can only function *in community*. They can't be practiced solo.

In this context, faith also functions to remind us that we are not in control of our lives, and that our life's direction is not our own to determine. Following Jesus' example of only doing and saying what we see the Father doing, we must take the risk of learning to hear the voice of God for ourselves. We are relinquishing control, our own need for safety and predictability, and seeking to be Spirit-led instead of program-driven. We will more closely resemble the kind of people Jesus described: "The wind blows wherever it pleases. You hear its sound, but you cannot tell where it comes from or where it is going. So it is with everyone born of the Spirit" (John 3:8).

In the conclusion to the Parable of the Widow and the Unjust Judge, Jesus sums up by asking, "However, when the Son of Man comes, will He find faith on the earth?" (Luke 18:8). At first, this seems like a strange way to end this parable, when the purpose of the parable was clearly stated at the beginning: "Then Jesus told his disciples a parable to show them that they should always pray and not give up" (Luke 18:1). If the point of the parable was that we should pray and not give up, then what kind of faith is Jesus talking about?

The juxtaposition of the unjust judge with a justice-loving God is not uncommon to Jesus' teaching style. He often used the lesser-to-greater approach in helping His disciples understand what His Father was like. What Jesus was emphasizing through this parable was basing our risk-taking in light of God's character. There is a rich sense of excitement in being able to point to something and say without reservation, "*God* did that".

Yes, we want to avoid the "over-promising" that has happened too often in charismatic circles. But on the other hand, to miss out on the genuine activity of the Spirit, which can be explained only by the intervention of God, would be a tragedy.

FAITH = VERB: JAMES 2

A faith that can be spelled R-I-S-K assumes a certain amount of action. Living by faith cannot be merely a mental activity to truly be consistent with Paul's words: "I have been crucified with Christ and I no longer live, but Christ lives in me. The life I live in the body, I live by faith in the Son of God, who loved me and gave Himself for me" (Galatians 2:20).

Again, as Galatians 2:20 points out, it starts with Jesus and His story, and follows with our Spirit-led role in that story.

No other passage on the topic of the connection between faith and works (or faith in action) has been debated as much as chapter 2 in the Epistle of James. Martin Luther was so disturbed by the emphasis on 'works' in James that he seriously questioned its inclusion in the Bible, although to his credit, he did not actually have it removed.

Luther's concern was that James' emphasis on works might lead some to believe that they could somehow 'earn' their salvation. Luther was particularly sensitive to anything that might contradict his assertion that "the just shall live by faith" (Romans 1:17; Galatians 3:11; Philippians 3:9; Hebrews 10:38).

The proverbial "straw that broke the camel's back" for Luther was the sale of 'indulgences' to the common folk. These indulgences basically functioned as buying forgiveness for sins committed by deceased loved ones, and perhaps avoiding/lessening time in purgatory.

James wrote his epistle, in part, to help his readers understand the intersection between faith and works. As mentioned earlier, faith is the Greek word *pistis*, meaning a deeply held conviction. The word translated 'works' is *ergon*, which can be an occupation, a product that is created by someone, or an act (deed). It literally means "work" – an action.

The context of James' discussion is very important. He has just finished admonishing his readers to:

- Humbly accept the word planted in them (1:21).

- Recognize that being only a "hearer of the word" is a form of deception, if hearing does not include "doing" (1:22).

- Remember that pure religion that God accepts is concerned with orphans and widows, and not being polluted by the world (1:27).

- Avoid giving special attention to rich people, which is a sign of being polluted by the world, as is treating poorer people with contempt (2:1-8).

- Be warned that fawning over the rich and despising the poor is just as sinful as murder and adultery (2:9-11).

- Speak and act as merciful people, because mercy triumphs over judgment (2:12-13).

With the echoes of being "doers of the word" ringing in his readers' ears, James then launches into the whole faith/works discussion. He begins with a rhetorical question: is it genuine faith if there are no "deeds" (NIV) or "works" (KJV, NASB)? The question is worded in such a way that a negative response is the only available option: *no*, faith without works cannot save.

It is interesting but perhaps not surprising – since James had just written about not looking down on poor people – that his illustration of faith at work is related to caring for the poor.

Charismatics have been good at "speaking blessing", and intercessors have been deeply committed to praying against poverty, and binding demons of poverty. And certainly, there is a sense of faith required to invest time praying for poor people and against the spiritual forces of darkness that are doubtless at work behind the scenes. (Although there is no evidence to suggest that there are literal 'demons of poverty' anymore than there are 'demons of gluttony', or lust, or whatever.)

Rather than viewing prayer/intercession and hands-on ministry to the poor as separate options, it is more biblically accurate to view them as partners in ministry. There is a need for people to pray in faith that God will overturn structures and disarm the enemy. But if these same intercessors hide behind their prayer meetings and do not get involved in hands-on ministry to the poor, we have the same problem that James is warning us against.

In *Loving Our Neighbor's Welfare*, Amy Sherman writes, "Often the church has been guilty of a cheap benevolence that wants only to *help* the poor, but isn't willing to *know* them."[73] (emphasis in original)

James reminds us that knowing about the needs of others immediately puts us into the position of exercising our faith by *doing something about it.*

James puts the stakes on this very, very high: "In the same way, faith by itself, if it is not accompanied by action, is dead" (James 2:17). The Greek word for 'dead' is *nekros*, which literally means 'a corpse'. There's no way to candy-coat the implications of James' assessment of faith that is not expressed in works. It's not useless; it's not deficient; it's not lacking in some way – it's a corpse, rotting in a grave somewhere.

It's amazing the lengths to which some people will go in order to find a way to excuse themselves from this passage. Some in the Word of Faith movement would blame the poor for being poor; they just need to claim the prosperity that God guarantees them. Others will attend conferences and prayer meetings till they have nothing else on their weekly schedules, and conclude that their intercessory work of prayer was all they were 'called' to do. (Do we need a specific 'call' to do something God has already commanded in His Word?)

Still others, in their concern to avoid the error of salvation by works, label all ministries to the poor as being "social gospel". By this, they mean that the Gospel message has been ignored in favor of caring for the needs of the poor.

I think that if more self-proclaimed intercessors and prayer warriors spent time with the poor directly, 'knowing' them, their prayer times would be much more focused and fervent. (I don't know about you, but I'm much more comfortable with people who just pray lots and pray for people, but don't feel the need to be identified and recognized as "intercessors" or "prayer warriors".)

"When we allow ourselves to be touched with the brokenness and pain of our needy neighbors, then an oh-so-needed holy discontent will begin to grow within us... There's not supposed to be discrimination. There's not supposed to be destitution. There's not supposed to be child abuse. There are not supposed to be hunger and privation. We are spiritually impoverished by this absence of agitation. We need the holy discontent we can gain by participating in the suffering of our neighbors."[74]

I can't help but wonder if Jesus felt this same 'holy discontent'? "When He saw the crowds, He had compassion on them, because they were harassed and helpless, like sheep without a shepherd" (Matthew 9:36).

A trap at the opposite extreme is also quite real: On one hand, those who have recaptured the hands-on dynamic are to be commended for escaping the prayer-meeting-only mentality. But at the same time, there is a danger that these practical efforts may ultimately become prayer-less and lacking any expectation of Divine intervention.

I once worked in closed-custody (medium security) detention center for teenagers. I have also spent time working as an outreach counselor on behalf of a local school board for teenagers who had been expelled from school. It was very hands-on, very James 2 in its practicality.

As time went on, however, I came to an inescapable conclusion: even in this brief lifetime – let alone eternity – these teenagers had zero hope at all, apart from literal divine intervention. Their dysfunctional family backgrounds and resulting choices/issues were simply far too immense and complex. Even with all the interventions and social services available to them (for which we should be grateful), the brokenness in their lives required a spiritual solution.

My prayer life for these teenagers was deeply affected by seeing the level of devastation in their lives. Before that, my prayers for the emerging generation would have been genuine and heart-felt, yes. But as a result of those years, my understanding of Romans 8:27 was heightened considerably:

Do we need a specific 'call' to do something God has already commanded in His Word?

"In the same way, the Spirit helps us in our weakness. We do not know what we ought to pray for, but the Spirit Himself intercedes for us with groans that words cannot express."

We need to develop a balance that embraces intercessory prayer and the need for divine intervention, but at the same time is living in the day-to-day practice of noticing and responding to the needs of those around us.

James goes on to dare us to demonstrate our faith without works (if possible). His premise and conclusion is the same: it can't be done. Faith by itself is not remarkable, as evidenced by James' somewhat sarcastic remark: "You believe that there is one God. Good! Even the demons believe that – and shudder" (James 2:19).

James has a word to describe anyone who thinks that intellectual faith is enough: "foolish" (James 2:20). This is the Greek word *kenos*, which means 'devoid of truth', or at times 'empty-handed'. *Kenos* is neither a compliment nor something to aspire to. James is making it clear that faith without action is an oxymoron with deadly consequences.

James concludes this short passage with the examples of Abraham and Rahab, whose faith was expressed in their actions: Abraham by being willing to sacrifice his own son Isaac, and Rahab by aiding and abetting the Israelite spies in Jericho (James 2:21-26). Both situations required a great deal of faith being spelled R-I-S-K. Their belief (conviction) in God was expressed by their actions, and God considered their faith-filled actions to be righteousness.

The absence of this risk-taking faith-in-action is spiritual death, according to James, when he concludes, "As the body without the spirit is dead, so faith without deeds is dead" (2:26). As previously mentioned, this means "a corpse". A cadaver, slated for burial.

However, it is not merely the hands-on nature of ministry that qualifies as faith expressed in deeds. If nothing that we are involved in requires risk-taking, but instead can be done all by ourselves with or without the Spirit's empowering, we have not yet found that all-important balance.

As John Wimber once wrote: "A disciple is always ready to take the next step. If there is anything that characterizes Christian maturity, it is the willingness to become a beginner again for Jesus Christ. It is the willingness to put your hand in His hand and say: 'I'm scared to death, but I'll go with You. You're the pearl of great price.'"[75]

FAITH = EXPECTATION

"The Lord replied, 'My Presence will go with you, and I will give you rest.' Then Moses said to Him, 'If Your Presence does not go with us, do not send us up from here'" (Exodus 33:14-15).

In any ministry setting –institutional church, house church, parachurch – the stories that give people the greatest sense of excitement, adventure and encouragement are the ones where there is no other possible explanation except: "God did it."

Nothing encourages people to take risks in their faith more than hearing other Christians – regular, everyday folk whom they know and trust – tell God-stories where He has clearly had a hand in whatever was happening. It is the same sense of wonder that the paralytic felt in Mark 2:1-12, after his friends had torn a hole in somebody's ceiling, lowered him through it, and hearing Jesus say: "Son, your sins are forgiven... I tell you, get up, take your mat and go home." And then *actually being able to get up and do just what Jesus said.*

Think of the many people Jesus healed from disease and/or delivered from demonic oppression (Matthew 8:16-17; Mark 1:32-34; Luke 4:40-41) who returned home completely changed. Imagine yourself as a jaded synagogue attendee, raised on stories of God's miraculous acts in the history of your people, yet having never seen anything like that in your lifetime – *until now.*

The charismatic movement, including but not limited to the Word of Faith subset, has been guilty at times of "over-promising". As Jason Clark writes: "I've also got memories of seeing dozens of people being prophesied over 'I see you changing a generation'. Given that maybe one or two people have that kind of influence historically, there are a lot of disappointed people out there, who that has not come true for."[76]

This "over-realized eschatology" in the Word of Faith movement contributes to the kind of thinking that pastor and writer Len Hjalmarson describes:

"We have moved from Christianity as a lifestyle to event-driven Christianity. Recently Chad Taylor, of Timothy's House, a discipleship house in Boise Idaho, wrote: 'What does it really cost to see a whole region shaken by God? Is it more than infrequent conferences and prayer meetings? Could it cost us our lives instead? Our dreams and aspirations? Would it require that we take up our cross and follow Him wherever He may be going?'"[77]

The good news is that many post-charismatics would read these words and resonate with that desire. Many post-charismatics are willing to invest themselves in the cause of Christ, but not in the hyped, over-promising way in which they perceive that many charismatic churches are currently functioning.

But to anchor this risk-taking, faith-as-verb approach in the leading of the Spirit, instead of works done only in our own strength, we must cultivate an expectation that God *will* intervene and use us in ways that defy natural explanations.

We *need* the stories where the only possible explanation is "God did it". And we will have a hard time living these stories if we do not cultivate an attitude of expectation, in faith, that God can and will intervene in supernatural ways.

For example, another area that is often over-promised is the whole area of healing. In the Word of Faith worldview, it is simply impossible to *not* be healed if one has enough faith, therefore any lack of healing must be a sign of inadequate faith.

There are numerous instances in the New Testament where people's faith was clearly a factor in their healing, and there are other instances where people with lots of faith were not healed.

For example, Paul's famous affliction from which he was not delivered (2 Corinthians 12:7-9), leaving his co-worker Trophimus sick in Miletus (2 Timothy 4:20), and even Paul's advice for Timothy to self-medicate some stomach troubles with a little wine (1 Timothy 5:23). It was certainly not because of Paul's lack of faith.

"Through his books *Power Healing* and *Power Evangelism* he *[John Wimber]* taught an entire generation of Christians about praying with faith for the miraculous, all the while trusting in the sovereignty of God."[78]

If faith is to be understood as a risk-taking action based on our confidence in God, then an expectation of His presence is basically a prerequisite to truly being the Body. It is the understanding of the

Kingdom of God as 'already and not yet' that guards us from over-promising, but at the same time, allows us to live with an expectation of Divine accompaniment as we take Spirit-led faith-risks.

CHAPTER NOTES

1. Grady, J. Lee - *What Happened to the Fire?*, page 132
2. McIntyre, Joe - *Plagiarism of E.W. Kenyon by Kenneth E. Hagin?*
3. Ibid.
4. *The New Dictionary of Pentecostal and Charismatic Movements*, page 992
5. McIntyre, Joe - *An Open Letter to the Critics of E.W. Kenyon*
6. *The New Dictionary of Pentecostal and Charismatic Movements*, page 819
7. Ibid. page 687
8. Ibid. page 687
9. Ibid. page 687
10. Kenyon, Essex William - *Claiming Our Rights*
11. Hagin, Kenneth E. - *Possessing the Promise of Healing,* page 11
12. Copeland, Kenneth - *The Laws of Prosperity,* page 90
13. Copeland, Gloria - *God's Will is Prosperity,* page 5
14. Hagin, Kenneth E. - *Knowing What Belongs to Us,* page 11
15. Kenyon, Essex William - *Claiming Our Rights*
16. *The New Dictionary of Pentecostal and Charismatic Movements*, page 993
17. *Ibid.,* page 993
18. Assemblies of God Position Paper: *The Believer and Positive Confession*
19. Copeland, Kenneth - *The Laws of Prosperity,* page 50
20. Ibid., page 32
21. Assemblies of God Position Paper: *The Believer and Positive Confession*
22. Kenyon, Essex William - *What We Are In Christ*
23. Kenyon, Essex William - *Underestimating Jesus*

24. Hagin, Kenneth E. - *How Faith Comes,* page 10

25. Copeland, Kenneth - *The Laws of Prosperity,* page 87

26. Assemblies of God Position Paper: *The Believer and Positive Confession,* page 3

27. Ibid. page 4

28. Kenyon, Essex William - *Claiming Our Rights*

29. Ibid.

30. Hagin, Kenneth E. - *How to Win your Unsaved Loved One, Part 2,* page 10

31. Kenyon, Essex William - *What We Are In Christ*

32. *The New Dictionary of Pentecostal and Charismatic Movements,* page 992

33. Ibid., page 992

34. Hagin, Kenneth E. - *Knowing What Belongs to Us*

35. Assemblies of God Position Paper: *The Believer and Positive Confession,* page 9

36. Kenyon, Essex William - *Jesus the Healer*

37. Hagin, Kenneth E. - *Possessing the Promise of Healing,* page 10

38. Ibid., page 10

39. Copeland, Kenneth - *The Laws of Prosperity,* page 61

40. Ibid., page. 32

41. Kenyon, Essex William - *Jesus the Healer*

42. Kenyon, Essex William - *What We are in Christ*

43. Copeland, Gloria - *God's Will is Prosperity,* page 1

44. Kenyon, Essex William - *What We are in Christ*

45. Copeland, Kenneth - *The Laws of Prosperity,* page 9

46. Hagin, Kenneth E. - *How to Win Your Loved Ones, Part 2,* page 11

47. Copeland, Kenneth - *The Laws of Prosperity,* page 26

48. Copeland, Gloria - *God's Will is Prosperity,* page 4

49. Copeland, Kenneth - *The Laws of Prosperity,* page 43

50. Assemblies of God Position Paper: *The Believer and Positive Confession,* page 2

51. Kenyon, Essex William - *Claiming our Rights*

52. Copeland, Kenneth - *The Laws of Prosperity,* page 88

53. Ibid., page 44

54. Hall, Franklin D. - *Atomic Power with God through Prayer and Fasting,* page 9

55. Ibid., page 37

56. Hagin, Kenneth E. - *How to Win your Loved Ones, Part 2,* page 11

57. Hall, Franklin D. - *Atomic Power with God through Prayer and Fasting,* page 40

58. Ibid., page 41

59. Assemblies of God Position Paper: *The Believer and Positive Confession,* page 3

60. Ibid., page 3

61. Ibid., page 6

62. Ibid., page 7

63. Ibid., page 7

64. Grady, J. Lee - *What Happened to the Fire?,* page 131

65. Assemblies of God Position Paper: *The Believer and Positive Confession,* page 9

66. Grady, J. Lee - *What Happened to the Fire?,* page 131-132

67. Hall, Franklin D. - *Atomic Power with God through Prayer and Fasting,* page 13

68. *The New Dictionary of Pentecostal and Charismatic Movements,* page 993

69. Hagin, Kenneth E. - *Possessing the Promise of Healing,* page 11

70. Assemblies of God Position Paper: *The Believer and Positive Confession (1980),* page 8

71. Wimber, John – *Power Evangelism,* page 125

72. Girard, Robert C. – *Brethren, Hang Loose (Or, What's Happening to My Church?),* page 65

73. Sherman, Amy L. – *Loving Our Neighbor's Welfare*

74. Ibid.

75. Wimber, John, as quoted by Steve Beard - *Good News Magazine, 1998*

76. Clark, Jason – *Over-Promising? (emergent.typepad.com/ jasonclark/2005/09/overpromising.html)*

77. Hjalmarson, Len – *Renewal: The Hype, the Hope, and the Reality (http://nextreformation.com/wp-admin/articles/renewal-hype.htm)*

78. Beard, Steve – *Remember John Wimber (http://web.archive.org/ web/20060819092655/http://www.thunderstruck.org/archivevault/ Wimber.htm)*

Chapter Five
COVERING & AUTHORITY

Jeremy and his wife were the kind of Christians that everyone enjoyed being with. Wendy and I would joke about inventing reasons to spend time with them. They were friendly, hospitable, and we always came away feeling encouraged, and just a little closer to Jesus.

Jeremy was a gifted worship leader, and there were few things he enjoyed more than worshipping God. The context wasn't important: a home group, a church gathering, or just by himself in his basement. For Jeremy, leading worship was just another way of expressing his love for Jesus.

We lost touch for a number of years, after Jeremy and his family got involved in a new church. They seemed happy at first, and would remark on the great things that God had promised for this church. We assumed, as anyone who knew Jeremy would, that he would be leading worship there within a reasonably short time.

Imagine our surprise when we learned that Jeremy had only been 'released' to be a worship leader after *eight years*. We were incredulous. Apparently, Jeremy was first required to prove his trustworthiness. His desire to lead worship was labeled 'worldly ambition', so he was placed 'under the covering' of an overseer until Jeremy was properly 'submitted'.

Now, eight years later, Jeremy had finally been released. His wife had stopped attending the church some years earlier, finding the atmosphere too oppressive. Jeremy shared with us, "He (the overseer) said, 'I feel that I can now release you to lead worship, because you've proven that you're submitted to my authority.'"

As I looked at him, a shell of whom he had been, the vibrancy and cheerfulness that both he and his wife had been known for now gone. I really did not know what to say. Finally, I simply asked, "And what did you say to him when he released you?"

He looked down at the ground, his whole demeanor suggesting weariness and resignation. "I thanked him," he finally said. Crossing his arms over his chest, he slowly shook his head in disbelief, not looking me in the eye. Softly but angrily, he continued through clenched teeth, "Can you believe that? I actually *thanked him*."

There is no teaching or practice that elicits stronger negative reactions from disillusioned Christians than being 'under a covering', or 'under authority'. Coupled with the teaching of 'touch not the Lord's anointed' (don't question your leaders), the covering doctrine has resulted in many charismatics abandoning the movement.

"The spiritual abuse perpetrated by authoritarian leaders in the Church has resulted in thousands upon thousands of wounded believers; people who can no longer trust the Church to be a sanctuary and who no longer expect pastors to be healers."[1]

The Shepherding Movement is probably the mot well-known group that popularized the covering and authority doctrines, although it would be inaccurate to assume that they created the teachings. The roots of the problem go much further back, and the Shepherding Movement is merely a fairly recent re-occurrence of an age-old problem. However, any mention of the Shepherding movement continues to elicit strong reactions, which have not dulled after the official dissolution of the movement.

NOTHING NEW UNDER THE SUN

The roots of the Shepherding movement go back into numerous sources, including the writings of Watchman Nee, a Chinese believer who was imprisoned and later martyred for his faith by the Maoist government in China. Watchman Nee's teachings in turn influenced the leaders of the Shepherding movement.

Another source of input was the Latter Rain, through the writings and teachings of Ern Baxter, one of the 'Fort Lauderdale Five' who gave leadership to the Shepherding movement. The most obvious contribution is the Latter Rain's belief that end-time Apostles were about to be released, who must be submitted to.

But the roots of the problem go much further back than Watchman Nee, or the Latter Rain. The problem of authoritarian leadership has been around for centuries. The prophets in the Old Testament regularly prophesied against the abuse that the Israelites were enduring under corrupt priests, false prophets and ungodly tyrants. For example:

We expect bullying in the corporate world, but we should not tolerate it among church leaders.

"Both hands are skilled in doing evil; the ruler demands gifts, the judge accepts bribes, the powerful dictate what they desire – they all conspire together" (Micah 7:3).

"Woe to those who make unjust laws, to those who issue oppressive decrees, to deprive the poor of their rights and withhold justice from the oppressed of My people, making widows their prey and robbing the powerless" (Isaiah 10:1-2).

"So the Lord will cut off from Israel both head and tail... the elders and prominent men are the head, the prophets who teach lies are the tail. Those who guide this people mislead them, and those who are guided are led astray" (Isaiah 9:14-15).

Jesus' words to His own disciples echo the same problem with the human tendency to want to have power over others: "You know that the rulers of the Gentiles lord it over them, and their high officials exercise authority over them. Not so with you..." (Matthew 20:25-26).

The problem still exists today. People use a ministry position to gain power over others, often ministering out of their own insecurities. Worse yet, young leaders are 'discipled' in a church system that demands and rewards hierarchical control, which they then replicate wherever they go. They are the 'dark side' of Jesus' words in Luke 6:40: "everyone who is fully trained will be like their teacher."

The irony is that most of these leaders would describe themselves as servant-leaders. It would never occur to them that their approach to leadership is at odds with the servant example of Jesus. As Brent Toderash *(a.k.a. Brother Maynard)* notes: "It is not possible to hold the thoroughly hierarchical view of Church authority necessary to support the doctrine of spiritual covering and still exhibit New Testament servant leadership. The two are incompatible."[2]

Peter also warned church leaders that they must act in a way that is "not lording it over those entrusted to you" (1 Peter 5:3). Author Lee Grady strongly states: "It is time we challenged authoritarianism and called it what it is: an illegitimate use of God's name and authority[3]... We expect bullying in the corporate world, but we should not tolerate it among church leaders."[4]

It would be shortsighted to place the responsibility for authoritarian leadership solely on the Shepherding movement, or Watchman Nee. The problem of authoritarianism predates the church age that began at the Feast of Pentecost, going back into the earliest history of the people of God.

At the same time, the pervasiveness of the terms 'covering' and 'under authority' – backed up by 'touch not the Lord's anointed' – gives us good reason to look more closely at the Shepherding Movement. While the movement has been *officially* over for years, the teachings have not gone away, and in recent times have been re-branded under the banner of a 'culture of honor'.

WATCHMAN NEE

The writings of Watchman Nee had a profound influence on the Shepherding movement, especially *Authority and Submission* (also published under the title *Spiritual Authority*). While Nee is best known for writing *The Normal Christian Life*, it is *Authority and Submission* that laid the groundwork for introducing the covering doctrine.

Watchman Nee was raised in a second generation Christian family, but it was not until he was seventeen that he became a professing Christian. His early influences were mostly Plymouth Brethren teachers and writers, although some of his later teachings do *not* reflect Brethren thought.

"In 1928, Watchman Nee settled in Shanghai where he based his own speaking and publication work, the Shanghai Gospel Bookroom, which published books by Watchman Nee and others..."[5] Nee's passion was for the local church, and many thousands of house churches in China can trace their lineage to Nee's influence and writings.

To be fair, it is important to acknowledge that much of Nee's emphasis on authority was a product of his time and place in history. "Nee's writings on spiritual authority and on the normal church life reflect the kind of Asian authoritarianism that prevailed before World War II."[6]

Watchman Nee was imprisoned in 1952 during the Communist revolution in China, and remained in prison until his death in 1972. Because of his steadfast faith during his imprisonment and subsequent martyrdom, his writings have been given a significant platform.

Nee's most famous book, *The Normal Christian Life,* does not typically cause concern for most Christians. Still, Nee writes some provocative and head-scratching things, especially his interpretation of the interaction between the soul and spirit of a man. Nee believed that the spirit of a man was good, responding to God appropriately, but that the soul was in rebellion against submitting to God's authority.

In reference to Adam's fall in Genesis 3, Nee suggests, "It is not merely that man has a soul, but that from that day on the soul, with its independent powers of free choice, takes the place of the spirit as the animating power of man."[7]

This wrestle between acting in the spirit (desirable), versus acting in the soul (basis of sin), dominates much of the rest of the writing of *The Normal Christian Life.*

Nee applies this to the temptation of Jesus: "That thing in Him which is in distinction from the Father is the human soul, which He assumed when He was 'found in fashion as a man'. Being a perfect Man our Lord had a soul, and of course a body, just as you and I have a soul and a body, and it was possible for Him to act *from the soul* – that is, from Himself."[8] *(emphasis in original)*

This, according to Nee, was the basis of Satan's temptation of Christ – whether Jesus would act from His soul, or from His spirit. The use of this spirit/soul dichotomy can be found in some charismatic circles – you often hear references to *soul-ish* attitudes or even soul-ish prayers, meaning that some people are acting, thinking or praying from their soul, not their spirit.

In some ways, this idea resembles another form of Gnostic dualism, where the body (flesh) was seen as evil and the spirit was good. These imaginative explanations of the difference between soul and spirit – usually an attempt to reconcile Hebrews 4:12 – are a man-made construct, not a definitive teaching from Scripture.

I do not want this to become a rabbit trail to the issue of submission and authority, but there is a connection to the teaching on covering. Simply put, when people question the inappropriate use of authority that is the fruit of the doctrines of covering and authority, the questioner is often dismissed as being 'in rebellion', or acting *soulishly*.

In *The Normal Christian Life*, Nee also puts forth the idea that Christians cannot be used by God until they have achieved some level of spiritual purity. (Some of Nee's apologists believe that Nee had achieved perfection and completely overcome Satan.)

Nee also suggested that whether or not we are 'raptured' at the return of Christ depends on how much we actually want to be raptured:

"If I mistake not, this is the one passage in the New Testament that tells of our reaction to the rapture call. We may have thought that when the Son of man comes we shall be taken up automatically, as it were, because of what we read in 1 Corinthians 15... Well, however we reconcile the two passages, this one in Luke's Gospel (17:31-32) should at least make us pause and reflect; for the emphasis is here very strongly upon one being taken and the other left. It is a matter of our reaction to the call to go, and on the basis of this a most urgent appeal is made to us to be ready."[9]

> "It is easy to be forgiven of sin. It is not easy to be forgiven of rebellion."
>
> - Watchman Nee

Again, this is not meant to divert us from our discussion of submission and authority. However, it should be pointed out that the emphasis on possibly missing what God was doing has also been used to keep people from questioning leaders. While Nee takes it to an extreme – missing the Second Coming – many charismatics have been effectively silenced by suggestions that they were acting soulishly and therefore might be passed over in the next great move of the Spirit.

WATCHMAN NEE ON SPIRITUAL AUTHORITY

Throughout the text of *Submission and Authority*, it becomes immediately clear that submission to authority is the lens through which Nee reads the entire Bible:

"In the old creation and in the new creation, the order of precedence is the basis of authority. Whoever is created first is the authority. Whoever is saved first is the authority. For this reason, wherever we go, our first thought should be to find those to whom the Lord wants us to submit."[10]

Much like his creation of a dichotomy between spirit and soul, Watchman Nee also separated God's holiness and authority into different categories:

"Violating God's authority is a matter of rebellion; it is more serious than violating God's holiness. Sin is a matter of conduct; it is easy to be forgiven of sin. But rebellion is a matter of principle; it is not easy to be forgiven of rebellion."[11]

Okay, you might think, Nee is talking about God's authority. We might not agree with Nee that God forgives some sins more easily than others, but what's the big deal? Ah, but this is where it gets interesting.

Watchman Nee taught that God had appointed 'delegated authorities' to express His authority on earth, and absolute, unquestioning obedience to these delegated authorities was required. Nee went as far as to state that rebellion against delegated authority was the same as rebellion against God, because all authority comes from God: "Not only did (Eve) transgress God's commandment, she also disregarded Adam's authority. Rebellion against God's deputy authority is rebellion against God Himself."[12]

In saying this, Nee has created *two* sins in the Fall: disobeying God by eating the forbidden fruit, and also disobeying Adam's 'deputy authority'.

Nee took his hierarchical approach to extreme lengths, even suggesting that it was more important than truth: "When a few brothers are together, they should know how to line themselves up immediately... With us there should never be right or wrong, good or evil. Wherever we go, we should first know who is the authority. If you know who you have to submit to, you will spontaneously know what position you should occupy in the Body, and you will stand in your proper position."[13]

Nee's insistence on submitting to delegated authority was based in his belief in a hierarchy of submission reflected in the Trinity. Nee believed that Jesus became *Lord* only after His ascension. Before that, in Nee's view, Jesus was not considered to have the attribute of Lordship – because He had not yet earned it.

"Being God is His (Jesus) original position. But His attainment of the position of Lord is based on what He has done. When He laid aside His divine form to fully maintain the principle of submission and subsequently ascended to the heavens, God accorded to Him the position of Lord... This lordship was not originally present in the Godhead."[14]

Even salvation depended on submission to delegated authority. Nee taught that only those who were in submission to their leaders truly understood – and had experienced – salvation. Hence the need for absolute obedience and submission to any earthly delegated authority.

"If we want to learn submission to God, we should know to whom the authority of God is entrusted. If we understand God's authority as being only in Himself, it is very likely that we will offend God's authority more than half of the time...[15] Man's rebellious nature likes to submit to God's direct authority but reject God's appointed deputy authority."[16]

This troubling statement seems to negate the Reformation doctrine that Christ Jesus alone is mediator between God and humanity, without the need for additional human intermediaries. The delegated authority teaching (or 'under-shepherds' as the Shepherding movement would refer to it) turns the clock back on the Protestant Reformation, and re-introduces the idea of a hierarchical system of intermediaries. The idea of mutual submission to each other as equal parts of the Body of Christ is rejected.

For Watchman Nee, submission to delegated authority was an unquestionable protocol: "Today many ask, 'Why do I have to submit?' They also ask, 'Why do I have to submit to you? I am a brother, and you are a brother.' Actually, men do not have a right to say such things."[17]

Nee did not take the responsibility of being a delegated authority lightly, however. He was concerned that delegated authorities, like the Old Testament kings and priests, could become corrupt and misrepresent God's authority: "It is imperative that an authority represent God properly. Whether in wrath or in compassion, he should be like God all the time. If we are wrong, we should confess that we are wrong; we should never drag God into our mistake."[18]

While it is commendable that Nee would want delegated authorities to be willing to admit their mistakes, it remains disturbing that he assumed that 'in wrath or in compassion', an human leader was capable of adequately representing God. That role was given solely to Jesus Christ.

HOW TO BECOME A DELEGATED AUTHORITY

In the gospel of Matthew, we find the story of James and John asking Jesus (through their mother) for the right to sit on His right and left side when the Kingdom came. The other disciples were indignant at their audacity, but Jesus used the opportunity to instruct His disciples to *not* lord it over their brothers and sisters, as the rulers of the Gentiles did.

Watchmen Nee, however, turns this passage around to mean just the opposite:

"James and John thought that they would acquire the place merely by asking. But the Lord told them that it was not a matter of asking but a matter of drinking the cup and partaking of the baptism...[19]

"This is why the Lord asked James and John, 'Are you able to drink the cup which I drink'? It seems that the Lord was saying, 'If a man wants to draw near to Me and receive a place in glory above that of the other children of God, he must be like Me, yielding to God's will and taking it as the unique goal. Only such ones can come near to Me and sit at My right and left hand.'"[20]

Jesus was saying no such thing. He was using this opportunity to teach His disciples that they should reject desires for hierarchical power positions in favor of mutual service. To be great in the Kingdom is to be a servant, not to seek the status of 'delegated authority'.

Watchman Nee also held out the possibility that those who followed his teachings could possibly earn the seats which James and John coveted:

"If the Lord gave the right and left places to James and John, these two seats would have been gone for the past two thousand years of church history... The Lord did not grant their request, and the two seats are still available. Some among us may still have a chance to take those two seats."[21]

One of the responsibilities that anyone seeking the two seats must be willing to accept: "...we must learn to bear all of God's children upon our shoulders. May the Lord make us gracious persons, those who can tolerate all of God's children and who can bear His children upon our shoulders."[22]

This kind of thinking should set off alarm bells for those familiar with Scripture, as Jesus is the only one who deserves this position. Of course, if anyone has already embraced the idea of delegated authority, then perhaps Nee's words make sense. But aside from not being a biblically sound idea, the acceptance of this paradigm gives leaders power over the church that they have no right to have; power that creates temptations towards authoritarianism which they seem incapable of resisting.

As Lee Grady notes, "Rather than see their role as that of a servant to encourage, strengthen and equip the people of God, authoritarian leaders inflate their own importance and view themselves as somehow 'owning' the people God has entrusted to them for spiritual oversight."[23]

Watchman Nee, however, takes this 'ownership' motif a step further by suggesting that any delegated authority will have unique insights into the hearts and motives of the people under his authority. (I am intentionally using non-inclusive language here because only men were allowed to be leaders in both Nee's and the Shepherding movement's understanding of covering and authority).

"If a man has met authority *[learned submission and become a delegated authority]*, any transgression in others will be detected by him immediately. He will see through many lawlessnesses and realize many rebellions. He will then come to know that the principle of lawlessness abounds everywhere, in the world as well as in the church."[24]

This type of omniscience is usually reserved for God. And it is also significant that Nee assumes the delegated authorities will discern only 'lawlessness'. Many can attest to the damage done by suspicious and paranoid leaders, who have bought into the idea that they have been given the ability to discern sin and rebellion in their congregations.

Nee takes this to a disturbing extreme: "It is also right for us to leave the denominations to stand as the testimony of oneness in the local church... Today's denominational organizations are overthrowing the Lord's glory. This is a blasphemy to the Lord."[25]

Lastly, Nee taught that delegated authorities possessed special revelatory knowledge of God's will that was not available to the average believer.

As such, these delegated authorities had the responsibility to inform believers under their care what God's will for them as individuals was.

"A person becomes an authority because of his knowledge of God's will, God's mind, and God's thoughts... God appoints a person to be a deputy authority because such a person knows His will and His thoughts more than others."[26]

Another area that affected the later Shepherding movement and still affects authoritarian leaders today is Nee's insistence on aloofness and separation of the delegated authority from the rest of the body:

"But if we vindicate ourselves to anyone, we are in effect making him our judge. If we seek understanding from anyone, we are falling under that person's feet. Hence, we must never vindicate ourselves and must never seek understanding from anyone."[27]

In other words, leaders never have to defend, explain or be accountable for anything they say or do. They are unassailable. This is a dangerous position for the leader to be in, and far more dangerous for anyone who has been convinced to submit his/her life to such a leader.

This aloofness inevitably results in an unhealthy distance between shepherds and those following them, destroying the fabric of community, and leaving these leaders vulnerable as a result of isolation and spiritual pride.

"In order for us to learn to be an authority, we can only fellowship with the brothers and sisters to a certain extent...[28] It will strip us of excitement. We will no longer dare to joke around the brothers and sisters...[29] We cannot enjoy what others enjoy, and we cannot rejoice in what others rejoice in. (God) has to separate the holy from the common..."[30]

"Authority is based on separation. Without separation there is no authority. If you crave the company of others, you cannot be an authority. The higher an authority stands, the greater is the separation...[31] Authority manifests itself in separation and distinction."[32]

This might come as a surprise to the Son of God. "The Word became flesh and blood, and moved into the neighborhood" (John 1:14 *The Message).* 'Aloof' is not a word that would accurately describe Jesus.

However, as the history of the charismatic movement has shown us, these ideas of delegated authority, hierarchical power, and a clergy/laity divide do not easily go away. As was mentioned earlier, Watchman Nee did not originate these ideas; even Jesus had to actively teach His own disciples against this kind of approach.

God has to separate the holy from the common... Authority manifests itself in separation and distinction.
- Watchman Nee

THE SHEPHERDING MOVEMENT

The Shepherding movement did not begin with any intention of becoming a *movement.* Nor were the original leaders pursuing power and control over others. The four men involved were simply responding to the recognition of their own human weaknesses, and humbly choosing to be transparent and accountable to each other.

However, the phrase 'shepherding movement' has since become synonymous with controlling and abusive leaders on hierarchical power trips. What happened?

Lee Grady writes, "Since the renewal blossomed in the late 1960s, many groups that began with vibrant faith degenerated quickly into legalism and authoritarianism."[33] There were many sociological as well as spiritual reasons for this troubling trend. Significantly, the cultural upheaval of the 1960s had left many exhausted and looking for stability and rest.

The failure of the 1960s cultural revolution to achieve its most cherished goals – ending the war in Vietnam, achieving enlightenment through experimentation with drugs and the occult, and ushering in a new era of world peace – left many young people disillusioned. But even as the 1960s were drawing to a close, God was supernaturally orchestrating a significant revival among the emerging generation of that day. Just when you would least expect it, there was a powerful move of God among the hippies and counter-cultural groups who had just recently been some of the harshest reactionaries *against* Christianity.

Literally thousands of counter-cultural youth and young adults became Christians in just a few years. They were called Jesus People and Jesus Freaks, and the movement was quickly dubbed the Jesus Movement, and was even featured on the cover of *Time* magazine. Calvary Chapel, a small church in Costa Mesa California, became one of the most recognizable centers for this revival. Calvary Chapel baptized thousands of young people in the Pacific Ocean in just a few short years. Similar to the cultural landscape of today, "the Jesus Movement was non-traditional and characterized by an emphasis on community, contemporary music, outreach activism, use of indigenous media and parachurch structures."[34]

On one hand, there was incredible excitement as literally thousands of young people came to faith in Jesus Christ in a relatively short time. On the other hand, discipleship for these decidedly 'un-churched' new converts provided some unique challenges.

"The 1960s cultural revolution, with its anti-institutional orientation, had been carried into the Jesus movement revival and left many young people 'leaderless'... The Jesus movement fostered a generation of energetic and idealistic young Christians in need of spiritual accountability and discipline."[35]

Not all of the Jesus People were necessarily charismatic, of course, but a great many were. The influence of Calvary Chapel, and later the Vineyard movement (an offshoot of Calvary Chapel), meant that a significant number of these Jesus People *were* charismatic in their understanding and practice of the faith.

This raised a sociological problem that many did not take into account at the time. David Moore, in his helpful book *The Shepherding Movement: Charismatic Ecclesiology and Controversy*, writes: "Since the Charismatic Renewal in part was a reaction to a lack of spiritual experience in the historic churches, many Charismatics responded not only by leaving their churches, but also by casting off any sense of ecclesiastical polity, tradition, or restraint, making themselves vulnerable to confusion and deception."[36]

So, then, we can see three contributing factors that created the kind of situation where a leadership and discipleship vacuum would emerge:

* A society that was in turmoil and wanting some sense of stability in the midst of significant cultural change.

* A movement of charismatics who, in their zeal to throw off dead systems of church, developed an instinctive distrust of denominational and clergy authority.

* An influx of counter-culture young people, with passion and zeal but little knowledge, who shared a similar distrust of authority.

An aside: I'd like to point out the remarkable similarity between the societal and church situation of the early 1970s and the dynamics that are present now in the early twenty-first century.

I believe that we may face another, possibly more damaging, version of the Shepherding movement if we do not learn from history's mistakes, and pro-actively develop a biblically-sound understanding of authority and discipleship. (Since the release of the first edition of this book, the 'culture of honor' has become the new face of the Shepherding-style teachings, only substituting submission to 'apostles' instead of 'delegated authorities'.)

Even as the 1960s were drawing to a close, older Christians recognized the need for these new converts to be properly discipled. They were deeply concerned that these new believers could end up falling away from the faith. The lessons from the Parable of the Sower and Seed, where the cares of this world or persecution would cause these tender plants to shrivel and die, was a very real concern.

One of these concerned believers was Eldon Purvis, a Christian businessman, who felt a deep unease about the lack of spiritual depth that he saw in the charismatic renewal of the 1960s. "From these Charismatic meetings Purvis and others became increasingly aware that there was a need for 'some kind of teaching mission' to tell others about the Holy Spirit's power. From this vision came the birth of the Holy Spirit Teaching Mission (HSTM)."[37]

The HSTM began in earnest in 1965, and held its first conference in Fort Lauderdale, Florida that same year. It quickly became a significant center of the charismatic renewal, with many well-known Pentecostal and charismatic speakers addressing the conferences. Some of the well-known speakers included David du Plessis and Dennis Bennett, whose book *Nine O'Clock in the Morning* (co-written with his wife, Rita Bennett) had become a classic text for the charismatic renewal and beyond. The primary motivation was to provide a teaching ministry, and as such Purvis and his colleagues were seeking to fulfill the mandate to be spiritual fathers (1 Thess. 2:10-12). The HSTM also made use of television and was granted its own broadcasting license in 1968.

"Of greater significance, the HSTM started *New Wine* in the spring of 1969. Purvis invited Don Basham and Derek Prince, both living in Ft. Lauderdale, to serve with him on the magazine's editorial board... Beginning with the magazine's second issue, Charles Simpson wrote a monthly Bible study, 'Breaking Bread', and also joined the editorial board in early 1970 along with Bob Mumford. At Purvis' invitation, Mumford moved to Ft. Lauderdale in August 1970."[38]

What makes this significant is that these four men – Prince, Basham, Simpson and Mumford – would become widely referred to, along with the later addition of Ern Baxter, as the 'Fort Lauderdale Five'. They would soon become the public face of the Shepherding Movement.

However, not long after the introduction of *New Wine* magazine, Eldon Purvis – the undisputed leader of the HSTM – was accused of 'serious misconduct', which he later admitted to, as well as confessing other problems. The HSTM's board called the four teachers associated with the ministry – Prince, Basham, Simpson and Mumford – to meet with them to work through the crisis.

The original accountability covenant was based on a bond of mutuality among equals.

It was during this time that the four teachers began to forge the bonds of relationship that would prove to be the genesis of the Shepherding movement: "As the four men discussed and prayed regarding the problems surrounding the crisis and particularly the unfortunate situation with Purvis, they recognized their own weaknesses... One by one the men acknowledged their own vulnerability to misconduct and confessed their fears and temptations to one another. The four knew they needed accountability and protection."[39]

The four men decided to form a mutual accountability group for themselves. They each had independent teaching ministries, although they were also commonly linked through *New Wine* magazine. But they also recognized that, as human beings who lived in the reality of Romans 7, they needed each other as a safeguard against falling into sin.

However, when well-known teachers, with the added public platform of a magazine and a regular conference, make such a commitment to each other, word spreads. And shortly after, a shift in emphasis would occur.

"Because these men had hammered out a special covenant among themselves, submitting their lives and ministries to one another, they taught that all Christians, in order to grow spiritually, should likewise submit themselves to a personal pastor or 'shepherd'."[40]

It should be noted that the original accountability covenant was based on a bond of mutuality among equals. The shift towards each person needing a personal shepherd – quite different from mutual accountability – would later prove to be the major contributor towards the controlling and abusive authoritarianism that the Shepherding became known for.

As David Moore writes in retrospect, "From this milieu a church movement was born as they tapped into a leadership vacuum within the Charismatic Renewal. Hundreds of leaders came running to find a pastor."[41]

Suddenly, the four teachers were thrust into the spotlight as the leaders of a new paradigm of leadership, which they themselves were still fleshing out. They had intended to encourage believers to be in accountability or 'covenant' relationships with each other, but the vacuum of leadership quickly pushed them into developing an ecclesiology to give language to this concept.

The mutuality of the original Fort Lauderdale Five gave way to a discipling 'method' which they hoped would function like John Wesley's Methodist small groups.

But almost from the beginning, there were some who sounded the warning that these leaders were covertly (or unwittingly) moving towards developing a charismatic denomination, with the Fort Lauderdale Five as its leaders.

They were an unlikely combination: Prince and Basham had a strong emphasis on deliverance ministry, including the controversial teaching that a born-again, Spirit-filled Christian could be demonized (literally, 'have a demon', not the same as demon *possession*).

Leaders such as du Plessis and Ralph Wilkerson expressed concerns to Mumford and Simpson about their association with the 'demon-chasers' (Prince and Basham), but they held fast to their bond of friendship and accountability. "These five very different men were drawn together because they were like-minded in their concern for the spiritual maturity of the Charismatic believers."[42]

According to Prince: "We saw a lack of spiritual growth in many Christians... Thousands of people were coming into the Charismatic Renewal, but most had little or no knowledge of Scripture, or how to live in the Spirit."[43]

The Fort Lauderdale Five did not become a quintet until 1974, when Ern Baxter approached them during one of the early conferences and asked to be directly included in their accountability group.

As a fifth teacher, Baxter fit in immediately. Despite the unsought label 'Fort Lauderdale Five', the five teachers never lived in Fort Lauderdale all at the same time. But four of them did, and *New Wine* magazine was based there, which gave impetus to the name sticking.

Ern Baxter brought an interesting mix of theological ideas to the group. Baxter was a Reformed pastor in a Pentecostal denomination, and had been a part of the Latter Rain Movement. He was also one of the Bible teachers traveling with William Branham in the 1950s, where Baxter also functioned as Branham's campaign manager. The Latter Rain influence on the Shepherding movement would be strengthened further by the presence of Baxter.

Bob Mumford was only one of five teachers, all of whom were considered gifted, but his personal charisma and eloquence resulted in him being seen as the *de facto* spokesman of the burgeoning movement.

"While some of the focus was on Mumford and Simpson joining with the 'demon chasers', Basham and Prince, the concerns went beyond that issue... As a consequence of the suspicions regarding their association and other issues that challenged the Charismatic Renewal's unity, Basham, Mumford, Prince, and Simpson were instrumental, along with Dennis Bennett, Harald Bredeson, and David du Plessis, in starting an annual 'Charismatic Leaders Conference'."[44]

The original intent of this Charismatic Leaders Conference was to provide an opportunity for charismatic leaders from across a wide spectrum of denominations to join together for fellowship and teaching.

The second reason was to demonstrate that the Fort Lauderdale Five were *not* starting their own denomination, which the inclusion of Bennett, Bredeson and du Plessis should have indicated.

However, the vacuum in leadership created a situation in which the anticipated numbers were dwarfed by the deluge of conference participants. "Expecting 75 charismatic pastors and lay leaders, the conference drew, by word of mouth, an attendance of over 450.

The second, in June 1974, held at Montreat NC, drew over 1,700 pastors and leaders."[45]

Watchman Nee's influence became evident very early on. After the spring Church Growth Ministries Conference in Miami in 1972, the next issue of *New Wine* included this quote:

"In past years God has laid the emphasis of teaching on the Baptism in the Holy Spirit, Water Baptism, The Gifts of the Spirit, and other topics usually associated with the Charismatic movement. This year the message came through loud and clear on a new area: AUTHORITY. God is beginning to place in His Church the authority that has been truly lacking for so many years. Along with this came a new understanding of the home and family relationship, divine order in the church, and a believer's personal relationship of submission to God."[46]

Watchman Nee's concept of delegated authority, coupled with Latter Rain teachings on the 'five-fold' ministry, quickly became a central part of a strategy that consisted of essentially three parts:

1. The need for submission to God's delegated authority.

"Another significant article in *New Wine* was Charles Simpson's 'Covering of the Lord' in the October 1972 issue. This article was a direct result of the HSTM leadership crisis in 1970 and focused on the 'covering' or protection provided by submitting oneself to God's delegated authority in the home, church, and civil government."[47]

2. An emphasis on the five-fold ministries – apostle, prophet, pastor, teacher and evangelist – as the key to equipping the body to be effective in ministry and grow in maturity.

Like the Latter Rain, there were assumptions made that the leaders of this movement were the apostolic and prophetic foundation. "Specifically, he (Prince) emphasized the roles of apostles and prophets as present-day ministries.

"Prince also presented an idealistic view of 'one city, one church' concept in which Christians should congregate not by any one denomination, but by geographical groupings of 'cells' or house churches, in which leaders emerge."[48]

3. The house church (or cell group) as the primary vehicle for these shepherding relationships to be practiced.

Each house group leader would be likewise submitted to another leader above him (women leaders were not allowed), and so on, up the hierarchical chain to the trans-local Fort Lauderdale Five.

Idealism was quite common among the leaders in the early months; it seemed that God was allowing them a precious opportunity to assist the charismatic renewal into a season of greater spiritual maturity. The developing ecclesiology that would give impetus to this ministry would be the house church or cell group. "Along with Basham, Mumford and Prince, Simpson became more convinced that house churches were central to New Testament ecclesiology and were the missing dimension in contemporary church practice."[49]

House churches were considered the primary building block to develop a relational basis for the movement. While there was emphasis on apostles and prophets in the five-fold ministry, there was also a deliberate focus on the pastoral role in bringing Christians into greater spiritual maturity.

"They saw shepherds as the most important of God's delegated authorities in mediating his government on the earth. Jesus as the Great Shepherd delegated to 'undershepherds' the care for his sheep. This concept of Shepherding was a logical next step in implementing the ecclesiologically oriented principles of authority and submission, covering, and fivefold ministry offices... Discipleship emphasized the need for mentoring by a more mature leader, and house groups provided the venue for building the accountability and community the four teachers believed so essential."[50]

The goal of these house groups, as they submitted to their delegated authority (under-shepherd), was simple: "Believers were not to be casual church participants who simply attended meetings. Each believer was a vital participant in the church...[51] *They hoped their teachings on submission to a shepherd and the importance of Christian community would help charismatic leaders draw independent charismatics into practical, committed church participation.*"[52] (emphasis added)

So far, it all sounds good, doesn't it? Mentoring, discipling, small groups, accountability, community – it's not difficult to see why many Christians wanted to become involved. How did it all go so wrong? And what was the key that derailed all the good intentions?

With the influence of Ern Baxter, the Latter Rain concept of a conquering end-times army became grafted into the teachings that were already heavily influenced by Watchman Nee's *Authority and Submission*. Baxter wrote *Thy Kingdom Come*, which helped set the Latter Rain agenda front and center: "Drawing from Psalm 110, the movement taught that Christ was to remain seated in heaven until His enemies in the earth were subdued by the activity of the 'redeemed community'... whereby He would establish God's sovereign right to reign in His own redeemed earth."[53]

The teachings of the Shepherding movement continued to develop into a stronger hierarchy of delegated authority – the Five would have shepherding relationships 'trans-locally' with other leaders, who would in turn be shepherds over others, and so on. As this happened, some Christian leaders began to express concern. At the same time, the zeal in the movement was becoming increasingly apocalyptic. "At one of the evening sessions, after Derek Prince had challenged the men, most of the 60 present made life or death 'military-type' commitments to the leaders."[54]

Part of the problem that developed – in hindsight – was the extreme lengths that these 'delegated authorities' would go in exercising their authority over their churches. "The movement taught that submission to a shepherd provided spiritual 'covering' by being in right relationship to God's delegated authority in the church. The shepherd assumed responsibility for the well-being of his sheep. This responsibility included not just their spiritual well-being, but for their full development emotionally, educationally, financially, vocationally, and socially."[55]

"This doctrine of discipleship and submission (is) going to bring absolute destruction to the Charismatic movement."

- Kathryn Kuhlman

The phrase that was often used – which may sound familiar to some – was having 'permission to speak into his or her lives'. The understanding was that anyone being shepherded, by requesting a discipling relationship, had given permission to the shepherd to 'speak into' every aspect of their lives. This differs from giving advice when requested; the under-shepherd was *responsible* to speak into anything that he thought might be problematic in the lives of his sheep.

If we recall Watchman Nee's teaching that delegated authorities would have God-like ability to discern the thoughts and motives of those being discipled, as well as knowing God's will better than anyone, it doesn't take a rocket scientist to see how this would become controlling and abusive.

"The movement's leaders failed to realize fully the strong desire people have to belong, and that many of their followers committed to the system without recognizing how it would work functionally."[56]

Shortly after the 'military-style' commitments in 1975, well-known Christian ministries began to publicly denounce the Shepherding movement. Initially, the first two that spoke up were the 700 Club's Pat Robertson, and the head of the Full Gospel Businessmen's Fellowship International (FGBMFI), Demos Shakarian.

"For what he called 'cultic' excesses, Robertson forbade Mumford and the others to appear on CBN-affiliated radio or TV stations and ordered that all CBN tapes of the teachers be immediately erased...[57] At about the same time, Full Gospel Business Men's Fellowship International (FGBMFI) founder Demos Shakarian joined the controversy by forbidding the five teachers or any teaching on shepherding or discipleship in any FGBMFI chapter."[58]

In the controversy that ensued, there were many accusations and counter-accusations. Bob Mumford expressed concerns that the Five were being publicly charged with serious error, yet had not been previously contacted in private to address these concerns. To Mumford, this meant that their critics had violated the teaching of Matthew 18 on handling discipline within the Body of Christ.

A meeting between all of the concerned parties, as well as other recognized leaders within the charismatic renewal, was called in the early part of 1975, in Minneapolis.

Of central concern was a letter that Pat Robertson had published, which "contained a long section contrasting the Shepherding teachings with Scripture and making serious charges of 'another Charismatic heresy in the order of the manifested sons, the latter rain and Jesus only teaching of the former days'."[59]

"'The shoot-out at the Curtis Hotel', as the meeting became known, was heated, with accusations flying back and forth, and accomplished little toward reconciliation and understanding."[60] Upset with the level of animosity in the room, Dennis Bennett decided to leave, but accidentally went into a broom closet instead of choosing the exit door. After some crashing around, Bennett came back into the room and left by the appropriate door. It should have been a moment of levity, but the stakes were high and the accusations pointed, and nobody laughed.

"(Brick) Bradford summarized the previous day's proceedings, saying that Robertson needed to publicly 'ask forgiveness for his handling of the situation that [contributed to the] controversy'. He called on Christian Growth Ministries (CGM) leaders to 'temper teaching in regard to controversial doctrine'. Bradford asked for a re-establishment of communication and recognition between ministries."[61]

Bradford's words were timely, but the sides were entrenched enough, and upset enough, not to listen. Don Basham later referred to the meetings as "a time of almost total frustration"[62], while Pat Robertson publicly announced: "My concern is for the gross doctrinal error and resulting practice which has been harming the body of Christ nationwide, and yet has been covered up by a cloak of deception of which we saw only part in Minneapolis."[63]

One of the immediate results of the Curtis Hotel meetings was that Basham, Baxter and Simpson all wrote letters to those they were shepherding and urged them to exercise caution in how they applied shepherding principles. It is to their credit that they were willing to admit that there was some legitimacy to the accusations, and to take action.

Mumford wrote: "These instances, as far as I know, are occasions of immature use and application of spiritual authority. Misuse and abuse are always wrong. However, the principles I understand to be correct and Biblical. I am not embarrassed to say 'we have not gone this way before', and some mistakes are unavoidable. We have, as well, sought to walk in all candor, openness and adjustment from responsible leadership – charismatic and non-charismatic."[64] Hindsight makes it clearer that the whole concept of 'spiritual authority' was dangerously unbiblical, but at the time, Mumford's candid comments were seen as an honest attempt to deal with problems within the movement. (At least, in the minds of the movement's supporters and participants.)

When healing evangelist Kathryn Kuhlman also took a public stand against the Shepherding movement, the spotlight became much brighter. Kuhlman stated, in part: "this doctrine of discipleship and submission must be stopped or it's going to bring absolute destruction to the great Charismatic movement."[65]

Jack Hayford, the well-known Foursquare pastor of Church on the Way in Van Nuys, California, was of the opinion that some of the judgments against the movement were unnecessarily harsh. At the same time, he was also concerned that the Fort Lauderdale Five had not adequately addressed some legitimate concerns, because they felt their accusers had not brought their concerns forward in an appropriate way. Hayford felt that they were dodging the real questions, even if they were correct about some of the accusers.

Chuck Smith, pastor of Calvary Chapel of Costa Mesa and one of the Jesus movement's most high-profile pastors, also strongly rejected the teachings of the Shepherding movement. "In answer to Mumford's request for 'time and patience to demonstrate the fruit of what are presently new Biblical concepts', Smith emphatically told him there already was more than enough evidence to reject the movement's teachings as Satan's deception."[66]

"(Dennis) Bennett feared that the movement was setting up a new hierarchy to be God's government in the last days."[67]

The perception and fear of a new charismatic denomination being created was one of the main reasons why Shepherding was not refuted as quickly as some thought it should have been. Some were already sounding the alarm about the heavy-handed discipling methods that put people in an extreme dependence on their 'shepherd'. Still others recognized the potential for abuse inherent in the discipling teachings, but the concern about a new denomination being formed eclipsed these concerns.

David du Plessis met with the Five and urged them to recognize that there had been problems with the practice of some of their shepherding concepts. Following this meeting, the movement's leaders issued the following statement in 1976:

"We realize that controversies and problems have arisen among Christians in various areas as a result of our teaching in relation to subjects such as submission, authority, discipling, shepherding. We deeply regret these problems, and insofar as they are due to fault on our part, we ask forgiveness from our fellow believers whom we have offended. We realize that our teachings, though we believed them to be essentially sound, have in various places been misapplied or handled in an immature way; and that this has caused problems for our brothers in the ministry. We deeply regret this and ask for forgiveness. Insofar as it lies in our power, we will do our best to correct these situations and to restore any broken relationships."[68]

Another complicating factor was that the Five were recognized teachers whose commitment to Jesus was without question. The accountability that existed between them was testimony to their integrity as Christians and as leaders. It proved difficult then, as it does today, for many believers to separate criticism of a teaching from criticism of the person.

"The consensus of the [1976 Charismatic leaders conference] meeting was that allegations of heresy were unfounded, that there was no reason to question the integrity of the teachers involved, and that, while many doctrinal differences remain among the groups represented, those differences fall within acceptable limits."[69]

However, immediately after this statement was released, Oral Roberts University professor "Dr. Ervin wrote to Kevin Ranaghan in April 1976 and challenged the Ann Arbor statement that said the movement's doctrines fell within acceptable limits."[70]

All of this contributed to creating a feeling among the Fort Lauderdale Five and their supporters of being persecuted for truth. The ferocity of the attacks made it seem like it was a form of spiritual warfare – possibly even direct demonic attack. This only served to strengthen and encourage the leaders to hold firm, although they did take steps to curb some of the fringes.

Bob Mumford met with numerous leaders in attempts to mitigate some of what were perceived to be legitimate concerns. "(Mumford's) group discussed authoritarianism, exclusivism, elitism, neglect of the female role, unbalanced use of metaphors, creation of a jargon, and *minimal biblical support for the degree of headship they taught*."[71] (emphasis added)

Meanwhile, the number of participants in the 'shepherding track' at the annual Charismatic Conferences continued to grow – as many as 4,600 pastors and leaders at one point, easily dwarfing the main conference workshops.

The perception that a new denomination was being covertly set up continued to plague the Five. Others more charitably took the Five at their word that they were not attempting to begin a new denomination, but still warned them that this would be the unavoidable end of their work.

Oral Roberts University professor Charles Farah "believed that the movement had certain institutional features that would inevitably lead to a denomination, even if the leaders did not want it."[72]

As the same accusations continued, the Five began to take steps to defuse these fears. "(Simpson) wrote in a 1976 newsletter: 'In the interest of hearing God, we are dismantling our property, offices, or concentration of influence here in Pascagoula that might smack of a headquarters for a new denomination'."[73]

The Shepherding movement's influence, meanwhile, had become international in its scope. For example, "Bob Mumford had a strong relationship with English and Canadian church leader Barney Coombs... However, according to Coombs, Mumford's leadership was personal and did not directly involve the churches Coombs led in England and Canada."[74] (Former members from the Canadian churches have privately expressed a strongly differing opinion.)

By 1980 many leaders and their followers were leaving the movement.

As much as Mumford and the others were attempting to listen to their critics and address some of the legitimate concerns, the ship that was the Shepherding movement proved difficult to turn. The momentum carried the group along despite the attempts to bring correction and balance.

"The other leaders shared Mumford's concerns, but they found it difficult to maintain their efforts to produce order, discipline, and maturity and, at the same time, avoid the aforementioned pitfalls. The very things they taught created a propensity toward an abuse of spiritual authority, especially among young immature leaders, or leaders who lacked character and integrity."[75]

The Shepherding movement felt a kinship with the Anabaptist understanding of the visible, believing community. Their emphasis on house churches and living separate from the world intersected smoothly with Anabaptist distinctives. The movement also felt that the persecution and misunderstandings that had plagued those Radical Reformers were very similar to the struggles and controversies they were experiencing.

By 1980, however, the stress was taking its toll, and cracks were beginning to show in the solidarity of the Five, as evidenced by the following quotes:

"The five teachers thereupon agreed to bring together all the movement's leaders for a Congress of Elders in Louisville, Kentucky, expecting several thousand men... Two months before the Congress, Mumford and Prince objected to the plan, feeling it was a move towards becoming a denomination, which Simpson adamantly denied was his intention. As a result of Mumford's and Prince's concern, the Congress was cancelled. Simpson was extremely frustrated, feeling that the other two men did not trust him, and he released both Mumford and Prince from their commitments to him."[76]

"Over the years, at least from 1977 on, Derek Prince had struggled with some of the movement's teaching... First, he felt the movement was 'by most generally accepted standards' a denomination. Further, Prince said he did not feel there was an adequate scriptural basis for the concept that 'every Christian should have a personal human pastor', or 'the practice of a pastor overseeing another pastor translocally'... The theological and geographical distance between Prince and the other four teachers culminated in March 1984 with Prince's formal disassociation from the Shepherding movement."[77]

There were also many defections from the ranks during that time: "By 1980 many leaders and their followers were leaving the movement."[78] This was due in part to the concerns being raised by other leaders, but also from a sense of disillusionment in the relationships with shepherds, and also a growing conviction that some of the teachings were being abused.

"Mumford and Simpson, in particular, were faced with many situations around the nation where leaders were accused of abusing their spiritual authority. Many other leaders and churches were leaving the movement disillusioned because of what they thought were extreme teachings and practices."[79]

The combined effect of these defections and accusations – and particularly Derek Prince's departure – brought the remaining four teachers to an almost inescapable crossroads. "In April 1986, at a meeting in Chicago, Basham, Baxter, Mumford and Simpson decided to dissolve their structural and governmental ties together as a movement."[80]

The Shepherding movement was officially at an end, but the teachings of covering, authority, and the concept of delegated authorities have continued to this day in many circles. Granted, some participants in the movement did not suffer the extremes of abuse that others did, and therefore their view is that the only real problem was immaturity in some leaders. But the fatal flaw was not that *some* leaders were authoritarian and abusive, but in the foundational teachings on submission and authority itself.

After the demise of the organizational structure of the movement, the Five adopted a variety of post-Shepherding postures. "In June 1987, Basham affirmed the Shepherding movement's good points and also acknowledged the movement's abuses. He apologized to any who had been hurt by the movement...[81] In 1988, he suffered a massive heart attack (and) on 27 March 1989, Basham died after suffering another heart attack."[82]

Ern Baxter continued to teach for a while, but failing health (he was the oldest member of the Five) slowed him down. "Baxter's health declined rapidly into the summer of 1993, and he died on 9 July."[83]

Charles Simpson remains the major proponent of the Shepherding teachings. He has restructured the movement into the *Fellowship of Covenant Ministers and Churches (FCMC)*, which "carried on many of the central themes of the Shepherding movement... discipleship, accountability, covenant, male government, kingdom of God, house groups, and servanthood...[84] Today, Simpson believes that he and those who continue in association have corrected many of the movement's extremes."[85]

Derek Prince took a much different direction. "After his departure in 1983-84, Prince seldom referred to his longtime relationship to the Shepherding movement. He publicly wrote in 1995 that he believed the movement was guilty of the Galatian error: 'having begun in the Spirit, we quickly degenerated into the flesh'...[86] 'I don't believe now, looking back, it was ever God's intention to start a movement... I think God wanted us to relate to one another as brothers.'"[87] Prince died in 2003.

The most comprehensive statement coming out of the post-Shepherding movement came from its most recognizable spokesperson: Bob Mumford. The cover of *Ministries Today* magazine featured an excerpt from Mumford's statement, which confirmed what the critics had been saying for some time, and which started the process of healing for many who had been injured in the movement.

"After a season he described as 'deep conviction from God' and counseling with leaders, including Jack Hayford, Bob Mumford issued a strong public statement of apology in November 1989: 'This statement of apology has two known motivations. First, I feel as though I have offended the Lord Himself, resulting in His resistance and conviction. Secondly, I am deeply convinced that only by my stating the truth can those who have been adversely affected be healed and released. The following statement represents my personal convictions, and I do not presume to speak for any other person... Accountability, personal training under the guidance of another and effective pastoral care are needed biblical concepts. True spiritual maturity will require that they be preserved. These biblical realities must carry the limits indicated by the New Testament. However, to my personal pain and chagrin, these particular emphases very easily lent themselves to an unhealthy submission resulting in perverse and unbiblical obedience to human leaders. Many of these abuses occurred within the spheres of my own responsibility. For the injury and shame caused to people, families, and the larger body of Christ, I repent with sorrow and ask for your forgiveness."[88]

"Mumford received hundreds of letters of support, including a letter from Dennis Bennett, affirming Mumford's courage to make a public apology. Bennett also apologized to Mumford for his own antagonism during the controversy."[89]

With Mumford's broken and humble public statement of repentance, the Shepherding movement was laid to rest in the public mind. I know I've said the before, but please allow me say it again: the teachings popularized by the Shepherding Movement during its hey-day of the 1970s *are still very much alive* in many charismatic churches and ministries.

THE NEW APOSTOLIC REFORMATION

We looked at some aspects of the NAR in the Latter Rain section, since the Latter Rain teachings form the foundation for the beliefs, practices and structure of the New Apostolic Reformation. However, there is significant overlap with this section, due to their belief that the end-time apostles form the 'new foundation' for the

21st century church, and therefore people need to be submitted under an 'apostolic alignment' to find their destiny in God.

In describing what he calls 'The Second Apostolic Age', self-proclaimed Presiding Apostle C. Peter Wagner proposes the following: "Apostolic-type churches make a different set of assumptions concerning the local church pastor:

- "The pastors cast the vision. Not the congregation.

- "Pastors major on leadership and minor on management.

- "Pastors make top-drawer policy decisions and delegate the rest.

- "Pastors build a solid management team of both elders and staff. The pastor is not subject to the authority of this team, but the team serves at the pleasure of the pastor. The staff members are employees of the pastor, not of the church.

- "Pastors are called for life.

- "Pastors choose their successors."[90]

In language that is startlingly reminiscent of the Shepherding movement, Wagner envisions 'translocal apostles' having authority over churches and pastors that voluntarily choose to be part of the network of the New Apostolic Reformation. "Local churches are autonomous, and, as I have said, pastors are the leaders. They decide whether or not to place themselves under the 'spiritual covering' of a translocal apostle based solely on their personal relationship with the apostle."[91]

If that sounds somewhat akin to the Shepherding movement's line of reasoning, it's probably because the terms are virtually verbatim from the teachings of that movement. In a statement that raises a red flag of warning in my mind, Wagner says of these apostolic 'coverings': "*[These pastors]* are convinced that they would not be able to reach their full destiny in serving God apart from their submission to the apostle. This allows them not only to contribute financially to the apostle's ministry, but also to be cheerful givers."[92]

And part of the New Apostolic Reformation's influence has included what is touted as a 'culture of honor', which is based on submission to modern apostles. Many charismatics who have had experience with the 'covering' teachings from the Shepherding movement recognized the same teachings in the culture of honor.

What is alarming is how many of the emerging generations, who weren't around for the original Shepherding movement, are being led into the same errors.

Danny Silk, one of the pastors at the prominent NAR church Bethel in Redding CA, has authored a book entitled *Culture of Honor: Sustaining a Supernatural Environment*, which follows the same 'submit to the apostle' motif. Silk acknowledges the importance of teachers and pastors, but insists that they cannot function properly unless they are first submitted to a recognized apostle.

In classic NAR fashion, Silk (and Bethel) believe that the role of prophets and apostles is to know what God is up to in 'the heavenlies', and (properly submitted) pastors, teachers, and evangelists carry out God's plans on an earthly level, in order to bring heaven to earth.

Ultimately, it doesn't solve anything to pin all the blame on the Fort Lauderdale Five, Watchman Nee, or the leaders of the New Apostolic Reformation. The answer is not demonizing the character of leaders who promote these teachings (many of them are probably nice people).

The problem, ultimately, is the teaching itself, and the solution will be found in addressing the teachings biblically.

216

A CLOSER LOOK

The more extreme application of the Shepherding concepts, even after "Mumford admitted that the Shepherding emphasis was heresy"[93], included leaders taking over virtually every aspect of their followers' lives. "Rather than see their role as that of a servant to encourage, strengthen and equip the people of God, authoritarian leaders inflate their own importance and view themselves as somehow 'owning' the people God has entrusted to them for spiritual oversight."[94]

In my personal experience, one of the verses that authoritarian leaders and teachers would often use is Hebrews 13:17: "Obey your leaders and submit to them, for they keep watch over your souls as those who will give an account. Let them do this with joy and not with grief, for this would be unprofitable for you" (NASB).

I have heard defenders of the 'covering' teaching quote Hebrews 13:17 and follow it with something like: "notice that it doesn't say 'obey if your leader is good' – it just says *obey...*"

It's amazing how effective that misapplication has been in silencing many people, who instinctively know that it's unbiblical but have trouble putting their finger on why.

By spending a brief amount of time looking at this verse, we can demonstrate a very different way of applying Hebrews 13:17.

1. Obey is the Greek word *peitho*, which can mean "to persuade, to be persuaded by, to co-operate with, to have confidence in, to trust, and to obey".

2. *Hegeomai*, from which we get the word 'leader', can be translated as "to have authority over" or "to go before, to lead". When coupled with the word *peitho*, it's a realistic interpretation to suggest that the writer of Hebrews was

instructing the people to trust, or co-operate with those who 'go before' them. (Or it could mean what others have suggested: you had better be under the authority of those God has placed above you, if you know what's good for you.)

3. *Hupeiko* – submit – can mean one of two things: to yield to authority, or to resist no longer as combatants. So far, we could interpret this verse to say "yield authority to the leaders above you", or "have confidence in those who have gone before, and stop fighting (being combative)".

4. "Keep watch" is a phrase that comes from the Greek *agrupneo*, which can be translated "to be sleepless, to watch" or "to be circumspect, attentive". Either way you want to translate this one, it describes leaders as someone who is genuinely committed to the spiritual health of those around them.

5. "Give an account" – *apodidomi* – can mean "to deliver (sell)", but I don't think leaders sell us back to God. Next possibility? It can also mean "to give back, restore", but I'd be on shaky ground if I suggested that anybody is going to 'give back' people to God; last time I checked, Jesus is the only Mediator between God and humanity. It can also be interpreted "to pay off a debt". Hmm... That doesn't fit the context either. Finally, it can simply be translated as it usually has been: "render (give) an account".

Eugene Peterson's *The Message* says it this way: "Be responsive to your pastoral leaders. Listen to their counsel. They are alert to the condition of your lives and work under the strict supervision of God. Contribute to the joy of their leadership, not its drudgery. Why would you want to make things harder for them?"

That is certainly quite different to a mindset that says, in effect, 'mindlessly obey'. It is more of an appeal to cooperation and trust within the Body.

An intriguing bit of context for this verse is found a bit earlier in the same chapter of Hebrews, where we read: "Remember your leaders, who spoke the word of God to you. Consider the outcome of their way of life and imitate their faith" (Hebrews 13:7).

This verse provides a clear implication that we are to actually *evaluate* the lifestyle of those in leadership, and follow their (good) example.

Of course, we need to also avoid the opposite problem: using "consider the outcome of their way of life" as a pretext for relentlessly nitpicking anyone in leadership. A suspicious and critical mindset is the antithesis and destroyer of true community, no matter if it's done by leaders, or by the congregation.

If we were to pair these verses from Hebrews sequentially, we would read: "Appreciate your pastoral leaders who gave you the Word of God. Take a good look at the way they live, and let their faithfulness instruct you, as well as their truthfulness... Be responsive to your pastoral leaders. Listen to their counsel. They are alert to the condition of your lives and work under the strict supervision of God. Contribute to the joy of their leadership, not its drudgery. Why would you want to make things harder for them?" (Hebrews 13:7, 17 *The Message*)

If anything, Hebrews 13:17 stands as a great example of how your assumptions can color your approach to God's Word. (Remember *eisegesis* - reading your own ideas into a biblical text?) You can quote it accurately but (intentionally or not) twist it to fit your worldview. We should *all* tread very carefully when using God's Word to set the culture of a church, a parachurch ministry, or even a home group.

COVERING

As many critics of the Shepherding movement are quick to point out, the term 'covering' – when used in the Bible – does not have the same meaning that it was given by the Shepherding Movement. Most Christians would agree that mutual accountability is a good thing, but they would stress the *mutual* aspect much more strongly.

It is fascinating to note that the Shepherding movement gained both popularity and notoriety among charismatics in the late 1970s and early 1980s, and in that same era, Bill Gothard's *Institute in Basic Youth Conflicts* became prominent among non-charismatics. Gothard also emphasized being under covering/authority.

One example was his teaching that a wife who sought employment outside of the home was therefore 'not under her covering' (husband), and therefore opened the entire family to Satanic attack.

Gothard was also accused of heavy-handed authoritarianism, and many churches that adopted the *Institute's* teachings produced similar spiritual casualties.

It should not be surprising that there was a non-charismatic version of shepherding occurring at the same time. The reaction to the societal changes that produced the Shepherding movement occurred everywhere, not just in the charismatic movement. It is more disturbing that so many churches and denominations (charismatic and non-charismatic) were so easily sucked in.

AUTHORITY

As you may remember, some years after the dissolution of the movement, Derek Prince observed, "I don't believe now, looking back, it was ever God's intention to start a movement... I think God wanted us to relate to one another as brothers."[95] The mutuality of the original four teachers in submitting to each other could have functioned as a great example for other Christians to follow. But by attempting to build a theological justification to place other believers *under* them in accountability – again, in the words of Prince – "the movement was guilty of the Galatian error: having begun in the Spirit, we quickly degenerated into the flesh."[96]

During the height of the Shepherding movement's influence, the Assemblies of God produced a statement in response: *The Discipling and Submission Movement (1976).* In this document, the authors wisely pointed out that the goal of the five-fold ministry is to equip the body to be mature; in other words, to work themselves out of a job. To use the Ephesians 4 passage to justify an increase in control over individual believers actually sets up a system that works directly against developing Christian maturity.

"However, when they rely altogether on another person to protect them from all error, they will cease searching the Scriptures and fail to develop their own ability to withstand false teaching."[97]

"Thus believers need more than a human shepherd to protect them. They need to develop their own ability to search and understand the Scriptures under the guidance of the Spirit, who alone can lead into all truth (John 16:13)."[98]

Inadvertently, George Mallone touched on this in *Furnace of Renewal: A Vision for the Church*: "In its extreme, it is extortion and domination of the worst variety. Seen in its best light it is a response to the crass individualism of many North American Christians. The question that is being asked is, *How are we to shepherd people unless they are responsive to our authority?*"[99] (*emphasis added*)

The question that immediately comes to mind is: Does 'shepherding' (pastoring) depend on authority?

PROTECTING THE FLOCK?

An argument that is often employed in defense of Shepherding-influenced leadership styles is that the pastor is to protect the sheep from false teachers (ironic, isn't it?). The belief is that, without appropriate pastoral oversight, individuals and groups will easily fall into doctrinal error or excesses.

In reality, this *is* a biblical function of elders in the local church. The error is to equate this necessity of pastoral discernment with demands for unquestioning subservience to leaders.

The Assemblies of God position paper also identified this problem in its response to the Shepherding movement: "Both Paul and Peter warn against false teachers, but the New Testament does not indicate that the answer is to get a human shepherd who will protect the believer."[100]

Perhaps the most bizarre twisting of Scripture that I have personally heard by a Shepherding-influenced speaker was Jesus' lament over Jerusalem: "For I tell you, you will not see Me again until you say 'Blessed is he who comes in the name of the Lord'" (Matthew 23:39, Luke 13:35).

Creatively (and without a shred of biblical support), the speaker twisted this verse to mean that unless believers give absolute, unquestioning submission to their leader – who 'comes in the name of the Lord' – God will never speak to them again. Another self-proclaimed apostle insisted that he was the 'Man of God' who must never be questioned, because questioning him was equal to rebellion against God (the influence of Watchman Nee is clear).

When I challenged this interpretation, the only response I was given was: "You're not arguing with me, you're arguing with God's Word. The Bible says that rebellion is like the sin of witchcraft, so if that's your choice..." (Gotta give 'em credit: they have their handy list of 'shut-up' lines well-practiced.)

A close second would be the time I listened to another speaker use Matthew 10:24 – "A student is not above his teacher, nor a servant above his master" – to bolster her assertion that leaders must be obeyed without question, since they are above us. (And, in her conclusion, lack of submission to leaders would lead to poverty instead of God's promised financial prosperity.)

If we read Matthew 10:24 in context, an entirely different scenario is painted for us: Jesus is warning His disciples that since He was being persecuted, they could expect persecution as well. It is definitely not a statement on submission, leadership or prosperity.

In regards to the issue of accountability within the body, the Assemblies of God also states: "The Bible does teach a submission to our leaders and to one another in love. But this is a matter of mutual concern and consideration for one another. The Bible also recognizes the need for leadership, but Jesus warned that whoever would be first should be the servant of all. There is no room in the church for anyone to lord it over another or over God's heritage (1 Peter 5:3)."[101]

> "What does it mean to be leading people who are supposed to be following Somebody else (Jesus)?"

Anyone who has experienced some level of abuse from the teachings of the Shepherding movement tends to flinch whenever they hear the word *control*. Many post-charismatics have developed a 'won't get fooled again' posture towards anything that even hints at authoritarianism and hierarchical power structures.

TOUCH NOT THE LORD'S ANOINTED?

When authoritarian leaders are questioned or – by the more daring of Christians – *confronted* about their abusive leadership, a common response is 'touch not the Lord's anointed'. This snippet from the Old Testament has been used many times to silence all questions and critiques.

The phrase 'touch not the Lord's anointed' (which is again dependent on the King James Version) first appears in 1 Chronicles 16:22, and actually reads: "touch not my anointed ones". This passage is the first psalm that King David gave to the worship leader Asaph (a percussionist, according to 1 Chronicles 16:15), as a part of the celebration when the Ark was returned to Jerusalem from Obed-Edom.

It should be noted that, even in English, *anointed ones* is plural, not singular, and in this psalm (part of which is also found in Psalm 105:1-15), *anointed ones* refers to the whole nation of Israel. Those who were being warned to "touch not" were foreign kings. Anyone who uses "touch not my anointed ones" to mean that leaders cannot be questioned is guilty of playing 'Twisted Scripture'.

The other Old Testament example that pro-Covering leaders will appeal to is David refusing to take matters into his own hands with King Saul (1 Samuel 26). David refused to kill Saul ('the Lord's anointed'), which has been twisted to mean that leaders are untouchable.

Some immediate thoughts on the misuse of this passage:

1. Pastors, leaders, and even self-proclaimed apostles are not 'kings'.

2. This is what is known as a 'descriptive' passage of Scripture (e.g. it tells us what happened historically), not a

'prescriptive' passage (e.g. it's not instructions for everyone to follow).

3. In David and Saul's case, David not "laying a hand on the Lord's anointed" was *refusing to murder Saul as he slept* (cf. David ordering the execution of the Amalekite youth who *did* kill Saul in 2 Samuel 1:1-16). Not murdering King Saul is light years away from questioning or not submitting to a spiritual bully in a leadership position.

J. Lee Grady has strong words for authoritarian leaders: "... because the pagan idea of leadership pervades our churches, many of us are in constant pursuit of celebrity status in the Kingdom of God."[102] Why? The answer isn't flattering: *celebrity* status means power and prestige. George Mallone adds: "Our Western philosophy, so steeped in competitive tradition, has done plenty to squelch true fellowship and love in our churches."[103]

Accountability has been one of the casualties of the covering and submission model. The Bible supports the idea of confessing our sins to each other, so that we can be set free (healed) from the effects of sin in our lives (James 5:15-16). However, many people later found, after confessing their struggles to their 'shepherd', that leaders used this insider knowledge (given in trust and in keeping with scriptural teaching) to exert control over them. Instead of freedom, they experienced more bondage.

Leadership has also become a dirty word for many Christians. Immature leaders and toxic understandings of what constitutes 'leadership' are at least partly to blame. But I recall something one of my professors at Bible college was fond of saying: "The answer to bad theology is not *no* theology, but *good* theology." The same principle applies to how we deal with inadequate, and at time abusive, models of leadership – we need to reconstruct good, biblically based models.

Bishop Todd Hunter (Anglican Mission in America) once mused, "What does it mean to be leading people who are supposed to be following somebody else *(Jesus)*?" Perhaps the best starting point for re-constructing a healthy understanding of leadership, accountability and authority is to look at Jesus' use of His authority, and how He taught His disciples to use the authority that He gave them (and us).

JESUS AND AUTHORITY

One of the most eloquent passages of Scripture that describes the earthly ministry of Jesus is Philippians 2:5-8:

"Your attitude should be the same as that of Christ Jesus: Who, being in very nature God, did not consider equality with God something to be grasped, but made himself nothing, taking the very nature of a servant, being made in human likeness. And being found in appearance as a man, he humbled himself and became obedient to death – even death on a cross."

In this passage Paul writes of Jesus emptying Himself of His divine prerogatives – as King of the universe – and becoming the suffering servant prophesied by Isaiah (Isaiah 53). The theological term is *kenosis* – taken from the Greek word *kenoo* which is translated 'emptied' in Philippians 2:7 – the idea that Jesus actually gave up some of His divine prerogatives during His earthly ministry.

We need to be careful, however, how we communicate what 'emptying' really means. Theologians like Wayne Grudem have proven very helpful in suggesting that this emptying does not mean that Jesus *gave up* some of His attributes. Grudem's legitimate concern is that the *kenosis* theory, as advocated by some German theologians in the 1800s, potentially forces us into a position where "we could no longer affirm Jesus was fully God while He was here on earth."[104] The early creeds of the church, if you recall, were written with extreme care to affirm that Jesus *was* fully God and fully man.

Grudem would suggest that the appropriate understanding of 'emptied' (*kenosis*) in Philippians 2 is that Jesus was at all times fully God, but willingly *chose to limit Himself* in the expression of His deity.

There are numerous examples in the Gospels that demonstrate the willingness of Jesus to limit the use of His attributes: Jesus was certainly not *omnipresent* in a physical sense; He had to travel from place to place. There were other times when He was also not *omniscient* (all-knowing), such as when the disciples questioned Him about the timing of His second coming. Jesus' answer, of course, was that He didn't know; only the Father knew (Mark 13:32).

Anyone who heard Jesus teach was amazed by the authority He exuded.

Grudem points us in a helpful direction – the willingness of Jesus to be a *servant*, when by rights, the people should have been serving *Him*. The focus of the Philippians passage is on the servant attitude that Jesus exhibited. And the introduction to this powerful passage on Jesus' servant example is simple and profound: "Your attitude should be the same as that of Christ Jesus…" (Philippians 2:1).

JESUS' AUTHORITY IN ACTION AND TEACHING

What is striking is the level of authority Jesus – even as the Suffering Servant – exhibited in His interactions with people. Anyone who heard Jesus teach was amazed by the authority He exuded. They commented on how He had an authority that the teachers of the law did not (Matthew 7:29; Mark 1:22), and even exclaimed, "A new teaching, and with authority! He even gives orders to evil spirits and they obey Him" (Mark 1:27).

His disciples saw examples of His authority in His miracles of healing (Matthew 4:23-24), deliverance (Mark 1:32-34), and divine provision (like the feeding of the five thousand in Matthew 14:15-21, Mark 6:35-44, Luke 9:12-17 and John 6:1-13). When Jesus calmed a storm on the Sea of Galilee, His astonished disciples asked each other, "What kind of man is this? Even the winds and the waves obey Him" (Matthew 8:27)!

The reaction of the Pharisees was quite the opposite: they wanted Jesus dead. He was a threat to their self-perception that they were the rulers of Israel. They recognized an authority in Jesus that they could not compete with, no matter how many times they tried to trap Him (Matthew 15:1-9, 22:15-22, for example). As a result, they feared and resented Him.

JESUS' CLAIMS OF AUTHORITY

For someone who had willingly humbled Himself to be a servant, Jesus still overtly claimed that He was an authority on more than one occasion. Many times in the Gospels, Jesus seemed to go out of His way to compare Himself with some of the 'greats' in the Old Testament – with Jesus always coming out the greater.

The Tabernacle had been the resting place of God's glory until the completion of Solomon's Temple (1 Kings 8:1-66), and even in Jesus' day, the Temple was the center of Israel's worship. (Despite the depiction of God's glory leaving the Temple in Ezekiel 10, there was still the hopeful expectation for the return of His glory, as foretold in Ezekiel 43:1-5). Yet Jesus, when questioned about His disciples breaking Sabbath laws, went beyond defending His disciples and claimed that He was not only greater than the Temple, but Lord of the Sabbath as well (Matthew 12:1-8).

King David's son Solomon, who was granted a gift of wisdom as king of Israel, had been chosen by God to build the Temple in the first place. Solomon was held in high esteem in the history of Israel. When the Pharisees demanded that Jesus do a miracle to prove His authority, He declined – although He had just healed a demon-possessed blind and mute man (Matthew 12:22) – but went on to say that He was greater than Solomon (Matthew 12:42).

Jesus further outraged the Pharisees and teachers of the law by claiming that He was "I Am" – Yahweh (John 8:52-59), and that Abraham was overjoyed when he saw Jesus' day (time) come.

The Jews understood *exactly* what Jesus meant, which explains why they responded by picking up stones to kill Him (the Old Testament punishment for blasphemy).

Jesus clearly established Himself as an authority in the minds of the people, and to His disciples – the ones who didn't desert Him after He upset their preconceived ideas (John 6:66-68) – and even in the minds of the Jewish leaders, who could not discredit Him with their traps and wanted Him silenced at any cost.

Jesus also demonstrated His authority over those afflicted with demonic spirits, over sickness, and even over death, by raising Jairus' daughter (Luke 8:49-56) and His friend Lazarus (John 11:41-44).

Jesus also quietly assumed authority in numerous areas of His ministry:

- The authority to expand their accepted interpretations of the Old Testament, in the *Sermon on the Mount*: "You have heard it said... but I say unto you..." (Matthew 5:21-48).

- The authority to forgive sins, after a paralyzed man had been lowered through the roof so that Jesus could heal him – offending the Pharisees yet again (Mark 2:3-12).

- The authority to pronounce judgment on cities (Korazin, Bethsaida, and Capernaum) because they had not received Him or His proclamation of the Kingdom of God (Matthew 11:20-24), and later on Jerusalem itself (Matthew 23:37-39).

- The authority to pronounce judgment on the Pharisees (to their faces, in public) for not only rejecting Him, but using their positions of influence to dissuade others from becoming followers of Jesus as well (Matthew 23:1-36).

- The authority to (a) make a home-made whip, (b) drive the money-changers out of the Temple, (c) over-turning tables while accusing them of making His Father's house a "den of thieves", and (d) silencing His Pharisaical critics when they tried to protest (Matthew 21:12-13; 23:27; Mark 11:15-18; 27-33; Luke 19:45-48; 20:1-8).

By this point, it may seem amazing to describe Jesus, as the Philippians 2 passage does, as *nothing* and a *servant*, when He clearly claims, exercises and is recognized as having incredible authority. Perhaps more amazing still would be what His full authority will look like when He is revealed as King of kings and Lord of lords.

As important as it is to understand Jesus' use of His own authority, it is equally important to understand what kind of authority He has given to His disciples.

DISCIPLES AND AUTHORITY

"Then Jesus came to them and said, 'All authority [Greek *exousia*] in heaven and earth has been given to Me. Therefore go and make disciples of all nations, baptizing them in the name of the Father and of the Son and of the Holy Spirit, and teaching them to obey everything that I have commanded you. And surely I am with you always, to the very end of the age'" (Matthew 28:18-20).

This short passage has been the driving force behind the evangelistic and missionary energy of recent centuries.

There was a time, believe it or not, when churches did nothing 'outside the walls', because the church building was perceived to be the most appropriate place for people to hear and respond to the gospel. For example, when John Wesley first began preaching the gospel in fields and town squares, his critics accused him of treating the Gospel with contempt. He endured verbal and even physical abuse because of this.

Even Wesley himself initially struggled with the idea of preaching outside the church, at one point writing in his journal, "I could scarce reconcile myself at first to this strange way of preaching in the fields... I should have thought the saving of souls almost a sin, if it had not been done in a church."

That may sound strange to us today, but it important for our discussion to understand that the authority Jesus conferred on His disciples *was for the purpose of evangelism and disciple making*. He gave them authority to preach the gospel, and to teach those who became followers of Jesus.

The Greek word *exousia*, which we translate as authority (authority and power, KJV), can mean:

1. The power of choice; liberty of doing as one pleases.

2. Physical and mental power (ability or strength which one possesses or exercises).

3. The power of authority (influence) and of right (privilege).

4. The power of rule or government *(Source: The NAS New Testament Greek Lexicon)*.

When Jesus uses *exousia* to describe His authority, any or all of the above definitions would fit. The significance is that the same word that describes Jesus' authority also describes the authority that Jesus has given to His disciples (including us).

Examples of how *exousia* is used to describe Jesus' authority include: the crowds recognized an authority in Jesus' teaching that their scribes didn't have (Matthew 7:29), Jesus' words regarding His authority to forgive sins as well as heal (Matthew 9:6), and the interaction between Jesus and the Pharisees about His authority (Matthew 21:23-27).

The same Greek word is also used regarding the secular authorities of the day: the governor (Luke 23:20), the local puppet-king, Herod (Luke 23:7), and any authorities that the disciples would be dragged in front of on account of Jesus (Luke 12:11).

AUTHORITY OVER WHAT?

It is vitally important to grasp that while the secular authorities used their *exousia* as power and control over people, the authority given to the disciples by Jesus was never intended to function that way.

Jesus' authority was clearly recognized by the people, who referred to him as Rabbi, which means 'teacher' (Matthew 26: 25; Mark 10:51; John 1:49), and Lord (Matthew 14:28-29; 17:4; John 6:68). Jesus referred to Himself as both during the Last Supper with His disciples (John 13:13).

But when we read about the authority given to the disciples in Matthew 28:18-20, it has to be said: it did *not* include power over people. One of the 'commands' Jesus instructed the disciples to teach would include His prohibition of lording it over others (Matthew 20:25-27). Instead, the authority given by Jesus was for a much nobler purpose: preaching the gospel of the Kingdom, and authority over sickness and the demonic. In other words, Jesus gave authority to the disciples (and us) for the proclamation and demonstration of the Kingdom of God (evangelism).

A parallel Great Commission passage is found in Mark 16:15-18. Both versions give absolutely no indication that Jesus was giving the disciples authority *over people*. Jesus remains Lord and Shepherd, and there is no conferring of Lordship to any 'delegated authorities' or 'under-shepherds'. Jesus remains the Authority.

This is an understanding that Paul expands upon in his writings on the body of Christ (1 Corinthians 12:12-17): Jesus is the Head (authority), and everyone else is a member of His body. Different parts of the body have varying functions as the Holy Spirit graces people with spiritual gifts for the common good (1 Corinthians 12:7), but Jesus is the undisputed Head.

There are two other instances recorded in the Gospels where Jesus conferred authority on some of His followers. The first is found in Luke 9:1-2: "And He called the twelve together, and gave them power and authority over all the demons, and to heal diseases, and He sent them out to preach the kingdom of God, and to heal the sick."

The parallel passage in Matthew 10 recounts the same story: authority to preach, authority to heal, and authority over unclean (evil) spirits. In Matthew's account, the twelve were commissioned and immediately sent on this mission.

In Luke's account, the twelve who would later became apostles (except for Judas, of course) witnessed more miracles and heard more of Jesus' teaching before they were sent out.

What is important is that the authority was identical in purpose: preaching the gospel, healing the sick, and authority to set people free from demonic bondage. Unique to Luke's Gospel is the second passage which recounts the second sending out of seventy-two of the disciples:

"After this the Lord appointed seventy-two others and sent them two-by-two ahead of Him to every town and place where He was about to go. He told them, 'The harvest is plentiful, but the workers are few. Ask the Lord of the harvest, therefore, to send out workers into His harvest field'" (Luke 10:1-2). Jesus instructed them to heal the sick (Luke 10:9), and later, "The seventy-two returned with joy and said, 'Lord, even the demons submit to us in Your name'" (Luke 10:17).

The same authority was given to the seventy-two that Jesus had earlier given to the twelve soon-to-be apostles. Later, as Luke recounts for us throughout the book of Acts, the number of people empowered for the Great Commission would continue to expand far beyond the original twelve disciples.

Two things that bear repeating regarding the authority that Jesus gave to His disciples:

1. The authority is given in connection with them participating in the advancement of the kingdom – evangelism, and

2. No authority over other Christians is even *hinted* at. The authority was the message, the healing, and the deliverance from demonic spirits.

Significantly, in both Luke and John's Gospels, the disciples are commanded to wait until the Holy Spirit was poured out before taking on the Great Commission. In Luke, Jesus refers to the promise of the Father, and that they will be clothed in power before being sent out (Luke 24:48-49). Luke picks up this same command to wait for the Spirit in Acts 1:5 and again in Acts 1:8.

In John's Gospel, we read of Jesus inviting "all who are thirsty" (John 7:37) to come to Him, and that whoever came would be given the promise of the Holy Spirit, who had not been poured out at that time (John 7:39). In language reminiscent of Luke's writing, John is anticipating the coming expansion of the circle of those who would get to 'do the stuff': participate in the spread of the Kingdom. Even after the Resurrection, we read in the Gospel of John that Jesus told the disciples that they would be sent, just as He had, but to wait for the Holy Spirit to be poured out first.

Finally, in preparation for His impending death at the Last Supper, Jesus showed all of His disciples, past and present, what "taking the very nature of a servant" looked like, when He washed His disciples' feet.

"Jesus knew that the Father had put all things under His power, and that He had come from God and was returning to God; so He got up from the meal, took off His outer clothing, and wrapped a towel around His waist. After that, He poured water into a basin and began to wash His disciples' feet, drying them with the towel that was wrapped around him..."

"When he had finished washing their feet, He put on His clothes and returned to His place. 'Do you understand what I have done for you?' He asked them. 'You call me "Teacher" and "Lord", and rightly so, for that is what I am. Now that I, your Lord and Teacher, have washed your feet, you also should wash one another's feet.

"I have set you an example that you should do as I have done for you. I tell you the truth, no servant is greater than His master, nor is a messenger greater that the one who sent him. Now that you know these things, you will be blessed if you do them'" (John 13:3-5, 12-17).

What a powerful picture of servant leadership! The ultimate Authority takes on a level of servanthood that His disciples couldn't even imagine themselves doing. Imagine the chagrin they must have felt as Jesus washed their feet, and then reminded them that, as Lord and Teacher, it would have been more appropriate that they wash His feet. (Which I would guess several of them would have sheepishly realized by this point.)

Jesus was emphatically clear about the meaning of this living parable: they were to serve, just as He had, and not fall again prey to the attitudes that prompted His teaching on authority in Matthew 20:25-28.

LET'S TALK ABOUT ELDERS

Leadership is one of the gifts listed in Romans 12:6-8, along with the gifts of apostle, teacher, encouragement and mercy. And not only did Paul make a habit of appointing elders in every church, he also instructed his colleagues Timothy and Titus to do the same (Titus 1:5), and even provided some helpful criteria in discerning and selecting them (1 Timothy 3:1-13; Titus 1:5-9).

One of the duties of the elders, according to Paul's instructions, was to safeguard the gathered Body from false teaching brought by false apostles. Significantly, "in the early church, *false apostles did not pioneer ministries;* they preyed upon ministries established by others."[105] (emphasis added)

Paul warned the Ephesian believers before his last trip to Jerusalem that false apostles would infiltrate the church after he'd left. Worse yet, some of them would even come from *within* the Body, whose ultimate motive would be "to draw away disciples after them" (Acts 20:30).

With Paul's warning about false apostles in mind, the admonition for an elder to be "able to teach" (1 Timothy 3:2) and able to "encourage others by sound doctrine and refute those who oppose it" (Titus 1:9) makes a lot of sense, doesn't it? If an elder can teach, it means that elder knows their Bible well – invaluable knowledge in weeding out false teachings and false teachers. Beyond the danger of false teaching itself, Paul realized these false apostles had a goal of manipulating people so that they could collect followers.

If you have ever been in a church where this has happened, you've seen the effect of these people 'gathering disciples'. They first become a relentless lobby group, dividing the Body, creating factions and divisions. If they don't get their way, they seldom repent. Instead, they leave, and their gathered disciples follow them.

Therefore, part of being entrusted with oversight as an elder includes guarding against false teaching. Check out Paul's admonitions to Timothy (1 Timothy 1:3-7, 4:11-16) and Titus (Titus 1:10-14), and particularly the cryptic instruction given Titus to "have nothing to do with" divisive people (Titus 3:9-11).

The two-sided coin of responsibility for elders/overseers is (a) guarding against false teachings/doctrine, and (b) guarding against false apostles whose goal and intent was to gather their own followers (some people might have good theology, but still be in the error of 'gathering followers').

It should be pointed out that the qualifications for elders and deacons, found in both Timothy and Titus, are moral and relational guidelines. These guidelines assume that elders and deacons understood Jesus' instructions regarding servant leadership. Paul is building on the foundation of Jesus' teaching, not the other way around.

Deacons are a little easier to figure out – even the word *diakonos* gives us a clue: it means someone who serves food and drink (i.e. a waiter). An early example is found in Acts 6:1-6, where the first deacons are commissioned to oversee food distribution. Not surprisingly, the word *diakonos* also carries the meaning of caring for the poor.

One of the unavoidable aspects of being an elder, entrusted with the responsibility to guard the 'safe place', will sometimes include the uncomfortable and unpleasant decision to exclude someone from the group. Whether in a small house church or a larger congregation, it's never a tidy, everyone-feels-the-same situation.

People are inter-connected. They have relationships, and if the church is even remotely healthy, disrupting these close-knit relationships is a sensitive matter, needing much wisdom and compassion. These times can be dangerously prone to producing a reactionary backlash, resulting in the dissensions and factions that Paul warns are not signs of the Kingdom (he calls them "acts of the sinful nature") in Galatians 5:20, which can tear the fabric of community apart.

Yet to *not* exercise what many call *church discipline* when it is required can actually result in the destruction of the faith community. The case of 1 Corinthians 5 is, of course, an extreme example (expelling a man who was in an incestuous relationship with his mother or step-mother). But the precedent is that in the case of serious and unrepentant sin, sometimes the only loving, Christ-honoring response is to exclude someone until they change (repent).

But also note that in 2 Corinthians 2:5-11, Paul instructs the church to welcome the repentant person back into the community, echoing the redemptive spirit of Jesus' teaching in Matthew 18:15-35.

This underlines the great importance for elders or overseers to be chosen based on their character and track record of serving the Body, not based solely on their talents or abilities in the business world. Many have quoted the saying 'Character before gifting', and this is especially crucial when appointing people to provide oversight and leadership.

Ideally, the role of elders/leaders was to safeguard (oversee) the purity of the teaching, as well as guarding the ethos of the community, while *at the same time* those gifted as apostles, prophets, teachers, pastors, and evangelists would be equipping and enabling people towards spiritual maturity.

ACCOUNTABILITY

Another casualty of the Shepherding movement is that it made 'accountability' into a panic-inducing word for many post-charismatics. When they read the epistle of James, they know what they're reading is true, but they struggle with how to apply it: "Therefore confess your sins to each other and pray for each other so that you may be healed. The prayer of a righteous man is powerful and effective" (James 5:16).

Knowing and practicing are two different things for those who have been wounded. People with background experience under spiritually abusive leaders understand all too well that 'accountability at gunpoint' doesn't work.

So how do we practice accountability in the healthy way that James assumes in his epistle? How do those who have been wounded by unhealthy models of accountability begin to function again as God intended?

As much as it is our human nature to set up defensive walls around ourselves for protection, these same walls thwart our desire for community. They make trust and vulnerability, transparency and risk-taking impossible.

In *Celebration of Discipline*, Richard Foster offers the following encouragement: "But if we know that the people of God are first a fellowship of sinners, we are freed to hear the unconditional call of God's love and to confess our needs openly before our brothers and sisters... In acts of mutual confession we release the power that heals."[106]

There is healing to be found in honest confession, prayer with others, and hearing 'the Lord forgives you' from our brothers and sisters in Christ. This stands in stark contrast to a view of accountability that gives one believer power and authority over another (which Jesus explicitly forbids).

This mutuality is simply the Body functioning as it was intended to. Jesus is the only Head, and the rest of the Body is arranged under Him. Elders and leaders (including vocational pastors) are tasked with creating this kind of 'safe place' where James 5:16 is normal. Grudem reminds us, "The metaphor of the church as the body of Christ should increase our interdependence on one another and our appreciation of the diversity of gifts within the body."[107]

John Stott writes in *Christian Counter-Culture*, "In all of our attitudes and behavior towards others we are to play neither the judge (becoming harsh, censorious and condemning) nor the hypocrite (blaming others while excusing ourselves), but the brother, caring for others so much that we first blame and correct ourselves and then seek to be constructive in the help we give them."[108]

In short, the healthier approach to accountability needs to reflect these values in order to follow the spirit of James 5:16:

- *It is invitational* – it cannot function arbitrarily as accountability at gunpoint, enforced by hierarchical power, structure or demand.
- *It is mutual* – the context is fellowship within the Body of Christ.
- *It is redemptive, not punitive*, in its intent and practice.

It really boils down to *trust*. Many people have had their trust in leadership damaged, and while forgiveness is where the healing begins, it will be the risk of trusting other people in the Body that will open doors for true community.

A pastoral friend, comparing the different models of church government that have existed for many years (Presbyterian, Episcopal, and congregational), observed: "there is room for abuse in any system – the success of government depends upon the trustworthiness and heart of the pastor or elders."[109]

George Mallone sums it up this way: "Contrary to what we would like to believe, elders, pastors and deacons are not in a chain of command, a hierarchical pyramid, which puts them under Christ and over the church. The leaders of a biblical church are simply members of the body of Christ, not an elite oligarchy."[110]

The antidote to bad theology is not 'no theology', but good theology. The antidote to controlling and abusive accountability is not 'no accountability', but biblical accountability. The antidote to false apostolic leadership is not 'no leadership', but biblical (servant) leadership.

Jesus is our model and our Teacher. The New Testament epistle-writers (Paul, Peter, John, James, and Jude) wrote to build on His foundation. Their instructions are Spirit-inspired, but always based on the teachings and example of Jesus, the Servant who washed the feet of His disciples.

CHAPTER NOTES

1. Grady, J. Lee – *What Happened to the Fire?*, page 145
2. Brother Maynard – *The Church Uncovered: A New Answer to the Question, 'Who is your covering?'*, page 2
3. Grady, J. Lee – *What Happened to the Fire?*, page 146
4. Ibid., page 148
5. Wikipedia – *Watchman Nee*
6. Vinzant, Don – *The Discipling Dilemma*, page 128
7. Nee, Watchman – *The Normal Christian Life*, page 95
8. Ibid., page 100
9. Ibid., page 107
10. Nee Watchman – *Authority and Submission*, page 6
11. Ibid., page 1
12. Ibid., page 8
13. Ibid., page 6
14. Ibid., page 19
15. Ibid., page 26
16. Ibid., page 32
17. Ibid., page 19
18. Ibid., page 80
19. Ibid., page 92
20. Ibid., page 95
21. Ibid., page 97
22. Ibid., page 73
23. Grady, J. Lee – *What Happened to the Fire?*, page 150
24. Nee, Watchman – *Authority and Submission*, page 52
25. Ibid., page 52
26. Ibid., page 55

27. Ibid., page 64

28. Ibid., page 102

29. Ibid., page 104

30. Ibid., page 105

31. Ibid., page 108

32. Grady, J. Lee – *What Happened to the Fire?*, page 141

33. Moore, S. David – *The Shepherding Movement: Controversy and Charismatic Ecclesiology*, page 20.

34. Ibid., page 43

35. Ibid., page 43

36. Ibid., page 26

37. Ibid., page 27

38. Ibid., page 29

39. Grady, J. Lee – *What Happened to the Fire?*, page 142

40. Moore, S. David – *The Shepherding Movement: Controversy and Charismatic Ecclesiology*, page 180

41. Ibid., page 41

42. Ibid., page 42

43. Ibid., page 48

44. *The New Dictionary of Pentecostal and Charismatic Movements*, page 1060

45. Moore, S. David – *The Shepherding Movement: Charismatic Controversy and Ecclesiology*, page 54

46. Ibid., page 55

47. Ibid., page 55

48. Ibid., page 53

49. Ibid., page 56

50. Ibid., page 56

51. Ibid., page 57

52. Ibid., page 61

53. Ibid., page 70

54. Ibid., page 89

55. Ibid., page 74

56. Ibid., page 75

57. *The New Dictionary of Pentecostal and Charismatic Movements,* page 1061

58. Ibid., page 1061

59. Moore, S. David – *The Shepherding Movement: Charismatic Controversy and Ecclesiology,* page 95

60. *The New Dictionary of Pentecostal and Charismatic Movements,* page 1061

61. Moore, S. David – *The Shepherding Movement: Charismatic Controversy and Ecclesiology,* page 104

62. Ibid., page 105

63. Ibid., page 105

64. Ibid., page 109

65. Ibid., page 110

66. Ibid., page 113

67. Ibid., page 114

68. Ibid., page 117

69. Ibid., page 119

70. Ibid., page 120

71. Ibid., page 148

72. Ibid., page 112

73. Ibid., page 141

74. Ibid., page 147

75. Ibid., page 149

76. Ibid., page 163

77. Ibid., page 165

78. *The New Dictionary of Pentecostal and Charismatic Movements,* page 1062

79. Moore, S. David – *The Shepherding Movement: Charismatic Controversy and Ecclesiology,* page 166

80. Ibid., page 168

81. Ibid., page 169

82. Ibid., page 170

83. Ibid., page 172

84. Ibid., page 177

85. Ibid., page 178

86. Ibid., page 174

87. Ibid., page 175

88. Ibid., page 173

89. Ibid., page 173

90. Wagner, C. Peter – *Spheres of Influence,* chapter 2

91. Ibid.

92. Ibid.

93. Grady, J. Lee – *What Happened to the Fire?,* page 143

94. Ibid., page 150

95. Moore, S. David – *The Shepherding Movement: Controversy and Charismatic Ecclesiology,* page 175

96. Ibid., page 174

97. Assemblies of God Position Paper: *The Discipling and Submission Movement (1976),* page 1

98. Ibid., page 2

99. Mallone, George – *Furnace of Renewal: A Vision for the Church,* page 83

100. Assemblies of God Position Paper: *The Discipling and Submission Movement,* page 2

101. Ibid.

102. Grady, J. Lee - *What Happened to the Fire?*, page 160

103. Mallone, George – *Furnace of Renewal*, page 83

104. Grudem, Wayne – *Systematic Theology*, page 551.

105. Assemblies of God Position Paper: *Apostles and Prophets (2001)*, page 11

106. Foster, Richard – *Celebration of Discipline* page 191

107. Grudem Wayne – *Systematic Theology*, page 859

108. Stott, John R.W. – *Christian Counter-Culture*, page 176

109. Bailey, Brad – *Our Leadership Structure* (http://www.vcfwestside.org/222911.ihtml)

110. Mallone, George – *Furnace of Renewal*, page 85

Chapter Six
AFTER THE MEETING

The chairs were stacked and put away, as were the folding tables. All the ceramic mugs had been scrubbed clean and returned to the worn cupboards in the galley kitchen adjacent to the meeting room. Floor swept, lights extinguished, and the front door locked until the next *Charismatics Anonymous* meeting.

Rick and Sandra had invited Justine out for coffee, at a retro 1950s-styled malt shop on the corner, about a half-block from the meeting hall. The narrow shop was crowded, even this late in the evening, but the three of them were able to find a booth near the front. Sandra and Justine sat together on one bench, while Rick sat across from them, jacket balled into the corner of the booth.

Justine was obviously feeling more relaxed than when she had first shared at the meeting, but Rick and Sandra wanted to spend just a little extra time with her.

"I guess one of the things that bothers me the most," she mused, after they'd placed their orders, "is that there were so many warning signs along the way, and I *knew* they were warning signs. But each time, they would give us some kind of reassuring slogan that seemed, somehow, *enough* to put aside my doubts."

Rick and Sandra exchanged a look across the table. They had heard this comment many times before. Rick could still remember the night Sandra had first voiced the same thing, almost verbatim.

"There are always red flags, if you are paying attention," suggested Sandra gently, laying her hand on Justine's arm. "I felt the same way when I first left our former church. How could I have missed it? What was I thinking? I'm a university graduate, after all!" The three of them shared a quiet laugh at Sandra's ironic comment.

"The most common one I've come across," Rick began, as their laughter faded, "is also probably the most effective. I've heard it from dozens of pastors, conference speakers, and read it in all kinds of books."

Anyone who mocks theology has a lie they want you to buy.

Rick leaned back against the wall of the booth as he continued. "They start by making fun of anyone who values theology and doctrine. They especially mock anyone with theological training. You've heard the terms: doctrine police, religious spirit, Pharisees, etc. The terms are designed to manipulate the audience into *distrusting* the very people who are best equipped to recognize the red flags."

Sandra picked up the train of thought as Rick paused; this was familiar territory for both of them. "If these speakers can convince their audience that theologians and doctrine are *anti*-Spirit, then anyone who raises a concern about what they're teaching is automatically discredited. And since I come from the same church as you, Justine, I know you've heard the threat – and that's what it is, a *threat* – that anyone who raises theological questions will *'miss the great move of God'*."

Justine was listening intently, eyes large as she recognized the dynamic that Rick and Sandra were describing. "I remember being told that pastors and teachers couldn't be trusted to get their doctrine right *unless* they were first submitted to an Apostle."

Rick sighed, shaking his head. "If I could sum up my thoughts on this in one sentence, it would be this:

"Anyone who mocks theology has a lie they want you to buy."

Leaning forward again, Rick continued, choosing his words carefully even as his voice betrayed his passion about the subject. "All the other 'red flags' more or less hang on that one. *Nobody* needs to mock doctrine and/or theologians, if what they're teaching is biblical. *Nobody*. Whenever you hear the mocking start, that in itself is a *huge* red flag. They want you to get on board with their 'new thing', and you can be pretty much guaranteed that it won't be biblical."

There was a moment of silence around the table, even amidst the boisterous noise of the malt shop. It was Justine who broke the silence once again.

"I remember you and Trevor both saying that it would be easier to just walk away from anything 'charismatic'. And believe me, I *totally* get that!" Justine laughed nervously, while her two companions smiled and nodded with understanding looks.

"It's harder work to separate the chaff from the wheat," agreed Sandra. "But in the end, it's the most rewarding and Spirit-honoring choice to make."

"But how does that work?" Justine wondered, shaking her head. "I don't know if I can trust my ability to 'discern'. I'm not sure I could ever trust leaders again. And this may sound awful, but I'm not sure I even trust the Holy Spirit anymore. Honestly, I think if I hear somebody say 'I've got a prophetic word for you' ever again, I might give them a good, swift kick!"

Their shared laughter lightened a profound moment. "That's the real question, isn't it?" asked Rick, as the waitress arrived with their orders. "Where do we go from here?"

* * *

A.W. Tozer wrote, prophetically, "Satan has opposed the doctrine of the Spirit-filled life about as bitterly as any doctrine there is. He has confused it, opposed it, and surrounded it with false notions and fears."[1]

Experiences of bad theology and spiritually abusive behavior, as found in the Latter Rain, Shepherding and Word of Faith movements, have created many spiritual casualties.

Part of the fallout has included many post-charismatics opting for *functional cessationism* – a belief in all of the *charismata* (spiritual gifts) 'on paper', but never using them.

As Tozer reminds us, however, there is the very real presence of an Adversary who would like nothing better than for post-charismatics to reject or suppress their spiritual gifts. If we were to become post-charismatic *and post-Spirit,* it would be a victory for the enemy of our souls.

Dr. John White had this to say about revival in general: "From a safe distance of several hundred years or several thousand miles, revival clearly looks invigorating. What could be more glorious than a mighty work of God in our midst, renewing thousands and converting tens of thousands? But when we actually look at a revival, we find... sin and infighting and doctrinal error. Why does our expectation not match the reality? Why is revival sometimes so messy?"[2]

As I mentioned in the first chapter, a popular phrase (this year, anyway) to describe those who believe that the Holy Spirit continues to give *all* the gifts listed in the New Testament is "continuationist". The term can be both helpful and unhelpful.

Unhelpful: Technically, *everybody* who isn't a cessationist fits. Pentecostals, Charismatics, Third Wave, Latter Rain, Word of Faith, televangelists, and snake-handling cults in the Appalachian mountains. It is too broad a term to really say much.

Helpful: It *does* describe the basic understanding that all the gifts of the Spirit are available and functioning today. And it doesn't have a lot of negative baggage associated with it (at least, not yet).

And is there anyone, identifying themselves as a continuationist, who would *not* want to see a genuine move of the Spirit that resulted in church renewal and the advancement of the Kingdom of God? Would we be willing to revisit and attempt to address some of the messiness that Dr. White describes, if we thought there was a chance of seeing the 'radical middle'?

SPIRITUAL GIFTS

One of the areas many post-charismatics are now beginning to wrestle with is the question of the *charismata* – grace gifts, or 'grace-lets' – in a post-charismatic setting. Many have been turned off by the hype that has surrounded spiritual gifts, and also with the elitism that prefers and honors some gifts above others.

John Wimber writes, "Some people think of the gifts as trophies, merit badges, or advanced degrees. They supposedly indicate an elite status in God's sight and higher level of spirituality. This mistaken point of view might tempt some people to show off their spiritual gifts like karate black belts or Olympic medals."[3]

Grudem has even stronger words: "If spiritual gifts are sought only so that the person may be more prominent or have more influence or power, this certainly is wrong in God's eyes. This was the motivation of Simon the Sorcerer in Acts 8:19..."[4]

And as you may recall, Peter basically told Simon to go to hell because of his mercenary attitude towards the power of the Spirit.

Many current models of exercising spiritual gifts seem to perpetuate the elitist attitude that Wimber and Grudem are urging us to avoid. Those with 'upfront' gifts, particularly prophetic people, seem to be the ones on stage, microphone in hand, much more prominently than others. This does nothing to dispel the idea that somehow those on stage are special and more 'anointed' than those sitting in the audience.

What if we took away the stage? I wonder what would happen if prophetic ministry happened in small groups only, led by people who valued and trusted Scripture as their grid?

If the stage and the spotlight were taken away, exercising spiritual gifts would become more grassroots in nature. This would be safer in some respects, yet at the same time, more risky. Safer, because these more intimate settings of house groups or new church plants don't have the same perceived glamor or power position.

(Although it should be noted that there are some people who deliberately prey upon house groups and new church plants because they are 'gathering disciples'.)

And also riskier: if you are the person giving the prophetic word, in a small group where everyone knows each other and words are 'weighed' as a community, you will find yourself in a very different spotlight. The dynamic is quite different from a large meeting with all the church props.

And there can be a much healthier dynamic of weighing prophetic words (1 Corinthians 14:29) in these smaller settings. "In a community which practices relational Christianity, such testing *[of prophecy]* is quite possible. But within the realm of media Christianity, globetrotting superstars, and oligarchic leadership styles, such a check is not possible."[5]

Creating a healthy environment for practicing spiritual gifts won't happen automatically. We first need to have a good understanding of what 'healthy environment' even looks like! There are two key verses in 1 Corinthians that I believe provide a framework for keeping the practice of spiritual gifts healthy and a source of life and encouragement.

The most gifted tongues-speaker, without love, is only a shrill annoyance.

1 CORINTHIANS 12:7

"Now to each one the manifestation of the Spirit is given *for the common good*" (1 Corinthians 12:7, emphasis added).

As Brent Toderash said regarding the five-fold ministries, spiritual gifts are for serving the rest of the body. The 'common good' is the ultimate goal. If we lose sight of *why* we have spiritual gifts in the first place, we have already lost the 'healthy environment'.

The Greek phrase 'common good' is *sumphero*, which means "to bear or bring together", based on the root word *phero* – "to carry a burden, to uphold (bear up)". The inference is clear: spiritual gifts are given to enable us to build up others.

Our motivation for having spiritual gifts must never be to enhance our own reputation, or a selfish desire for recognition or position. The gifts are given to individuals in order to bless others.

The common good of the rest of the Body is the goal. Spiritual gifts are merely tools to be used towards that goal.

If I may be permitted to over-state this (but not by much): Show me somebody who thinks their identity is connected to their spiritual gifts, and I'll show you someone who doesn't know what spiritual gifts are for.

Really, it's not about us. It's about the Body of Christ being built up.

1 Corinthians 13

It is no accident that Paul, writing under the inspiration of the Holy Spirit, includes the famous 'chapter of love' in between his teaching on the Body needing all its parts, and his teaching on how spiritual gifts best operate among the gathered Body.

The most gifted tongues-speaker, without love, is only a shrill annoyance. The most amazing prophetic voice in the church, without love, is a zero *(loose paraphrase of 1 Corinthians 13:1-2)*.

Whenever gifts are put on display for those seeking attention or to establish a 'pecking order' of importance, they have been corrupted by human pride and elitism (the prevailing problem in the Corinthian church, as we saw earlier).

While we often use the middle part of 1 Corinthians 13 in wedding ceremonies, try to read it again with fresh eyes. This was written as part of Paul's instruction on how the gifts of the Spirit were *meant* to function in the Body of Christ:

"Love is patient, love is kind. It does not envy, it does not boast, it is not proud. It does not dishonor others, it is not self-seeking, it is not easily angered, it keeps no record of wrongs. Love does not delight in evil but rejoices with the truth. It always protects, always trusts, always hopes, always perseveres.

"Love never fails. But where there are prophecies, they will cease; where there are tongues, they will be stilled; where there is knowledge, it will pass away. For we know in part and we prophesy in part, but when completeness comes, what is in part disappears. When I was a child, I talked like a child, I thought like a child, I reasoned like a child. When I became a man, I put the ways of childhood behind me. For now we see only a reflection as in a mirror; then we shall see face to face. Now I know in part; then I shall know fully, even as I am fully known.

"And now these three remain: faith, hope and love. But the greatest of these is love" (1 Corinthians 13:4-13).

This is the 'healthy environment' in which spiritual gifts are used as God intended!

1 CORINTHIANS 14:12

"Since you are eager to have spiritual gifts, try to excel in gifts that *build up the church*" (1 Corinthians 14:12, emphasis added).

Paul instructs us to 'eagerly desire' spiritual gifts (1 Corinthians 12:31; 14:1; 14:39). The phrase is the Greek word *zeloo* – "to burn with zeal, to desire earnestly". Passivity towards spiritual gifts is not what Paul has in mind; we are to burn with zeal regarding spiritual gifts (perhaps the first and most difficult step for post-charismatics).

But this zeal for gifts is based in looking around the gathered church, and recognizing where the Body most needs to be built up, to become more in tune with the Head. Spiritual gifts do not separate us into the 'haves' and 'have-nots'. When they function as the Spirit intended in the first place (1 Corinthians 12:11), the Body is encouraged (built up).

Some have suggested that spiritual gifts can be understood as 'situational gifting', meaning that the 'best gifts' to be eagerly pursued are the ones which would address specific needs in that group, in a specific situation. And once the situation passed, the spiritual gifts might change. Certainly, this view would lend itself more readily to a servant dynamic, although it would not be wise to limit our understanding of spiritual gifts as being situational only.

A discussion of the whole list of spiritual gifts would be too long for the purpose of this writing, but let's look at prophecy as an example, for two reasons:

1. Paul urges us to pursue this gift in order to be an encouragement to others.

2. It's easily one of the most abused gifts, between the elitism and theatrics that have often surrounded prophetic ministry, and the damage inflicted by bogus prophetic words (perhaps more accurately called "pathetic words").

For years, Wimber encouraged the Vineyard movement to avoid loaded phrases such as "thus saith the Lord", preferring to use a more humble approach, such as, "I think the Lord may be saying _____; what do *you* think?"

This approach is helpful a couple of ways:

First, it is invitational. It invites the interaction of the person receiving the 'word'; passivity is not a good thing, as we are instructed by Paul to weigh prophetic words (1 Corinthians 14:29). "True prophecy submits gladly to the final authority of Scripture, for it is not new revelation of truth for the church but a harmonic expression of that truth."[6]

Second, it downplays the importance of the person delivering the prophetic word. The focus shifts to the encouragement of the receiver, and to the fruit of the 'word' (1 Corinthians 14:3).

"Given that prophecy was tested within the meeting itself (1 Corinthians 14:29), there probably was a greater sense of humility than we might think pervading prophecy in the early church. It is easy to say 'thus says the Lord' when there are not spiritual people around to judge the word. But when such individuals are present, the environment for receiving prophecy changes."[7]

DISCERNMENT, DISCERNMENT, DISCERNMENT

To pretend that there are no risks in encouraging the *charismata* would be naive and ultimately dangerous. After all, Paul wrote long letters (twice!) to the church in Corinth to correct, warn, and encourage them in the use of spiritual gifts. We aren't any more immune to pride, excess or deception than the Corinthian church.

The problem is never the Holy Spirit.

And yet the apostle Paul – under the inspiration of the Holy Spirit – *didn't* write to the Corinthians and say, "It's too much chaos. It can't be done. Just forget the gifts."

The problem is never the Holy Spirit, nor His decision to give people the *charismata* according to His will (1 Corinthians 12:11).

The problem is always with us. When we turn our brains off, we are in trouble. When we allow pride to creep into the expression of a genuine gift of the Spirit, what He meant for good becomes corrupt (that's a truism for most things, isn't it?). When we stop using our discernment – another of the *charismata,* ironically – it's not surprising that all hell breaks loose.

Here's a quote that really made me stop and think:

"The more highly valued a word of prophecy is by the church, the more open is that church to deception, the more liable it is to be led astray by false prophecy. Failure to recognize the role of discerning of spirits means failure to recognize the character of prophecy and prevents the gift of prophecy functioning properly. As in the worshipping assemble tongues without interpretation is in fact only half a gift, *so prophecy without evaluation is in effect only half a gift.*"[8] *(emphasis added)*

The opposite extreme, of course, is to be so paranoid about false prophecy or false expression of spiritual gifts that they are ignored or deliberately suppressed.

The Scriptural balance is to "eagerly desire" (with burning zeal) the gifts of the Spirit (1 Corinthians 14:1), to exercise these gifts in the "most excellent way" (1 Corinthians 13), and practice discernment with the same care that the Bereans were commended for (Acts 17:11). The more highly valued Scripture is, and the more diligent we are to *obey* it by discerning and 'weighing' prophecy, the healthier the expression of the Spirit's gifts will be.

It's safe to say that we **will not** quench the Spirit by obeying His instructions in the Book that He co-authored: "Do not quench the Spirit. Do not treat prophecies with contempt, but **test them all**; hold on to what is good, reject every kind of evil" (1 Thessalonians 5:19-22).

"To be, or not to be," said Hamlet. We might paraphrase: "To *charismata*, or not to *charismata*." As continuationists, who believe that all of the Spirit's gifts are available today, the question has already been answered. All that remains is how we will go about it.

* * *

As late as the meeting had gone, it was much later still when they finally left the malt shop. Standing now on the sidewalk, coats buttoned against the cool of the night, Sandra and Rick watched as Justine hopped into her compact car across the street.

"Well, what do you think?" Sandra queried, hands once again tucked into her pockets for warmth. "She seems really open, in spite of everything."

Rick nodded, a little surprised to see his breath frost the air in front of him as he exhaled deeply. "The grace of God is remarkable. I wouldn't have blamed her – or you, back in the day – for just walking away completely. Thank God that she's willing to do the hard work of sorting through the good, the bad and the ugly."

Sandra chuckled, "Well, as the old and over-used expression goes, there *is* a 'baby in the bathwater'. She's tasted enough of the Spirit's goodness that she's willing to work through all the junk in the bathtub. Are you taking the bus tonight?"

Rick shook his head, "No, I'm parked just down the road. But I'll walk you to your car first; it *is* getting pretty late." And with that, the two began walking back the way they came.

"Do you think," Rick wondered aloud, "that people like Justine, and Trevor, and the rest of our little group, can see beyond the first steps of recovery from charismania?"

Sandra caught on immediately to his unasked question. "You mean, that there's more to being a post-charismatic continuationist than just spiritual gifts?"

Rick nodded wordlessly as she continued, "Well, that's hard to say. I guess it's the best place to start. But eventually, as they weed out all the unbiblical teachings they've been inundated with, they'll have to reconsider what the Kingdom of God is *really* all about."

Rick nodded once again, as they stopped beside Sandra's car, and he opened the door for her. "My thoughts exactly. Recovery is the priority right now, including discerning and weeding out the unscriptural teachings. But it's just the start of the journey. For every twisted teaching that gets weeded out, there needs to be biblical teaching planted in its place."

"True that," agreed Sandra brightly, as she started her car. "Until next week, then!" Rick closed her door and waved in response. And with a guttural roar from her engine, she was off.

Rick glanced back at the nondescript entrance to the meeting room as he walked to his own vehicle. *That's really what it all boils down to, isn't it?* He mused to himself.

Post-charismatic, but not post-Spirit.

CHAPTER NOTES

1. Tozer, A. W. – *Life in the Spirit,* page 23
2. White, John – *When the Spirit Comes with Power,* page 35
3. Wimber, John – *The Dynamics of Spiritual Growth*, page 158
4. Grudem, Wayne – Systematic Theology, page 1029
5. Mallone, George – *Those Controversial Gifts*, page 44
6. Mallone, George – *Those Controversial Gifts*, page 42
7. Mallone, George – *Those Controversial Gifts*, page 37-38
8. Dunn, James – *According to the Spirit of Jesus,* page 17

About the Author

Robby McAlpine is a husband, father, son, brother, writer, pastor, blogger, missionary, and bass guitarist. In his spare time, he loves to read and -- wait for it -- play his bass. He has a Bachelor of Arts in Biblical Studies from Providence University College, and a Masters of Theological Studies from Tyndale Seminary. Robby and his wife Wendy live with their children in beautiful British Columbia, Canada, and enjoy good times with good friends and good coffee.

Robby's other books include: *The Genesis Cafe: Conversations on the Kingdom* and *Detoxing from Church*.

Visit Robby's blog @:
www.robbymcalpine.com

from the back cover:

"the kingdom of God is near." - Jesus of Nazareth

The message of Jesus Christ was the "Gospel of the Kingdom", and wherever His disciples went, they spread that same message given to them by their Teacher and Messiah.

Today, there is nothing more foundational to understanding and living our faith than to know and embrace this same Gospel of the Kingdom.

So what, exactly, did Jesus *mean* when He said, "The Kingdom is near, repent and believe the good news"?

The Younger & the Elder, together with author Robby McAlpine, set out together to explore what Jesus meant. Drawing on the Gospels and the book of Acts, as well the writings of George Eldon Ladd, their animated conversations (and interactions with the Crusty Irish Barkeep, the shrewd but wary Proprietress, and the irrepressibly artistic Barista) make for a lively, thought-provoking, and spiritually invigorating journey of discovery.

Coffee's on at The Genesis Café. Consider yourself warmly invited.

Sample Chapter:

the
genesis cafe

conversations on the Kingdom

"This problem must not be solved by abstract theological reasoning but by the exegesis of the Scriptures. The point of departure must always be, 'What do the Scriptures teach?' rather than, 'What does logic allow?' We shall turn therefore to the New Testament, particularly to the teachings of our Lord, for the answer."

George Eldon Ladd, 1952

chapter One
the gathering

It was a near-perfect summer's afternoon, with just the right combination of bright, warm sunlight and a gentle, cooling breeze rustling the leaves of the medium-sized trees lining the boulevard. The timeworn bricks of the early-twentieth-century buildings, so drab and colorless during the cold, wet winter, now cheerfully soaked in and reflected the warm rays of the sun.

After satisfying the unspoken but unmistakable demand of the roadside parking meter for some of my coins, I threaded my way through the bustling pedestrian traffic on the sidewalk, my eyes scanning ahead down the block. There were many cafés to choose from in this busy downtown district, but like most people, I had my own favorite spot in mind.

In one of life's happy coincidences, the traffic light changed just as I arrived at the intersection. Thankful for my good fortune, I joined the crowd briskly striding across the street, the familiar sign over the door of my destination, *The Genesis Café*, beckoning me.

Stepping inside, I quickly glanced around the interior, and discovered that, as was often the case, I was the first to arrive.

Spotting a table near the open windows at the front (the one with a great view of the street and blessed by the summer's breeze), I quickly ordered a *café americano* from the barista behind the counter. She was at her usual welcoming, cheerful and efficient best, which was part of what made the *Genesis* such a great place. The Barista, consciously or not, defied the typical stereotypes: black-clad and multi-pierced, yet cheerful and professional in her work.

I had barely seated myself after claiming the window-side table, when the door burst open again and the two friends I was expecting came noisily inside, already involved in animated conversation. I half-rose from my seat, waving to let them see where I was, and they cheerfully waved in return, en route to the espresso bar. After purchasing their drinks, they joined me with the smiles and greetings of long-time camaraderie.

"I really must apologize for our tardiness," began the Elder, almost before he was seated. "I truly believe the City is gradually *shrinking* the parking spaces on the street, which makes my choices for parking more and more limited as the years go by."

The Younger made a theatrical show of stifling a choking cough. "The problem," he suggested to the Elder, "is that your car is a behemoth-sized land-yacht." Shifting his gaze to me, he added, "I'm starting to think that when 'Leviathan' is mentioned in the book of Job, they were talking about his car."

"I had a car like that once," I sighed, remembering fondly. "A '71 Dodge Monaco, with a 360 cubic inch engine. It was only a two-door, but it was longer than my dad's station wagon. I could fit my entire *life* into the trunk. It was a total rust-bucket, but it was *my* rust-bucket."

The Younger laughed in appreciation, although I knew his mind was racing to convert cubic inches to liters. The Elder pretended to be completely fascinated with his coffee as he ignored both of us.

They were an interesting duo, these two friends of mine. The Elder, content in his early retirement, was nonetheless still very much the embodiment of his former occupation as a teacher of classical literature. His fondness for the classics, coupled with his childhood in England (although his accent was barely noticeable these days), gave him a unique and endearing way of expressing himself.

To the surprise of many who made his acquaintance, the Elder had never spent a day in seminary. He was simply an avid reader, and his fascination with learning more about his faith led him to describe himself as an 'amateur theologian'.

"Remember," he was known to say with a mischievous twinkle, "the original meaning of 'amateur' meant *for the love of it.* Hence my love for learning more about God makes me a truly *amateur* theologian."

The Younger was as restlessly energetic as the Elder was contentedly calm. Still at the beginning of his career, having graduated from university less than a decade earlier, the Younger was also intensely curious about the intersection between faith and everyday life.

For as long as the Younger could remember, the Elder had been a family friend, but as an adult, he had come to appreciate their friendship on an entirely new level. (Not that this prevented the Younger from enjoying some vigorous teasing of his older friend from time to time.) Their animated conversations about life, spirituality, and justice were a source of enjoyment and challenge that the Younger thrived on.

"Okay, you said you wanted to bounce some ideas around with us. So, here we are. Let's do it," suggested the Younger, abruptly shifting gears and drawing my wandering thoughts back to the present. Leaning forward, elbows on the table, he unconsciously adopted his signature look of intense curiosity. Very few people possess the unwavering eye contact of the Younger. Or his profound sense of inquisitiveness, for that matter.

The Elder smiled as if he'd just heard a private joke, or perhaps something amusing had occurred to him. "Well, no-one has ever accused us of hiding behind small talk, eh? Even about the era of classic cars."

"Or accused us of subtlety," I replied, saluting them with my *americano*. "That's why I like hanging out with the two of you. Nobody else could put up with us." Taking a brief breath to collect my thoughts, I launched into the topic that captured my attention in recent weeks.

"I've been thinking about writing another book," I began, noting that the Younger's studious expression did not change, while the Elder nodded slightly as if he wasn't altogether surprised. "And, since you guys have always been such a good sounding board, I thought I'd get your input on it."

The Elder raised his eyebrows, as if surprised by my invitation. "I'm more than willing to help in any way that I can," he offered, clasping his hands around his coffee mug. "Although I'm not sure a single conversation would be adequate."

"Which means you'll be buying us a lot of coffee?" suggested the Younger slyly, sensing that an opportunity had presented itself.

"I've been considering what would make the most sense, after writing *Post-Charismatic*," I continued, addressing the Elder and pretending I hadn't heard the Younger's not-so-subtle suggestion. "I mean, after writing something like that, where do I go next?"

Leaning back in his chair, without breaking eye contact, the Younger became serious again as he wondered aloud, "Is it important that your next book be connected somehow? Couldn't you just write something completely fresh?"

Having already wrestled with that same question, I hastened to clarify. "No, I'm not feeling constrained or putting pressure on myself to do a sequel. And the last thing I want to do is to get stuck in a rut. But, the longer I thought about it, the more I became convinced about the importance of the *foundations* of our beliefs.

"What we believe isn't neutral – it can either be healthy, or dysfunctional. For example, if our understanding of the Kingdom of God is skewed, then everything we do based on that skewed assumption will be, for lack of a better word, *skewed*."

"Just don't call it *Post-Skewed* and you'll be fine," quipped the Younger, shifting in his chair, as the breeze from the open window suddenly moved all of our napkins six inches to the right. "Is that the topic you're thinking of? The Kingdom of God?"

"Well, it certainly was central to Jesus' teaching," I responded, as each of us collected our wayward napkins, "and even the gospel that spread during the book of Acts was known as the 'gospel of the Kingdom'. So, I think it's a very foundational question: what did Jesus *mean* when He said 'the Kingdom is near'?"

The Elder looked thoughtful as he sipped his coffee – black, 'the way God drinks it', as he was fond of saying. "What kind of questions do you think need to be asked?" he began, ever mindful of the big picture. "And who is looking for those answers?"

The Younger broke eye contact with me to look at the Elder, as if he were about to say something, thought better of it, and ended by frowning thoughtfully into space. Or perhaps it was the creaky ceiling fan over our table that had captured his attention.

"Well," I began, pausing to take another sip of my *americano*, "part of the larger problem is that a lot of people seem to be throwing around the phrase 'Kingdom of God' these days, but I don't think many of us mean the same thing when we say it. And more importantly, I don't know if many of us are using the term in the way that Jesus used it."

"Ah," replied the Elder, shifting forward in his chair, "so are you planning to focus on the eschatological end-of-the-world aspects, or the present-day stewardship implications, or what exactly?"

"I think I would start by explaining that *eschatological* refers to our beliefs about the future, and humanity's destiny," I suggested with a laugh.

The Younger's gaze refocused itself from space – or the ceiling fan – and settled again on the Elder. "Hang on a second, professor. Can you really separate them," he asked doubtfully, "without missing something important?"

The Elder surreptitiously moved his coffee mug beyond the reach of his young friend's animated hand gestures, smiling at the Younger's familiar nickname for him. "That's precisely the question I was about to ask," he replied. "There are so many emphases on different aspects of the Kingdom going around these days, that it would be tempting to only deal with one of them. And that, in my opinion, would be a disservice to the totality of what Jesus meant."

"That's probably the most daunting thing in this writing project," I admitted, taking the opportunity to finish the remainder of my *americano*. "The Kingdom of God is a massive topic, on so many levels. I don't want to gloss over anything, but at the same time, I need to have a fairly tight focus to keep it from getting too long."

"What's the title going to be?" asked the Younger, almost interrupting in his eagerness.

Taken aback slightly, I had to admit that I hadn't thought that far in advance. "I'm assuming that a title will make itself known as the material is created," I replied with a shrug. "Choosing a title is usually one of the last things for me, when I write."

The Elder frowned thoughtfully, before adding, "At the same time, a title could serve as a thesis statement, which can help you sharpen your focus." I nodded in agreement, seeing the merit in his suggestion, although I didn't want to get hung up on the title before even beginning the writing.

"It's about the Kingdom, stupid!" exclaimed the Younger loudly, slapping his hand on the table for emphasis. The condiments on the table, gathered in their usual formation next to the wall under the open window, rattled in protest.

The Elder attempted to mollify him. "Yes, obviously it's about the Kingdom. We just said that. I see no reason to be insulting."

"No, no, no," the Younger disagreed amiably, becoming more animated by the minute. "I meant that's what the *title* should be: 'It's About The Kingdom, Stupid!' When I was in university, I remember learning about a politician who campaigned successfully on the slogan: 'it's the economy, stupid'. It was his way of stating what the important issues really were. So, for your book, this title would be a great way to let people know, right from the beginning, that the Kingdom of God is the basis for everything."

I had to laugh. "Yes, that would be a very direct, in-your-face way of summing up the book. And for the record, I *do* plan on emphasizing that the Kingdom of God is our foundation. *That's* why we need to make sure we understand what Jesus really meant when He spoke about the Kingdom. But as the title of the book? I'm not convinced."

The Elder nodded vigorously. "You would do well to avoid the appearance of insulting the intelligence of people who haven't read anything beyond the front cover. Not everyone will recognize or understand the historical reference to an old politician."

"And you should never mix politics and religion, I know, I know," the Younger conceded with a chuckle, although you could tell that his enthusiasm for the title suggestion had barely subsided. "But still, you never know... people might pick it up out of curiosity *because* they thought it was offensive!"

I wished that I still had some of my *americano* left to drink, if only to buy a little time as I considered how to respond. Out of the corner of my eye, I could see the Elder intently studying the slight quivers of coffee in his mug, and I realized he was trying to stifle laughter.

At last, he simply took a deep breath and remarked, "*This* is what happens when you have several voices speaking into the same situation."

The Younger looked as if he were about to defend his suggestion once more, but I took advantage of the turn of events to voice the request that I'd come prepared with.

"And that's why I wanted to talk to both of you," I quickly interjected, looking back and forth at each of them. "I don't want to be the only voice in this. I'd like the two of you to be a part of telling this story." Both of them were looking intently at me by this time, expressionless. "I'm inviting the two of you to be a part of writing this book."

The two of them glanced at each other, the Elder with raised eyebrows, and the Younger uncharacteristically waiting to see what his long-time friend would say first, before committing himself. Before either of them could disagree, I pushed on.

"You both have an interesting take on things," I continued, leaning on the table, which shifted slightly on the uneven flooring. "When I listen to your conversations, I hear two voices expressing concepts in a way that anyone can understand and relate to. And sometimes," I admitted, somewhat sheepishly, "I can come across as a little too theologically verbose."

"I didn't say that," protested the Younger, holding up his hands in mock surrender, but making no attempt to disguise a wide grin.

Before I could respond, the Elder spoke up. "Well, if you think a couple of rabble-rousers like us could be of service, then by all means, I'd love to help in any way I can."

"Count me in," the Younger chimed in, serious but still grinning.

Leaning forward across the table, folding his hands in front of him, the Elder was suddenly all business. "Who is your target audience? And getting back to my earlier query, what questions do you think most need answering?"

Thankful for the Elder's practical bent, I replied, "I'm hoping to write something that will be accessible to the average layperson who is interested in knowing more about the Kingdom of God, that doesn't require a degree in theology first."

"As far as which questions need answering," I paused for a deep breath, "I'd want to start with what Jesus meant when He preached 'the gospel of the kingdom', and how the early disciples understood and spread that message after Jesus left."

"Absolutely *crucial*," concurred the Elder, nodding emphatically. "Jesus didn't begin to mention His crucifixion to the disciples until much later in His earthly ministry, which begs the question of what the 'gospel of the kingdom' that He taught at the beginning actually meant."

"Don't forget the justice issues," the Younger insisted. "There has to be a practical dimension to the Kingdom in the here and now. Jesus had a *lot* to say about ethics."

I nodded in agreement, "And the ethical/justice issues are as much personal as they are communal. In other words, what are the personal *and* corporate implications of being 'in the Kingdom'?"

"And what constitutes participation in the Kingdom?" added the Elder, finishing his coffee and replacing his mug on the wooden tabletop. "And let's not forget, *how* and *when* does the Kingdom come?"

As we looked back and forth at each other, all three of us began to laugh. It was a good moment – the realization that we were all excited about diving into the topic as a little community of friends.

As the moment passed, I suggested, "I'll start putting together a framework for the book, and you two can, well, just do what you do best: have a couple of pints and talk."

The Younger and Elder exchanged conspiratorial looks, yet neither seemed able to come up with a suitable retort.

As the after-work crowd began to line up at the counter, we stood to make our table available. Gathering our coffee mugs together and depositing them into the bin next to the espresso counter, the Elder again became quite serious as he asked, "I assume you'll be referencing the work of Ladd on this topic, am I right?"

The Younger looked puzzled, but I answered the Elder, "Of course. The 'already and not yet' Kingdom of God. Ladd's writings on the Kingdom are brilliant."

The Elder turned to the Younger, noticing his friend's perplexed silence. "Are we dating ourselves – revealing our advanced age? Have you heard of George Eldon Ladd? Or his influential book: *Jesus and the Kingdom*?"

The Younger just shook his head, holding his hands out in a gesture of helplessness.

"It's actually been re-titled *The Presence of the Future*, in recent years," I amended, although I could see that the Younger appeared as unenlightened as before.

This confirmed something that had been percolating in the back of my mind for some time, and now seemed as good a time as any to mention it. "Perhaps it's time to re-introduce Ladd's writings on the Kingdom to the next generation," I said, addressing the Elder. "We tend to assume that everyone is familiar with Ladd and his work on the Kingdom because he is quoted by so many other authors, but I'm meeting a lot of younger people who have never heard of Ladd or his books."

"You can include me on that list," agreed the Younger, with a self-deprecating shrug. "I've never heard of him, but it sounds like that's all about to change." Holding the door open, he gestured us through. "Allow me to show respect to the *older* generation."

"Psalm 71:18: 'Till I declare your power to the next generation, your might to all who are to come,'" quoted the Elder, as he led the way outside. "Although I hesitate to place myself in the role of the Psalmist, who described himself as 'old and grey'."

"But with the wisdom of Solomon," I hastened to add, schooling myself to keep a straight face, and pretending not to notice the Younger's barely-stifled guffaw. "Why don't we each invest some time reading *The Presence of the Future* before we meet again, as the basis for our conversations?"

The Elder nodded as he adjusted his cap. "Yes, I'll dig out my old, *original title* copy, and the two of us will put our heads together. And perhaps a copy of the newer edition needs to be purchased by the young and uninitiated among us."

The Younger looked momentarily offended, but then nodded sheepishly in agreement. "I'll get my own copy. I like to make notes and comments in the margins, and I know how much it drives him crazy when other people write in his books," he said, jerking his thumb in the Elder's direction. The Elder merely tipped his hat in response.

And with a few warm farewells, we parted ways, the two of them setting off in the opposite direction from where I'd parked earlier.

The afternoon sun had moved on, allowing long shadows to overtake the interlocking brick sidewalks, but the trees still sighed and rustled in the cool breeze. I was pleased to see that there was still time remaining on the parking meter as I returned to my car. And as I settled behind the steering wheel, probing with my key for the ignition, I recognized the familiar feeling of anticipation, discovery, and excitement that accompanies the first steps in writing a book.

And I sensed, as the engine came to life and I signaled my turn into traffic, that our journey into understanding what Jesus meant when He said 'the Kingdom is near' was going to be *life changing*.

the
genesis cafe

conversations on the kingdom

Now available at Amazon.com

CPSIA information can be obtained at www.ICGtesting.com
Printed in the USA
LVOW13s1518230314

378575LV00002B/495/P